Regulatory Compliance: Insurance and Annuity Products

Second Edition

LOMA (Life Office Management Association, Inc.) is an international association founded in 1924. LOMA is committed to a business partnership with its worldwide members in the insurance and financial services industry to improve their management and operations through quality employee development, research, information sharing, and related products and services. Among LOMA's activities is the sponsorship of the FLMI Education Program—an educational program intended primarily for home office and branch office employees.

The ***Associate, Insurance Regulatory Compliance (AIRC) Program*** is designed to educate insurance professionals about regulatory compliance issues that affect companies in the life and health insurance and annuity industry. To earn the AIRC designation, a student must complete all required courses as outlined in LOMA's most current *Education and Training Catalog*. Upon successful completion of the required courses, the student receives a diploma awarded by LOMA and is entitled to use the letters *AIRC* after his/her name.

Statement of Purpose: LOMA Educational Programs Testing and Designations

Examinations described in the *LOMA Education and Training Catalog* are designed solely to measure whether students have successfully completed the relevant assigned curriculum, and the attainment of the FLMI and other LOMA designations indicates only that all examinations in the given curriculum have been successfully completed. In no way shall a student's completion of a given LOMA course or attainment of the FLMI or other LOMA designation be construed to mean that LOMA in any way certifies that student's competence, training, or ability to perform any given task. LOMA's examinations are to be used solely for general educational purposes, and no other use of the examinations or programs is authorized or intended by LOMA. Furthermore, it is in no way the intention of the LOMA Curriculum and Examinations staff to describe the standard of appropriate conduct in any field of the insurance and financial services industry, and LOMA expressly repudiates any attempt to so use the curriculum and examinations. Any such assessment of student competence or industry standards of conduct should instead be based on independent professional inquiry and the advice of competent professional counsel.

Regulatory Compliance: Insurance and Annuity Products

Second Edition

Harriett E. Jones, J.D., FLMI, ACS
Monica R. Maxwell, J.D., FLMI

Information in this text may have been changed or updated since its publication date. For current updates, visit www.loma.org.

LOMA's Associate, Insurance Regulatory
 Compliance Program
Atlanta, Georgia
www.loma.org

PROJECT TEAM:

Authors:	Harriett E. Jones, J.D., FLMI, ACS
	Monica R. Maxwell, J.D., FLMI
Project Manager:	Joyce R. Abrams, J.D., FLMI, ACS, AIRC, AIAA, PAHM, ALHC, HIA, MHP
Production Manager:	Michelle Stone Weathers, ACS
Print Buyer:	Audrey H. Gregory
Copyeditor:	Sally M. Farnham
Index:	Robert D. Land, FLMI, ACS
Permissions Coordinator:	Iris F. Hartley, FLMI, ALHC
Production/Print Coordinator:	Amy Souwan
Administrative Support:	Aurelia Kennedy-Hemphill
Interior Design:	Amy Souwan
Cover Design:	Allison Ayers
	Amy Souwan
Cover Photo:	comstock.com

Copyright © 2002 LOMA (Life Office Management Association, Inc.) *All rights reserved.*

10 09 08 07 06 05 04 03 02   10 9 8 7 6 5 4 3 2 1

This text, or any part thereof, may not be reproduced or transmitted in any form or by any means, electronic or mechanical, including photocopying, recording, storage in an information retrieval system, or otherwise, without the prior written permission of the publisher.

While a great deal of care has been taken to provide accurate, current, and authoritative information in regard to the subject matter covered in this book, the ideas, suggestions, general principles, conclusions, and any other information presented here are for general educational purposes only. This text is sold with the understanding that it is neither designed nor intended to provide the reader with legal, accounting, investment, marketing, or any other types of professional business management advice. If legal advice or other expert assistance is required, the services of a competent professional should be sought.

Library of Congress Cataloging-in-Publication Data

Jones, Harriett E.
    Regulatory compliance: insurance and annuity products / Harriett E. Jones, Monica R. Maxwell.-- 2nd ed.
       p. cm.
    Includes bibliographical references and index.
      ISBN 1-57974-168-1 (pbk.)
     1. Insurance, Life--United States--State supervision. 2. Insurance, Health--United States--State supervision. I. Maxwell, Monica R., 1972- II. Life Office Management Association. III. Title.
HG8958 .J66 1998
368.3′00973--dc21

                                                                2002023590

ISBN 1-57974-168-1

Printed in the United States of America

Contents

Preface ix

Chapter 1: Regulation of Individual Life Insurance Products 2

Life Insurance Product Development 3
    Policy Form Development 4
    Actuarial Considerations 18
    Distribution Method 20
    Underwriting Considerations 23
Regulation of Specific Products 24
    Variable Life Insurance 24
    Universal Life Insurance 30
    Industrial Life Insurance 34

Chaper 2: Life Insurance Advertising and Disclosure Requirements ... 38

Unfair Trade Practices Act 39
Regulation of Life Insurance Advertising 43
    Regulatory Requirements 44
    Insurers' Compliance Responsibilities 47
Life Insurance Sales Illustrations 48
    Contents of Basic Sales Illustrations 50
    Contents of Supplemental Illustrations 53
    Delivery of Illustrations 54
    Periodic Reporting Requirements 55
Disclosure Requirements 56
    General Disclosure Requirements 56
    Variable Life Insurance Disclosure Requirements 58
    Pre-Need Funeral Contracts 60
Emerging Market Conduct Issues 61

Chapter 3: Regulation of Individual Health Insurance Products 64

Health Insurance Product Development 66
    Policy Form Development 66
    Mandated Benefits 84
Actuarial Considerations 92
    Minimum Reserve Standards 92
    Premium Rate Filing Requirements 93

Chapter 4: Health Insurance Advertising and Solicitation Disclosure Requirements 96

Regulation of Health Insurance Advertising 97
- Advertising Requirements 99
- Insurer's Compliance Responsibilities 105

Solicitation Disclosure Requirements 107

Chapter 5: Regulation of Specific Health Insurance Products 110

Medicare Supplement Insurance 111
- Required Policy Provisions 112
- Benefit Standards 113
- Standard Benefit Plans 114
- Advertising Requirements 116
- Marketing Standards 116
- Disclosure Requirements 117
- Additional Requirements 118
- Health Insurers' Compliance Responsibilities 120

Long-Term Care Insurance 121
- Policy Provisions 123
- Standards for Benefit Triggers 125
- Requirements for Application Forms 126
- Advertising Requirements 127
- Marketing Standards 127
- Solicitation Disclosure Requirements 129
- Suitability Standards 131
- Additional Requirements 133
- Insurers' Compliance Responsibilities 133

Chapter 6: Regulation of Managed Care Plans 136

Regulation of HMOs 139
- Licensing of HMOs 141
- Solvency Requirements 142
- Enrollee Contracts 143
- Filing and Reporting Requirements 144
- Disclosure Requirements 145
- Regulatory Supervision and Enforcement 145

State Regulation of Managed Care Plans	145
Regulation of Preferred Provider Arrangements	148
Legislative Concerns	149

Chapter 7: Regulation of Reinsurance Agreements ... 152

Types of Reinsurance Agreements	154
Assumption Reinsurance	154
Indemnity Reinsurance	160
Business Purposes for Reinsurance	162
Relief of Surplus Strain	162
Meeting Marketing Objectives	165
Regulation of Reinsurance Intermediaries	166

Chapter 8: State Regulation of Group Life and Health Insurance ... 170

Group Insurance Product Development	173
Eligible Groups	173
Dependent Coverage	181
Standard Policy Provisions	181
Regulation of Insurance Issued to Small Groups	191
Regulatory Jurisdiction	195

Chapter 9: Federal Regulation of Group Life and Health Insurance Plans ... 198

Consolidated Omnibus Budget Reconciliation Act	201
Qualifying Events	202
COBRA Continuation Coverage	203
Notice Requirements	206
Election Period	207
Enforcement Provisions	207
Health Insurance Portability and Accountability Act	208
Preexisting Conditions	208
Special Enrollment Period	215
Nondiscrimination Requirements	217
Guaranteed Availability Requirement	217
Guaranteed Renewability Requirement	219
Enforcement Provisions	219
Other Federal Requirements	221

Chapter 10: Regulation of Credit Life and Health Insurance 224

Product Development 231
- Policy Form Development 231
- Actuarial Considerations 240
- Marketing Considerations 241

Disclosure Requirements 244
Claims Handling 245
Insurer's Compliance Responsibilities 245

Chapter 11: Regulation of Annuities and Retirement Products ... 248

State Regulation of Annuities 250
- Product Development 250
- Advertising and Disclosure Requirements 255

Regulation of Specific Annuity Products 257
- Variable Annuities 257
- Modified Guaranteed Annuities 257
- Equity-Indexed Annuities 259

Regulation of Retirement Products 260
- Individual Retirement Plans 260
- Group Retirement Plans 264
- Other Types of Retirement Plans 272

Appendix A 275
Appendix B 281
Glossary 285
Index 313

Preface

The purpose of *Regulatory Compliance: Insurance and Annuity Products* is to describe how the state and federal governments regulate the life insurance, health insurance, and annuity products that are offered by insurance companies in the United States. This book has been designed for students who are preparing for LOMA's AIRC 420 examination.

Several features have been included in each chapter to help you organize your studies, reinforce your understanding of the materials, and prepare for the examination. As we describe each of these features, we offer suggestions for studying the material.

Learning Objectives. The first page of each chapter contains a list of learning objectives to help you focus your studies. Before reading each chapter, review these learning objectives. Then, as you read the chapter, look for material that will help you meet the learning objectives.

Key Terms and Concepts. This text assumes that you have a basic knowledge of the key terms and concepts associated with insurance principles and products and the key terms and concepts that were introduced in the AIRC 410 text, *Regulatory Compliance: Companies, Producers, and Operations*. In some cases, these basic terms and concepts are also reviewed and explained in this text. All "new" terminology introduced in this text is defined or explained when it is first used. Important terminology is highlighted in ***italic, boldface type*** when the term is first used or defined and is included in a list of key terms and concepts at the end of each chapter. All key terms are also included in a comprehensive glossary at the end of the book; each glossary entry identifies in brackets the number of the chapter in which the term is defined. As you read each chapter, pay special attention to these key terms, some of which are defined in Figures and Insights.

Insights. Excerpts from industry publications and other sources appear throughout the text and are designed to amplify the text's descriptions of certain topics. These Insights should help you get a better feel for compliance in life and health insurance companies.

Test Preparation Guide (TPG) assignment. In addition to this textbook, LOMA's *Test Preparation Guide for Regulatory Compliance: Insurance and Annuity Products* (TPG) is assigned reading for students preparing for the AIRC 420 examination. Used along with the textbook, the TPG will help you master the course material. Included in the TPG are practice exam questions for each chapter, a full-scale sample examination in both paper and electronic format, and answers to all of the questions in the TPG.

LOMA recommends that you use the Test Preparation Guide for this course. **Studies indicate that students who use LOMA study aids consistently perform significantly better on LOMA examinations than do students who do not use study aids.**

Acknowledgments

No matter how much work the authors put into developing a book, many other individuals provide valuable expertise and assistance that make the book possible. Developing and revising *Regulatory Compliance: Insurance and Annuity Products* required the combined efforts of many highly qualified experts in the insurance industry. On behalf of LOMA and its membership, the authors would like to express appreciation to those individuals who generously gave their time and energy and shared their considerable expertise for the development of this textbook.

Textbook Development Panel

Members of the textbook development panel reviewed each chapter as it was written. These individuals have overseen the entire project from beginning to end and have made many valuable contributions. Their critical judgment, diligence, patience, and technical expertise were essential to the book's accuracy and completeness. The members of the textbook development panel include:

- Robert M. Ahlschwede, CLU, FLMI, AIRC,
  RMA Consulting, LLC

- Marc E. Cavadel, J.D., FLMI, AAPA, AIRC, AIAA, ARA, ACS, CSF, Director of Compliance, Investment Products Division, Protective Life Insurance Company

- Paul Clark, CLU, FLMI, ACS, AIE, Insurance Policy Analyst, Office of the Commissioner of Insurance for Georgia

- Karen A. Johnson, Second Vice President, New England Life Insurance Company

- James R. Ruegg, CLU, FLMI/M, AIRC, AIAA, ARA, ACS, Assistant Vice President, Amica Life Insurance Company

We also would like to thank Sara Livergood, ACS, FLMI, ASF, Compliance Supervisor, Woodmen of the World Life Insurance Society and Karen J.

Alvarado, Assistant Vice President, Regulatory Affairs, Pacific Life Insurance Company.

With permission from the publisher, this second edition of *Regulatory Compliance: Insurance and Annuity Products* draws heavily upon research originally conducted for the first edition of *Regulatory Compliance: Insurance and Annuity Products*. For this reason, we would like to thank the industry experts who served on the textbook development panel and contributed to the first edition of this textbook:

- Robert M. Ahlschwede, CLU, FLMI, AIRC
- Karen Allen
- Suzanne Arundale, FLMI, ACS
- Lynn Carlson
- Paul Clark, CLU, FLMI, ACS, AIE
- Mindy K. Elfand
- Karen Frick, FLMI, ACS, HIA
- Carol Fritchie
- Joy Herman, FLMI, ACS, HIA, AIAA
- Peggy L. Johnson, FLMI
- Donna L. Kaywood
- Peter Larson, CLU
- William F. Megna
- Marguerite Menefee, FLMI
- Eric S. Miller, FLMI
- Timothy D. Morris, FLMI
- G. Thomas Roberts
- Julia B. Roper, CLU, ChFC
- James R. Ruegg, CLU, FLMI/M, AIRC, AIAA, ARA, ACS
- Lillie Schlessinger, FLMI
- June Stracener, FLMI
- Wayne G. Vosik
- John Weynand

LOMA Staff/Consultants

All textbooks developed by LOMA are team projects. The following individuals deserve special mention for the work they performed on this text. Joyce R. Abrams, J.D., FLMI, ACS, AIRC, AIAA, ALHC, HIA, PAHM, MHP, Assistant Vice President, Education & Training Division, served as project manager. LOMA consultant Sally M. Farnham served as copyeditor. LOMA consultant Iris F. Hartley, FLMI, ALHC, obtained the permissions for use of copyrighted material. LOMA consultant Robert D. Land, FLMI, ACS, developed the index. Aurelia K. Hemphill, Administrative Assistant III, Education & Training Division, provided administrative support. Amy Souwan, Production Coordinator II/Scheduling Coordinator, Production Department, designed the interior layout of the textbook, typeset the textbook, coordinated printing, and assisted in designing the cover for the textbook. Allison Ayers, Production Coordinator II, Production Department, assisted in designing the cover for the textbook. Michelle Stone Weathers, ACS, Manager, Production Department, guided the project through production.

Special thanks must go to Katherine C. Milligan, FLMI, ACS, ALHC, Second Vice President, Education & Training Division, and William H. Rabel, Ph.D., FLMI, CLU, Senior Vice President, Education & Training Division for their encouragement and support throughout the text's development.

Harriett E. Jones, J.D., FLMI, ACS
Monica R. Maxwell, J.D., FLMI
Atlanta, Georgia
2002

CHAPTER 1

Regulation of Individual Life Insurance Products

LEARNING OBJECTIVES

After studying this chapter, you should be able to

- Identify the types of regulatory requirements insurers must consider as they create individual life insurance policy provisions, policy forms, pricing structures, and underwriting guidelines

- Identify the provisions state insurance laws require individual life insurance policy forms to include, as well as the provisions that may be included at the insurer's option and the provisions that are prohibited

- Recognize regulatory requirements imposed on specific life insurance policy provisions, including requirements imposed by the Standard Nonforfeiture Law for Life Insurance, the Model Policy Loan Interest Rate Bill, and the Accelerated Benefits Model Regulation

- Identify the requirements insurers must meet in order to market variable life insurance policies and the provisions insurers are required to include in variable life insurance policies

- Identify the provisions insurers must include in universal life insurance policies

- Recognize regulatory requirements imposed on industrial life insurance policies

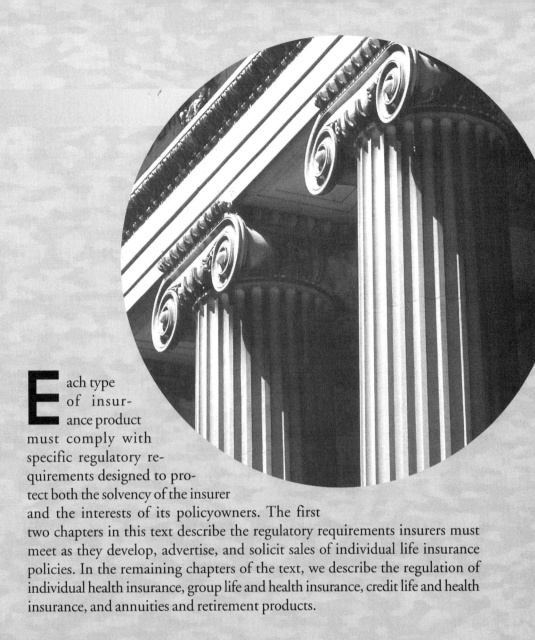

Each type of insurance product must comply with specific regulatory requirements designed to protect both the solvency of the insurer and the interests of its policyowners. The first two chapters in this text describe the regulatory requirements insurers must meet as they develop, advertise, and solicit sales of individual life insurance policies. In the remaining chapters of the text, we describe the regulation of individual health insurance, group life and health insurance, credit life and health insurance, and annuities and retirement products.

LIFE INSURANCE PRODUCT DEVELOPMENT

In this section, we describe the compliance issues that insurers must consider as they develop new life insurance products. By *new product*, we mean a product that is new in any way for the insurer concerned. Thus, a new product can be (1) a product that is new to a particular company, but has been available from other companies; (2) a currently offered product that the insurer is modifying, revising, or improving in some way; or (3) a totally new product that has never been conceived of or previously offered by any insurer.

The work of designing insurance products is typically performed by the members of a product development team. Team members represent every area of technical expertise important to insurers, including actuarial, marketing, underwriting, claim administration, investments, information systems, policyowner service, accounting, legal, and compliance. Figure 1-1 provides an overview of the process that insurers typically use to develop insurance products. In this chapter, we focus on the technical product design stage in which the product development team creates the individual life insurance policy form, prices the product, and develops underwriting and issue guidelines.

An individual life insurance policy usually must be filed with and approved by the state insurance department of each state in which the policy will be marketed and sold. During the product implementation stage, the insurer's product development team puts together a submission package that contains all required information for a policy form filing. Figure 1-2 lists the types of materials that often must be included in a policy form filing submission package. If the product will be marketed and sold in more than one state, the insurer must make appropriate modifications to the policy form and the submission package to ensure that they comply with the regulatory requirements of each state.

Life insurance products take a variety of forms, but most products can be classified into two broad categories: term life insurance and permanent life insurance. *Term life insurance* provides a death benefit if the insured dies during a specified period. If the insured survives until the end of the period, the life insurance coverage generally ceases without value. *Permanent life insurance* provides coverage throughout the insured's lifetime as long as premiums are paid when due and also usually provides a "savings" element that builds a cash value. Permanent life insurance includes products such as whole life insurance, endowment insurance, universal life insurance, and variable life insurance.

Regulatory requirements vary depending on the type of insurance plan a policy provides. In this section, we describe the regulatory requirements that generally apply to all individual life insurance policies. Later in the chapter, we describe regulatory requirements that apply to specific products, including universal life insurance and variable life insurance. In Chapters 8 and 9, we describe the requirements that are imposed on group life insurance plans.

Policy Form Development

For each new individual insurance product it develops, a life insurer develops a policy form and adapts that form to meet all regulatory requirements of each state in which the policy will be delivered or issued for delivery. When it issues a policy, the insurer tailors the policy form by adding information that identifies the policyowner, the person insured, and the amount of coverage provided. This customized policy represents the contractual agreement between the insurer and the policyowner.

FIGURE 1-1 Overview of the Insurance Product Development Process.

Idea generation is the phase in which the insurer gathers ideas for new products that will meet the needs of both the insurer and specific segments of the market for insurance.

 Idea screening is a weeding-out process designed to evaluate new product ideas quickly and inexpensively in order to determine which ideas warrant further investigation.

Comprehensive business analysis is the phase in which the insurer analyzes the feasibility of each product idea by conducting market analyses, preparing preliminary sales forecasts, performing actuarial calculations to evaluate whether the product can be priced so that it is both competitive and profitable, determining whether the insurer's operating and distribution systems can accommodate the product, and determining the type of investments the insurer must make in order for the product to be successful.

 Technical product design is the phase in which the insurer creates the product provisions, product language, pricing and dividend structures, and underwriting and issue specifications.

Product implementation refers to the phase in which the insurer files the policy form, application, and other related documents with appropriate state insurance departments; receives required regulatory approvals; and creates advertising and other sales and marketing materials. In some states, advertising materials must be filed with, and sometimes approved by, the state insurance department. Variable products that are subject to federal securities laws also must be registered with the Securities and Exchange Commission (SEC).

 **Product introduction** refers to the phase in which the insurer begins advertising and marketing the product.

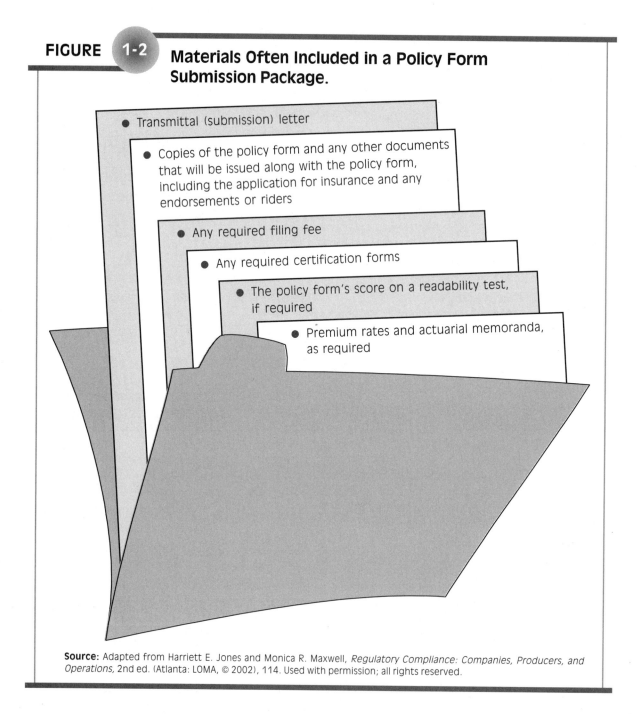

FIGURE 1-2 Materials Often Included in a Policy Form Submission Package.

- Transmittal (submission) letter
- Copies of the policy form and any other documents that will be issued along with the policy form, including the application for insurance and any endorsements or riders
- Any required filing fee
- Any required certification forms
- The policy form's score on a readability test, if required
- Premium rates and actuarial memoranda, as required

Source: Adapted from Harriett E. Jones and Monica R. Maxwell, *Regulatory Compliance: Companies, Producers, and Operations,* 2nd ed. (Atlanta: LOMA, © 2002), 114. Used with permission; all rights reserved.

In developing a policy form, an insurer must meet regulatory requirements concerning readability, required and optional policy provisions, and prohibited policy provisions. (The requirements regarding required, optional, and prohibited policy provisions are summarized in Figure 1-3.) The insurer also must develop all other documents that may be attached to the policy when it is issued.

FIGURE 1-3: Required, Optional, and Prohibited Life Insurance Policy Provisions.

REQUIRED PROVISIONS

All individual life policies:
- Free-look provision
- Entire contract provision
- Grace period provision
- Incontestability provision
- Misstatement of age provision
- Reinstatement provision

Participating policies:
- Dividend provision

Permanent policies:
- Nonforfeiture provision
- Policy loan provision

OPTIONAL PROVISIONS
- Assignment provision
- Accelerated death benefit provision
- Exclusions, such as a suicide exclusion, war exclusion, or aviation exclusion

PROHIBITED PROVISIONS
- Backdating beyond a specified period

Readability Requirements

In most states, insurers must comply with regulatory requirements based on the *Life and Health Insurance Policy Language Simplification Model Act* developed by the National Association of Insurance Commissioners (NAIC). Laws based on this model are designed to simplify the language used in individual life and health policies so that consumers are better able to understand the terms of their policies. Most states require individual life insurance policies—other than variable life policies—to achieve a minimum score on a readability test such as the Flesch reading ease test or a comparable test that has been approved by the state insurance department. In these states, a policy form filing submission package usually must include a certification stating that the policy form meets the minimum score.

Policy Face Page Requirements

Although requirements vary somewhat, many states require the face—or first—page of an individual life insurance policy to contain a title or other description of the type of life insurance product the policy represents. Some states require this description to include a statement as to whether the policy is a participating or nonparticipating policy. In addition, the face page of an individual life insurance policy usually must include the following information:

- The name and address of the insurer issuing the policy

- The *insuring clause*, which contains the insurer's contractual promise to pay the policy benefits in accordance with the provisions contained in the policy

- The signature of officers of the insurer—usually the president and secretary—evidencing that the insurer has issued the policy and intends to be bound by its terms

The policy form number the insurer has assigned to the product must appear in the lower left-hand corner of each page of a life insurance policy, including on the face page. Most states require individual life policies to include on the face page a *free-look provision* that allows a policyowner a specified period—usually 10 days—following delivery of a policy within which to cancel the policy and receive a refund of all premiums paid. Although the other states also require a free-look provision, these states do not require the provision to be on the policy face page. The free-look period allows a policyowner time to review the policy and evaluate whether it is the policy applied for and is the product best suited to his needs. Finally, term life insurance policies that include a renewal provision must include that provision on the policy face page. The *renewal provision* gives the policyowner the right, within specified limits, to renew the insurance coverage at the end of the specified term without submitting evidence of insurability.

Policies typically include a separate policy data page that follows the face page and that contains the following information:

- The name of the person who is insured by the policy and the name of the policyowner

- The amount of insurance coverage provided by the policy, often referred to as the *face amount* of the policy

- The date the policy takes effect, usually known as the *policy date*

Provisions Required in All Individual Life Insurance Policies

Most states have enacted laws that spell out the required wording of standard provisions that insurers must include in individual life insurance policies. Insurers, however, have the right to include provisions that are more favorable to policyowners than those required by law. As part of the policy form approval process, the state insurance departments review policy provisions to ensure compliance with applicable laws.

We mentioned earlier that most states require individual life insurance policies to include a free-look provision. The following provisions also generally must be included in all individual life insurance policies: an entire contract provision, a grace period provision, an incontestability provision, a misstatement of age provision, and a reinstatement provision. In addition, participating life insurance policies must include a dividend provision.

Entire contract provision. The *entire contract provision* defines which documents constitute the contract between the insurer and the policyowner. The specific wording of the entire contract provision varies depending on whether the policy is a closed contract or an open contract. With the exception of fraternal insurers, U.S. insurers issue individual life insurance policies that are closed contracts. A *closed contract* is a contract for which only those terms and conditions that are printed in—or attached to—the policy are considered to be part of the contract. In a closed contract, the entire contract provision states that the contract consists of the policy, any attached riders and endorsements, and the attached copy of the application. As a result of the entire contract provision, if a copy of the application is not attached to a policy, then the insurer is prohibited from contesting the validity of the policy based on information contained in the application.

Fraternal insurers issue life insurance coverage in the form of an *open contract*, which is a contract that identifies the documents that constitute the contract between the parties, but the enumerated documents are not all attached to the contract. Typically, policies issued by a fraternal insurer state that the entire contract between the parties consists of the following documents:

- The policy and any attached riders and endorsements
- The fraternal society's charter, constitution, and bylaws
- The application for membership in the society
- The declaration of insurability, if any, signed by the applicant

Typically, the fraternal insurer attaches a copy of the application for membership and the declaration of insurability to the policy delivered to an insured member. Although the fraternal's charter, constitution, and bylaws are not attached to the policy, those documents are available to society members, and the terms of those documents are enforceable by the parties as part of the contractual agreement.

Grace period provision. The *grace period provision* allows a policyowner to pay a renewal premium within a stated time following a premium due date. Life insurance coverage continues in force throughout the policy's grace period, regardless of whether the renewal premium is ever paid. The insurer, however, is entitled to deduct the amount of any premium due from the death benefit payable when a covered loss occurs during the grace period. For term and whole life insurance policies, the grace period usually is 31 days. Universal life policies usually include a 61-day grace period.

Incontestability provision. The *incontestability provision* limits the time during which the insurer may contest the validity of the insurance contract on the ground of a material misrepresentation in the application for insurance. Most states also require policies to specify that statements an applicant makes in an application for life insurance shall be treated as *representations* rather than *warranties*. A *representation* is a statement made by a party to a contract that will invalidate the contract if the statement is not *substantially* true. A *warranty* is a statement made by a party to a contract that will invalidate the contract if the statement is not *literally* true. A **material misrepresentation** in an application for life insurance is a misrepresentation that is relevant to the insurer's evaluation of the proposed insured. A misrepresentation is material when, if the truth had been known, the insurer would not have issued the policy or would have issued the policy on a different basis, such as for a higher premium or for a lower face amount. Some examples of misrepresentations are given in Figure 1-4.

Rules of contract law give the insurer the right to contest the validity of a life insurance policy, and the incontestability provision limits the time during which the insurer may exercise that right. States typically impose a maximum period of two years during the life of the insured and following policy issue in which an insurer has the right to contest an individual life insurance policy.

Misstatement of age provision. The *misstatement of age provision* describes how the policy death benefit will be adjusted if the age of the insured has been misstated. The misstatement of age provision generally must provide that the amount of benefit payable will be adjusted to the amount of insurance that the premiums paid would have provided had the insured's age been stated correctly.

FIGURE 1-4 Examples of Misrepresentation.

EXAMPLE 1

In her application for life insurance, Joy Kagelmacher stated that she had seen her doctor on July 10 for treatment of a broken bone in her left foot. In fact, she was treated for a broken bone in her right foot.

Ms. Kagelmacher's misrepresentation probably was not a material misrepresentation. Although her statement was not literally true, her statement was substantially true and provided the insurer with the material facts it needed to evaluate her insurability.

EXAMPLE 2

In his application for life insurance, Cicero Degolian stated that he saw his doctor on September 1 for a routine physical examination. In fact, the appointment had been for treatment of heart disease and Mr. Degolian did not otherwise disclose that he had been treated for heart disease.

Mr. Degolian's misrepresentation was probably a material misrepresentation because the fact that he had been treated for heart disease is likely to affect the insurer's decision as to whether to insure him and, if so, the premium rate to charge him.

The misstatement of age provision included in life insurance policies also may include requirements concerning how the insurer will treat a misstatement of the insured's sex. In these cases, the provision is known as the *misstatement of age and sex provision*. All states but Montana permit—but do not require—insurers to include a misstatement of sex provision stating that, if the insured's sex has been misstated, then the insurer will adjust the amount of the policy death benefit to the amount the premiums paid would have provided had the insured's sex been stated correctly.[1]

Reinstatement provision. The *reinstatement provision* gives the owner of a policy that either has lapsed for nonpayment of premium or has been continued under the extended term or reduced paid-up nonforfeiture options the right to reinstate the policy by meeting specified requirements. Note, however, that a policy that has been surrendered by the owner in return for payment of the cash value is not eligible for reinstatement. State laws require policies to provide at least a specified period—usually three years—in which to reinstate a policy that has lapsed or continued under a nonforfeiture option.

Participating policies. Participating life insurance policies also must include a *dividend provision* that describes the policyowner's right to share in the insurer's divisible surplus and the dividend payment options available to the policyowner. Insurers generally include five dividend payment options in their participating life insurance policies: the cash dividend option, the premium reduction option, the accumulation at interest option, the paid-up additional insurance option, and the additional term insurance dividend option.

Provisions Required in Permanent Life Insurance Policies

In addition to the provisions just described, permanent life insurance policies that build a cash value generally must include a nonforfeiture provision and a policy loan provision.

Nonforfeiture provision. The *nonforfeiture provision* specifies the nonforfeiture benefit options available to a policyowner who elects to stop paying renewal premiums. State laws generally require insurers to provide a cash surrender value after a permanent life insurance policy has been in force for a specified minimum time, typically three years. All states have enacted laws based on the NAIC *Standard Nonforfeiture Law for Life Insurance*, which specifies how a policy's minimum cash surrender value is calculated.

Policy loan provision. The *policy loan provision* specifies the terms on which a policyowner may obtain a policy loan. Almost all states have adopted requirements based on the NAIC *Model Policy Loan Interest Rate Bill*, which places a maximum limit on the interest rate that may be charged on policy loans and requires insurers to state the applicable interest rate in their policy forms.

Optional Policy Provisions

In addition to policy provisions that are required to be included in individual life insurance policies, a number of provisions may be included in such policies at the insurer's discretion.

Assignment provision. Most individual life insurance policies include an *assignment provision* that describes the policyowner's right to assign the policy and the responsibilities of the insurer and the policyowner when the policyowner exercises this right to assign the policy. An *assignment* is an agreement under which one party transfers some or all of his ownership rights in a particular property to another. A policyowner might, for example, assign some of his ownership rights in a life insurance policy as security for a loan.

General rules of property law give the owner of a life insurance policy the right to assign policy ownership rights. As a result, a policyowner has the right to assign ownership rights without regard to whether the life insurance policy contains an assignment provision. An insurer, however, may restrict or prohibit a policyowner from exercising this right by including such a restriction in the policy. Industrial life insurance policies often contain a provision restricting the policyowner's right to assign the policy. (Industrial life insurance will be described later in the chapter.) Other individual life insurance policies generally do not prohibit assignments.

Accelerated death benefit provision. Individual life insurance policies may include an *accelerated death benefit provision* that gives the policyowner the right to receive a portion—usually between 50 and 80 percent—of the policy benefit during the insured's lifetime when the insured is terminally ill as defined in the policy. Typically, the policyowner is also the insured and policy benefits are paid to the policyowner-insured. Sometimes, an accelerated death benefit is provided by a separate rider attached to a life insurance policy. (We describe policy riders later in the chapter.)

A number of states have adopted requirements based on the NAIC *Accelerated Benefits Model Regulation*, which is designed to regulate accelerated death benefit provisions and to impose disclosure standards on insurers that provide such benefits. According to the Model Regulation, policies must provide that the policyowner is entitled to receive the accelerated death benefit upon the occurrence of any of the following qualifying events:

- The insured has a medical condition that will drastically limit her life span as specified in the policy—for example, the insured is expected to live 24 months or less.

- The insured has a medical condition that requires extraordinary medical intervention, such as a major organ transplant or continuous artificial life support.

- The insured has any condition that requires continuous confinement in an eligible institution, as defined in the policy, and the insured is expected to remain there for the rest of her life.

- The insured has a medical condition that, without extensive medical treatment, would drastically limit her life span.

If a policy has been assigned or is payable to an irrevocable beneficiary, the Model Regulation requires the insurer to obtain written permission from the assignee or beneficiary before paying an accelerated benefit. The policyowner must be given the right to take the accelerated benefit as a lump sum, and the insurer may not place restrictions on how the recipient uses the proceeds.

As noted, the Accelerated Benefits Model Regulation imposes a number of disclosure requirements on insurers that include accelerated benefits provisions in their life insurance policies. As they solicit the sale of policies that include an accelerated death benefit provision, insurers must comply with the following requirements:

- The applicant for insurance must be given a written disclosure that describes the accelerated benefit and the events that qualify for payment of accelerated benefits. When the policy is solicited by an insurance producer, the producer must provide this disclosure no later than when the application is completed; the applicant and producer must sign an acknowledgement of the disclosure. When the policy is solicited by direct response methods, the insurer must provide the disclosure when the policy is delivered to the applicant.

- If the policyowner is charged an additional premium for an accelerated death benefit, then the insurer must provide the applicant an illustration that demonstrates how payment of accelerated death benefits will affect the policy's cash value, death benefit, premium, and policy loans. This disclosure must be provided at the time of application if an insurance producer is involved or at the time of policy delivery in the case of direct response sales.

- The insurer must disclose to the policyowner any administrative expense charges that will be imposed on the payment of accelerated death benefits.

When a policyowner requests the payment of accelerated death benefits, the insurer must send the policyowner a statement showing how the payment of an accelerated benefit will affect the policy's cash value, death benefit, premium, and policy loans.

The Model Regulation also imposes actuarial standards on how insurers calculate the premium charged for an accelerated death benefit and requires insurers to include actuarial information about accelerated death benefits as part of the policy form filing submission package.

Policy exclusions. Individual life insurance policies may include provisions known as *exclusions*, which describe situations in which the insurer will not pay policy proceeds following the death of the insured. The primary exclusion currently included in individual life insurance policies is a *suicide exclusion provision*, which states that policy proceeds will not be paid if the insured dies as the result of suicide within a specified period following the date of policy issue. Insurance laws in most states protect policyowners and beneficiaries by limiting the length of the suicide exclusion period to a specified maximum, usually two years. Policies are permitted to include other exclusions, including the following:

- Death resulting from war and acts of war may be excluded from coverage. Although the basic coverage provided by a life insurance policy is rarely subject to a war exclusion, insurers often include a war exclusion for additional benefits provided by life insurance policies, including accidental death benefit and waiver of premium coverages. Rather than including a war exclusion in their policies, insurers typically refuse applications for life insurance from military personnel when the United States is involved in an armed conflict.

- A life insurance policy may exclude from coverage death resulting from specified aviation activities. Typically, insurers issue coverage to proposed insureds who engage in aviation activities and, if necessary, increase the premium rate charged for the increased risk presented by such activities. Insurers generally include an aviation exclusion in a life insurance policy only when the proposed insured's aviation activities present a risk that is too great for any coverage or that is too uncertain to measure.

- When a proposed insured engages in a hazardous occupation or avocation, such as parachute jumping or auto racing, the insurer may exclude the specified activity from coverage.

Laws in most states require insurers that include an exclusionary provision in their policies to also include a provision specifying the insurer's obligation to return the premiums paid for a policy in the event the insured's death is excluded from coverage. State requirements vary somewhat. The insurer may be required to return all premiums paid, plus interest, less the amount of any outstanding policy loans. Alternatively, the insurer may be required to return the amount of the policy's net cash value. Some policies provide that the insurer will pay whichever of these two amounts is larger.

Prohibited Policy Provisions

States prohibit insurers from including specified provisions in individual life insurance policies because the provisions are deemed to be against public policy.

Most states, for example, prohibit insurers from backdating individual life insurance policies for a period of more than six months. ***Backdating*** is a practice by which an insurer makes the effective date of an insurance policy earlier than the date of the application. Backdating typically is used either to reduce the premium rate payable for a policy or to comply with a legal requirement, such as a divorce decree or a business buy-sell agreement that required coverage to begin by a specified date. When a policy is backdated, however, a premium is payable for a period of time during which no coverage was provided. Other prohibitions vary a great deal from state to state, but they generally are designed to prevent insurers from unfairly limiting the rights of policyowners and policy beneficiaries.

Application for Insurance

The application form for an individual life insurance product is created along with the policy form and must be designed to provide the insurer with the information it will need to evaluate and underwrite the application. When they issue policies, insurers attach a copy of the policyowner's application for insurance to the policy delivered to the policyowner, and the application becomes a part of the contractual agreement between the policyowner and the insurer. As a result, the insurer has the right to contest the validity of the contract on the ground of material misrepresentation in the application. Most states require insurers to file the application for an individual life insurance policy with the state insurance department as part of the policy form filing submission package. Thus, the application may not be used in the state until it is approved by the state insurance department.

Although requirements vary, most states impose regulatory requirements on information contained in applications for individual life insurance. The following types of requirements are imposed:

- Many states require applications to include a fraud warning, which notifies the applicant that knowingly presenting false information is a crime.

- All states require the name of the insurer to be included on application forms, and many states require application forms to contain the insurer's home office address.

- Some states require an application to include the name and state license number of the insurance producer who assists the applicant in completing the application.

- Most states require applications to contain specific questions about whether the policy applied for will replace an existing policy or contract.

Premium Receipts

The rules of contract law impose a number of requirements for the creation of an individual life insurance contract. One such requirement is that the initial premium must be paid before the contract becomes effective. Applicants often pay the initial premium when they complete the application for insurance. In exchange for an initial premium payment, the insurance producer generally gives the applicant a *premium receipt*, which provides the proposed insured with some type of temporary insurance coverage while the application is being underwritten. A premium receipt may be either a binding premium receipt or a conditional premium receipt.

A *binding premium receipt*, also known as a *temporary insurance agreement (TIA)*, provides temporary insurance coverage from the time the applicant receives the receipt. If the proposed insured dies before the insurer completes its evaluation of the application, the receipt generally provides a death benefit. Temporary coverage under a binding premium receipt typically remains effective until the earliest of the following occurrences: (1) the insurer issues the applicant a policy, (2) the insurer declines the application, (3) the insurer terminates or suspends coverage under the receipt, or (4) a specified time—usually 45 to 60 days—expires.

Other premium receipts, known as *conditional premium receipts*, specify certain conditions that must be met before the temporary insurance coverage provided by the receipt becomes effective. One type of conditional receipt, known as an *approval premium receipt*, specifies that the temporary coverage provided by the receipt becomes effective when the insurer approves the application; should the proposed insured die before the application is approved, the receipt provides no coverage. The other type of conditional receipt, known as an *insurability premium receipt*, specifies that the temporary coverage becomes effective when the receipt is issued *if* the insurer finds the proposed insured to be insurable. Should a proposed insured die before the application is approved, the insurer completes the underwriting process as if the insured were still alive. If the insurer determines that the proposed insured was insurable at the time of death, then the receipt provides coverage and a death benefit is payable. Note that the terms of an insurability premium receipt are more favorable to an applicant than the terms of an approval premium receipt.

In designing an individual life insurance policy form, an insurer must decide which type of premium receipt it will issue when the product is applied for and must ensure that the terms of the receipt are clear and unambiguous. The insurer also must consider how state courts have dealt with premium receipts. Courts in many states enforce the provisions of a premium receipt in accordance with the terms of the receipt. Courts in other states, however, interpret conditional premium receipts as if they were binding premium receipts.

Although state laws usually do not require insurers to file premium receipts for regulatory approval, insurers sometimes include a premium receipt as part of a policy form submission package.

Policy Riders

A *policy rider* is an amendment to an insurance policy; the rider becomes a part of the insurance contract and either expands or limits the benefits payable under the contract.[2] In all but a few states, exclusions may be contained in a policy rider. Riders are commonly used to provide some type of supplementary benefit, such as a waiver of premium for disability benefit, or to increase the amount of the death benefit provided by a policy. Any rider an insurer plans to attach to a new life insurance policy form must be filed with the state insurance department as part of the policy form filing submission package. In most states, a rider attached to a life insurance policy, even if it provides accident and health insurance benefits, must comply with the state insurance laws applicable to life insurance policies, and the rider is exempt from complying with regulatory requirements imposed on health insurance.

Actuarial Considerations

Actuaries are responsible for developing the mathematical features of life insurance products and for establishing the prices the insurer will charge for those products. Although actuaries focus on product pricing and related mathematical calculations, they are involved with all aspects of technical product design because those other aspects may affect the product's price. Each change to the design of a product may affect the product's actuarial calculations.

Insight 1-1 describes some basics of life insurance pricing and introduces basic terminology. Although state insurance laws do not directly regulate individual life insurance premium rates, various policy features that affect premium rates are regulated by state insurance laws. For example, permanent life insurance policies must provide nonforfeiture values, and those values must be calculated in compliance with applicable nonforfeiture laws. As described in Insight 1-1, policy reserves affect life insurance premium rates, and those reserves must comply with state requirements. *Reserves* are liabilities that represent amounts an insurer expects to pay to meet its future business obligations. State insurance laws in most states also give the state insurance department indirect authority to regulate life insurance premium rates. In these states, the insurance department is authorized to disapprove a policy form filing if the department determines that the benefits provided by the product are insufficient for the premium rates the insurer will charge for the product. In practice, state insurance departments rarely disapprove a policy form filing because the benefits provided are insufficient for the premium rates that will be charged.

> ### INSIGHT 1-1 Some Basics of Life Insurance Premiums.
>
> The amounts insurance companies charge for insurance products are known as *premiums*. The premium rates that actuaries establish for life insurance coverage are often expressed in terms of the charge per $1,000 of life insurance coverage. In reference to life insurance, $1,000 of coverage is known as a *unit of coverage*. The premium actuaries establish per unit of coverage in the process of rate making is usually a gross premium. A product's *gross premium* is the amount the insurer charges a policyowner for that product and is composed of two elements: the net premium and the loading. The premium is also influenced by another important element—the product's required reserves.
>
> **The Net Premium:** One of the first steps in pricing insurance products is to estimate the cost of benefits. A product's *cost of benefits* is the total amount the insurer is expected to pay out in contractually required benefits for the product. A *net premium* is the amount calculated to cover a product's expected cost of benefits. The cost of benefits generally is not equal to the net premium because expected investment earnings are used to partially offset the cost of benefits. The net premium is the amount per unit of coverage that will precisely pay for the product's cost of benefits, net of expected investment earnings. Net premium calculations are based on actuarial assumptions as to mortality rates, investment earnings rates, and policy lapse rates.
>
> **The Loading:** In addition to the cost of benefits, the gross premium charged for an insurance product must cover the expenses the insurer incurs in issuing the product and the cost of the insurer's operations. To pay for the expenses of doing business, insurers add to the net premium an amount called the *loading*. The amount of loading added to the net premium is based on an estimate of the company's operating expenses and product distribution expenses.
>
> **Policy Reserves:** When establishing the premium for an insurance product, actuaries consider the rate at which the product will accumulate policy reserves. A *policy reserve* is a liability that identifies the amount that the insurer expects to need in order to pay future policy benefits. Because they take into account *future* income expected to be earned from premiums and investments, policy reserves are generally less than the amount of death benefits provided by the policies. For permanent life policies, the policy reserve generally is lowest in a policy's early years, increasing over time. The difference between the amount of the policy death benefit promised and the policy reserve is known as the *net amount at risk* and represents the insurer's unfunded exposure to contractual liabilities. For permanent life insurance policies, the net amount at risk is generally highest in a policy's earliest years, decreasing over time as the policy reserve grows. For term life policies, the net amount at risk is generally high both at the beginning and at the end of the term. In calculating gross premiums, actuaries consider the rate at which policy reserves accumulate and the effect of this growth on the timing of a product's earnings.

Actuaries also assist in creating the policy form filing submission package. As stated earlier, insurance laws in most states do not require insurers to obtain state insurance department approval of life insurance premium rates. A significant exception to this general rule is that most states do require insurers to file credit life insurance premium rates. (We describe the regulatory requirements that are imposed on credit life and health insurance in Chapter 10.) Most states require the submission package for an individual life insurance policy form to include an actuarial memorandum showing that the policy complies with state actuarial requirements. A qualified actuary also must certify that the filing complies with applicable state laws and regulations. Actuaries who specialize in performing calculations and making decisions relating to designing and pricing insurance and other financial products are referred to as product actuaries, product design actuaries, or pricing actuaries. Whether an actuary is qualified to prepare an actuarial memorandum and sign such a certification depends on the actuary's work experience and professional qualifications.

Requirements as to what information must be included in the actuarial memorandum for a policy form filing vary from state to state, and they vary depending on the features of the policy form. The memorandum describing a permanent life insurance policy that provides nonforfeiture benefits must demonstrate how the policy's nonforfeiture values were calculated and that those values comply with applicable requirements. If a policy form provides supplementary benefits, such as accelerated death benefits, then those benefits must be described in the actuarial memorandum. For example, if a policy form contains an accelerated death benefit feature, then states that have adopted the Accelerated Benefits Model Regulation require the actuarial memorandum to describe the accelerated benefits, the risks, the expected costs, and the calculation of statutory reserves.

Distribution Method

During product development, an insurer must decide which method or methods it will use to market the product. Insurers primarily use two distribution methods to market individual life insurance.

1. Most individual life insurance is sold through personal selling distribution systems. *Personal selling* is a marketing method that uses commissioned or salaried sales personnel to sell products through oral presentations made to prospective purchasers; presentations usually are made face to face, but also are often made in telephone conversations. Various written materials may be presented to the prospect as part of such a presentation.

2. Some types of individual life insurance are often sold through direct response marketing. *Direct response marketing* is a marketing method that uses one or more media to elicit an immediate and measurable action—such as an inquiry or a purchase—from a customer. No agents or other

salespersons visit customers to induce sales, and no face-to-face contact occurs between consumers and the insurer or its insurance producers. The consumer purchases the product directly from the insurer by responding to the insurer's advertisements, mailings, or telephone solicitations. In order to be suitable for sale through direct response marketing, an insurance product must be designed for this type of distribution.

New distribution methods are constantly being created. For example, many insurers now use a combination method in which the initial contact is made through direct response marketing, which is followed by a personal contact by a licensed producer. State insurance regulators sometimes must adapt existing laws or create new laws in order to regulate new insurance distribution methods. Insight 1-2 describes some of the regulatory issues presented by insurers conducting business on the Internet.

INSIGHT 1-2   The Internet: A Sales and Regulatory Frontier.

The **Internet** is a worldwide collection of interconnected networks and computers that enables users to share information electronically and provides public, non-secured digital access to a wide variety of services. Users can access information on the Internet in a number of ways. One of the most popular access methods is the **World Wide Web (WWW)**, which is a section of the Internet that offers easy access to text, graphics, sound, and other multimedia resources. Each computer connected to the Internet has its own address, enabling it to send messages and receive messages from other addresses; these messages are typically referred to as **e-mail**. Internet capabilities allow insurers to (1) generate sales leads, (2) provide service to their customers, (3) establish companywide communications through intranets, and (4) better manage outsourced functions via extranets. An **intranet** is a private, Web-based network that connects employers and employees to vital corporate information. **Extranets**, also known as **field intranets**, are secure intranets made accessible to authorized users via the Internet for business-to-business communications.[3]

The marketing and sale of insurance on the Internet pose a variety of regulatory questions, and some of these questions are beginning to be answered. For example, most states require an applicant for an insurance policy to sign the application for insurance. With the enactment of state and federal laws, it has now become clear that insurers and purchasers can enter into insurance contracts electronically by means of electronic signatures, or E-signatures. A number of states have enacted laws, and most of those laws are based on the **Uniform Electronic Transactions Act (UETA)**.[4] The federal **Electronic Signatures in Global and National Commerce Act (ESIGN)**, which was enacted in 2000, basically mirrors the UETA.[5] The federal law will preempt only those state laws that conflict with the UETA. According to these laws, an electronic signature is given the same legal effect as a manual signature. In addition, these laws provide that records of electronic commerce can be stored electronically, rather than in paper form. Because E-signatures will reduce the time needed to complete the sale of insurance over the Internet and will eliminate

> **Insight 1-2. The Internet: A Sales and Regulatory Frontier,** *continued.*
>
> certain paperwork requirements, they also will reduce the costs involved in conducting such transactions.
>
> In a model bulletin adopted in 2000, the NAIC has set out the following guidelines for state insurance department regulation of electronic commerce.[6]
>
> - A state should not assert jurisdiction over a Web site that merely includes insurance content. Thus, the owner of a Web site that includes insurance advertisements is not "doing business" in a state if the owner does not otherwise solicit, negotiate, or sell insurance to individuals in that state.
> - As a general rule, advertising included in a Web site is subject to the same state regulatory requirements as are advertisements included in other media that are disseminated within a state.
> - Specific format requirements for printed documents are applied to Web content so as to ensure that the regulatory goals are met. Thus, for example, if a state requires that a document include information printed in a specific size font, then that content on a Web site is in compliance with the requirement if it is presented in a size that provides the same emphasis relative to the rest of the document as would be presented in a paper document.
> - An insurer can meet applicable record-keeping requirements if it can reassemble the original information upon request.
> - An insurer can meet requirements for the delivery of specific documents to customers by means of electronic communications. The insurer, however, must actually deliver such documents, must maintain such records as required, and must be able to provide an electronic or paper copy of such documents upon request. Customers are not required to accept such electronic communications unless they agree to do so.

In selecting the distribution method to use for a new life insurance product, an insurer must ensure compliance with regulatory requirements. For example, when a new product will be sold by personal selling, the insurer must ensure that its insurance producers are properly licensed to sell the product and, where required, that each producer has been appointed to represent the insurer. The insurer also must provide whatever training is necessary to ensure its insurance producers understand the regulatory requirements that apply to sales of the product.

Regardless of the distribution method selected, the insurer is responsible for all advertising and sales materials used in connection with individual life insurance products and must establish procedures to ensure all such materials comply with regulatory requirements. In addition, the insurer must establish procedures to ensure that, regardless of the distribution method, all required disclosures and information are provided to applicants and policyowners. We describe the advertising and disclosure requirements that the states impose on sales of individual life insurance in the next chapter.

Underwriting Considerations

An insurer's *underwriting philosophy* is a body of standards and goals for guiding all of the insurer's risk selection and risk classification procedures. The underwriting philosophy generally reflects the insurer's strategic business goals and the company's conservative or aggressive attitudes toward risk taking. The underwriting philosophy generally guides product pricing decisions and strongly shapes the underwriting guidelines established for each product.

Underwriting guidelines are general rules that the underwriting staff uses in assigning applicants to the different risk classifications. The product design team works with the actuarial and underwriting staffs to set underwriting guidelines for the product being developed. Such underwriting guidelines are intended to ensure that the underwriting staff's decisions are consistent with the risks that the insurer anticipated when it priced the product. Underwriting guidelines for a product define

- The level of risk the insurer will accept as standard, preferred, or rated
- The insurer's retention limits, indicating the level of risk the insurer will reinsure
- The level of risk the insurer will decline

Insurers must carefully review each state's regulatory requirements when establishing underwriting guidelines for new life insurance products. Although insurers generally are free to develop their own underwriting guidelines, state insurance laws impose requirements on life insurance underwriting to prevent insurers from *unfairly* discriminating against proposed insureds because of factors such as race, national origin, marital status, sex, sexual orientation, and certain physical and mental impairments. In addition, insurers must establish procedures to ensure that the underwriting process is handled in compliance with state and federal laws designed to protect the privacy of individuals.

Some states place restrictions on the amounts of insurance that may be issued on the lives of specified individuals. Such restrictions are designed to protect insureds—generally minors under specified ages. The state of New York, for example, places maximum limits on the amount of insurance coverage that may be issued on the life of minors who are under age 14½.[7] An insurer is prohibited from knowingly issuing a policy in New York insuring such a minor if total coverage on the child exceeds a specified amount. The maximum amount of coverage prohibited gradually increases as the minor's age increases.

REGULATION OF SPECIFIC PRODUCTS

As insurers have created new types of life insurance products, state regulators have enacted additional insurance laws and regulations designed to govern aspects of such products to which existing requirements did not apply. The specific products we describe in this section generally are subject to the same state insurance laws as other individual life insurance products. In this section, we describe some additional regulatory requirements imposed on variable life insurance and universal life insurance. We also describe how the states regulate industrial life insurance.

Variable Life Insurance

Variable life insurance policies are insurance products governed by state insurance laws, and they are securities subject to federal securities laws. Figure 1-5 summarizes the federal requirements imposed both on variable life insurance policies and on insurers that market those policies. In this section, we describe state insurance requirements that apply specifically to variable life insurance policies. Most states have adopted regulations based on the NAIC *Variable Life Insurance Model Regulation*, which establishes qualifications an insurer must meet in order to market variable life insurance within a state and specifies requirements variable life insurance policies must meet. For purposes of the Model Regulation, a *variable life insurance policy* is an individual policy that provides life insurance coverage which varies in amount or duration according to the experience of one or more separate accounts established and maintained by an insurer. The Model Regulation distinguishes between *scheduled premium variable life policies*—those under which both the timing and amount of premium payments are fixed by the insurer—and all other variable life policies, referred to as *flexible premium variable life policies*. Flexible premium variable life insurance is often known as *variable universal life insurance*.

Qualifications of Insurer

Before delivering or issuing a variable life insurance policy for delivery in a state, an insurer must obtain a *certificate of authority*, or *license*, from the state insurance department granting the insurer the right to conduct a life insurance business in the state. In addition, the Variable Life Insurance Model Regulation requires that an insurer receive the insurance commissioner's written approval to market variable life insurance in the state. Before granting such approval, the insurance commissioner must find that (1) the insurer's

FIGURE 1-5 Federal Regulation of Variable Life Insurance.

Federal securities laws are designed to protect investors by requiring that consumers receive specified types of information about securities being offered for sale to the public and by ensuring that companies and individuals engaged in the issuance and sale of securities conduct their businesses fairly and in accordance with regulatory requirements. Insurers that sell variable life insurance and variable annuities must comply with three federal laws: the Securities Act of 1933, the Securities Exchange Act of 1934, and the Investment Company Act of 1940.

The **Securities Act of 1933** requires that each security be registered with the Securities and Exchange Commission (SEC) before it is offered for sale to the public.[8] The issuer of a security registers the security by filing a registration statement with the SEC. A **registration statement** is a written statement containing detailed information about the issuer and the security, including specified financial statements. The SEC reviews each registration statement for accuracy and completeness. If a statement is not complete or contains inaccuracies, the SEC may require the issuer to amend the statement before it will become effective. A communication that offers a security for sale, known as a **prospectus**, must contain most of the information that was in the security's registration statement.

The **Securities Exchange Act of 1934** created the SEC and granted it authority to regulate the securities industry.[9] Sales of securities must be conducted by a securities broker or an individual who acts as an agent for a broker. Before selling variable life insurance, individuals must register with the SEC and become members of the National Association of Securities Dealers (NASD). The NASD is a nonprofit organization of securities dealers responsible for regulating sales of securities other than sales through a stock exchange. Individuals engaged in the sale of variable life policies must conduct business in accordance with all statutory requirements and in compliance with SEC and NASD rules and regulations.

The **Investment Company Act of 1940** regulates the conduct of **investment companies**, which are entities that issue securities and engage primarily in investing and trading securities.[10] An insurer's separate account maintained to fund a variable life product is an investment company subject to the Investment Company Act. An investment company must register with the SEC and must comply with requirements of the Investment Company Act.

operating plan for the sale of variable life insurance is not unsound, (2) the character and experience of the insurer's management are such as to reasonably ensure competent operation of a variable life insurance business, and (3) the insurer's financial condition and method of operation are unlikely to render its operation hazardous to the public or policyowners.

The procedural requirements for obtaining regulatory authority to market variable life insurance are somewhat different in the various states. In a number of states, a certificate of authority to conduct a life insurance business automatically includes the authority to market variable life insurance. In other states, an insurer must specifically apply for authority to sell variable life insurance as required by the Model Regulation. In these states, if the state insurance department approves an insurer's application to sell variable products, the insurance department either amends the insurer's certificate of authority to include variable life insurance or issues the insurer a letter granting the additional authority to market variable life insurance.

The Model Regulation requires the insurer to establish and maintain a written statement specifying the *standards of suitability* the insurer will follow when selling variable life insurance policies. The standards of suitability must specify that the insurer will not issue a variable life insurance policy or recommend such a policy without reasonable grounds to believe the policy is not unsuitable for the applicant. In order to establish reasonable grounds for such a belief about the suitability of a variable life insurance policy, the insurer must obtain information from the applicant about his insurance and investment objectives and his financial situation and needs. If the insurer or insurance producer has any other relevant information about the applicant, that information also must be considered in evaluating the product's suitability for the applicant.

Policy Requirements

In a state that has adopted the Variable Life Insurance Model Regulation, an insurer is prohibited from delivering or issuing for delivery in the state a variable life insurance policy unless the policy has been filed with and approved by the state insurance department. The Model Regulation also lists the minimum requirements that all variable life insurance policies must meet, including the following:

- Mortality and expense charges must be borne by the insurer, and the amounts of those charges must be subject to maximums stated in the policy. In other words, the insurer must bear any mortality and expense costs that exceed the maximum charges specified in the variable life policy.

- Scheduled premium policies must provide a minimum death benefit that is at least equal to the initial face amount of the policy. Reserve liabilities for any guaranteed minimum death benefits must be maintained in the insurer's general account.

- The policy must reflect the investment experience of one or more separate accounts. The insurer must demonstrate that the method used to reflect the investment experience of each separate account is actuarially sound.

- Changes in the amount of variable death benefits must be calculated at least annually.

- The amount of the policy's cash value must be calculated at least monthly and in accordance with specified requirements.

The Model Regulation also specifies that the face page of a variable life insurance policy must contain the following information:

- A prominent statement—in either contrasting color or boldface type—that the amount or duration of the death benefit may be variable or fixed under specified conditions

- A prominent statement—in either contrasting color or boldface type—that cash values may increase or decrease in accordance with the experience of the specified separate account subject to any specified minimum guarantees

- For scheduled premium policies, a statement describing any minimum death benefit that will be provided as long as premiums are paid when due

- The method that will be used to determine the amount of insurance payable at the insured's death or a reference to the policy provision that describes the method

- As permitted by state law, a provision giving the policyowner the right to return the policy within 10 days of receiving it and to receive a full premium refund

- Any other items that state laws require an insurer to include on the face page of fixed-benefit life insurance policies

States' standard life insurance policy provisions laws typically apply to variable life insurance policies. We have already described the entire contract, incontestability, misstatement of age, and free-look provisions that all individual life insurance policies—including variable policies—must contain. The

Variable Life Insurance Model Regulation specifies the following additional provisions that variable life insurance policies must include:

- Like other individual life policies, scheduled premium variable life policies must provide a grace period of at least 31 days. This grace period requirement has been modified to reflect the operation of flexible premium policies, which do not specify regular premium due dates. Instead, flexible premium policies specify dates, referred to as *policy processing days*, on which authorized charges are deducted from the policy's cash value to continue coverage in force. Such a policy must provide a grace period that begins on the policy processing day when the total charges authorized by the policy—and necessary to keep the policy in force until the next policy processing day—exceed the amounts available under the policy to pay such charges. The insurer must send the policyowner a report that specifies the minimum payment required to keep the policy in force and the length of the grace period that is available. The grace period must continue for at least 61 days following the date the insurer mails the required report to the policyowner.

- The policy must fully describe the **benefit base**, which is the amount to which the policy's net investment return will be applied periodically. It also must describe how the amount of variable benefits payable under the policy will be calculated.

- The policy must specify the separate account in which the policy values will be invested. In practice, insurers usually state the various investment options in the policy, and they attach to the policy a separate statement that identifies the specific separate accounts in which the policy values will be invested.

- The policy must state that the investment policy of the separate account will not be changed without the approval of the insurance department of the insurer's domiciliary state.

- If the policy includes a settlement option provision, it must provide at least one fixed benefit option.

Separate Accounts

State insurance laws allow life insurers to establish and maintain separate accounts and impose various requirements on the insurers' handling of those accounts. We noted earlier that variable life policies must state that the investment policy of the separate account will not be changed without the approval of the insurance department of the insurer's domiciliary state. The insurance department may disapprove any such change if it would be harmful to policyowners.

In each separate account, the insurer must maintain assets with a value at least equal to the greater of (1) the valuation reserves for the variable portion of variable policy values or (2) the benefit base for those policies. The assets in each separate account must be valued at least monthly at their market values. The Variable Life Insurance Model Regulation places maximum limitations on separate account ownership of any one security. The Model Regulation also prohibits an insurer from buying, selling, or transferring assets to a separate account or between separate accounts. In other words, the assets of each account must remain separate. The insurer must submit to the state insurance department an annual statement of the business of its separate accounts on a form prescribed by the NAIC.

The insurer's board of directors must adopt a written statement specifying the standards of conduct the insurer will follow with respect to the purchase or sale of investments of its separate accounts. A code of ethics that meets the requirements of the federal Investment Company Act of 1940 will satisfy this requirement. Insight 1-3 describes the code of ethics requirements of the Investment Company Act.

INSIGHT 1-3 Code of Ethics Requirements of the Investment Company Act.

Conflicts of interest between an investment company and its personnel, such as its portfolio managers, can arise when these persons buy or sell securities for their own accounts ("personal investment activities"). A **portfolio manager** is a professional who is responsible for managing a specific group of assets, known as a **portfolio**. These conflicts of interest arise because investment company personnel have the opportunity to profit from information about investment company transactions, often to the detriment of investors. Such activities are referred to as **insider trading**. SEC Rules adopted to implement the Investment Company Act address these conflicts of interest by

- Prohibiting fraudulent, deceptive, or manipulative acts by investment company affiliates and certain other persons in connection with their personal transactions in securities held or to be acquired by the investment company;

- Requiring investment companies and their investment advisers and principal underwriters to adopt codes of ethics containing provisions reasonably necessary to prevent their **access persons**—generally, those personnel involved in the portfolio management process—from engaging in the prohibited conduct; and

- Requiring access persons to report their personal securities transactions to the investment company.[11]

Application for Insurance

According to the Variable Life Insurance Model Regulation, the application for a variable life insurance policy must contain a prominent statement indicating that the death benefit may be variable or fixed under specified conditions. The application also must contain a prominent statement that cash values may increase or decrease in accordance with the investment experience of the separate account and, if applicable, subject to any minimum guarantees provided by the policy. Finally, the application must include questions designed to provide the insurer with information from which it can determine the suitability of the policy for the applicant. Figure 1-6 includes a portion of an application including questions relating to the suitability of the policy for the applicant. Applications for variable life insurance policies must be filed with and approved by the state insurance department before they are used in a state.

Universal Life Insurance

A number of states have adopted regulations based on the NAIC *Universal Life Insurance Model Regulation*, which is intended to provide states with a means to supplement their insurance laws and regulations to accommodate the issuance of universal life insurance. The Model Regulation defines a ***universal life insurance policy*** as any policy for which an insurer periodically makes separately identified (1) interest credits, other than credits for dividend accumulations, premium deposit funds, or other supplementary accounts; (2) mortality charges; and (3) expense charges. The Regulation applies to all individual universal life insurance policies except variable universal life insurance policies. Most universal life policies are flexible premium policies, and, thus, the Model Regulation contains provisions that allow the issuance of such products and that seek to ensure the insurer's solvency and to protect policyowners.

The Model Regulation specifies the minimum valuation standards and minimum reserve requirements for universal life policies. It also specifies minimum nonforfeiture values for both flexible premium and fixed premium universal life policies.

Required Policy Provisions

According to the Universal Life Insurance Model Regulation, universal life insurance policies must provide guarantees of minimum interest credits and maximum mortality and expense charges. All values and data shown in a universal life policy must be based on guarantees. Policies must describe how cash surrender values will be calculated and must include the following information:

- The guaranteed maximum expense charges and loads

FIGURE 1-6 Suitability Questions Contained in an Application for Variable Life Insurance.

APPLICATION FOR VARIABLE LIFE INSURANCE

Owner: _____ Joint Owner: _____
Address: _____ Address: _____
_____ _____
Occupation: _____ Occupation: _____

Investment Objectives (Check one):
- ☐ Safety of principal
- ☐ Long-term growth
- ☐ Retirement income
- ☐ Other (Please describe): _____

Financial Situation (Check one):
- ☐ Under $50,000   ☐ $50,000–100,000   ☐ Over $100,000

Household income _____
Net worth _____
Life insurance _____
Tax bracket: _____ %
Dependents: Number _____ Ages _____

Signature of Owner: _____ Signature of Joint Owner: _____
Signature of Registered Representative: _____

- Any limitation on the crediting of additional interest
- The guaranteed minimum rate or rates of interest
- The guaranteed maximum mortality charges
- Any other guaranteed charges
- Any surrender or partial withdrawal charges

If the policyowner has the right to change the basic coverage provided by a universal life policy, then any limitation on the amount or timing of a coverage change must be stated in the policy. If the policyowner has the right to *increase* the amount of coverage the policy provides, then the policy must state whether a new contestable and/or suicide exclusion period will apply to the additional coverage.

According to the Model Regulation, the grace period provision of a universal life policy must provide for the insurer to send written notice to the policyowner's last known address at least 30 days before coverage under the policy terminates. Flexible premium policies must provide for a grace period of at least 30 days after lapse. Unless otherwise defined in the policy, a universal life policy lapses on the date on which the net cash surrender value equals zero.

Interest-Indexed Universal Life Policies

The Universal Life Insurance Model Regulation contains separate policy form filing requirements for *interest-indexed policies*, which are universal life insurance policies that provide for interest credits to be linked to an external standard. Interest-indexed policies typically are linked to *Standard & Poor's 500 (S&P 500)* index, which measures changes in stock market conditions based on the performance of 500 selected stocks. The submission package prepared for filing an interest-indexed policy form must include the following information:

- A description of how the interest credits are determined

- A description of the insurer's investment policy for the assets supporting interest-indexed products

- A description of any interest guarantee provided in addition to or in lieu of the index

- A description of any maximum premium limitations and the conditions under which they apply

- If policies are linked to an index for a specified period that ends before the policy maturity date, a description of the method used to determine interest credits after the end of the specified period

The Model Regulation also requires an insurer that issues interest-indexed policies to submit to the state insurance department a Statement of Actuarial Opinion similar to the one shown in Figure 1-7. The insurer also must submit on an annual basis a description of the amount and type of assets it currently holds with respect to its interest-indexed policies. Before making any material change in the insurer's investment strategy or method of determining the interest credits, the insurer must submit to the insurance department a description of the change. A change is considered to be material if it would affect the form or definition of the index or would significantly change the amount or type of assets held for interest-indexed policies.

FIGURE 1-7 **Statement of Actuarial Opinion for Interest-Indexed Universal Life Insurance Policies.**

I, _____ (name), am _____ (position or relationship to Insurer) for the XYZ Life Insurance Company (The Insurer) in the state of _____ (State of Domicile of Insurer).

I am a member of the American Academy of Actuaries (or if not, state other qualifications to sign Annual Statement actuarial opinions).

I have examined the interest-indexed universal life insurance policies of the Insurer in force as of December 31, 20xx, encompassing _____ number of policies and $_____ of insurance in force.

I have considered the provisions of the policies. I have considered any reinsurance agreements pertaining to such policies, the characteristics of the identified assets, and the investment policy adopted by the Insurer as they affect future insurance and investment cash flows under such policies and related assets. My examination included such tests and calculations as I considered necessary to form an opinion concerning the insurance and investment cash flows arising from the policies and related assets.

I relied on the investment policy of the Insurer and on projected investment cash flows as provided by _____, Chief Investment Officer of the Insurer. (If the actuary does not choose to rely on an investment officer for the projected investment cash flows, this statement should be modified to show the extent of the actuary's reliance.)

The tests were conducted under various assumptions as to future interest rates, and particular attention was given to those provisions and characteristics that might cause future insurance and investment cash flows to vary with changes in the level of prevailing interest rates.

In my opinion, the anticipated insurance and investment cash flows referred to above make good and sufficient provision for the contractual obligations of the Insurer under these insurance policies.

_____
Signature of Actuary

Source: Excerpted from NAIC, *Universal Life Insurance Model Regulation* § 10C, 2001. Reprinted with permission from the National Association of Insurance Commissioners.

Industrial Life Insurance

Industrial life insurance, which is also known as *home service insurance* or *debit insurance*, is usually defined for regulatory purposes as life insurance that is paid for by weekly or monthly premiums, which are collected by an agent of the insurer. A few states prohibit the sale of industrial life insurance within their jurisdictions.[12] Other states allow its sale in accordance with regulatory requirements and have enacted laws based on the NAIC *Industrial Life Insurance Model Bill*. In addition to the required life insurance policy provisions we described earlier in the chapter, all industrial life insurance policies issued in a state that has enacted the Model Bill must include the following provisions:

- A *grace period provision* granting a grace period of at least 31 days

- A *facility of payment provision* stating that, under specified conditions, the insurer may pay policy benefits to the executor or administrator of the insured's estate, relatives of the insured, or any other person who is equitably entitled to the benefits or has incurred expenses for the care or burial of the insured

- A *discount for advance payment of premium provision* stating the amount by which premiums due will be reduced if premiums are paid at least a specified time in advance

The Industrial Life Insurance Model Bill also prohibits industrial policies from excluding or restricting the payment of policy death benefits if the insured's death results from the act of another. Each optional benefit provided by an industrial policy must be priced separately, and such prices must be clearly set forth in the policy.

To ensure that applicants for industrial life insurance have enough information on which to base their decision about the purchase of an industrial life policy, the Model Bill requires insurers to include the following information in the application for an industrial life insurance policy:

- An acknowledgement by the applicant that he has reviewed his life insurance program

- Disclosures by the applicant of the total face amount of insurance and the number of policies that are in force on the applicant or on the named insured if that is someone other than the applicant

- An acknowledgement that the applicant understands the relationship between the cost of the policy and the applicant's total income

In states that have enacted laws based on the Model Bill, an insurer may not deliver an industrial life insurance policy in the state unless the insurer has taken a written application for the policy and that application contains the foregoing information.

KEY TERMS AND CONCEPTS

term life insurance
permanent life insurance
Life and Health Insurance Policy Language Simplification Model Act
insuring clause
free-look provision
renewal provision
entire contract provision
closed contract
open contract
grace period provision
incontestability provision
representation
warranty
material misrepresentation
misstatement of age provision
reinstatement provision
dividend provision
nonforfeiture provision
Standard Nonforfeiture Law for Life Insurance
policy loan provision
Model Policy Loan Interest Rate Bill
assignment provision
assignment
accelerated death benefit provision
Accelerated Benefits Model Regulation
exclusion
suicide exclusion provision
backdating
premium receipt
binding premium receipt
conditional premium receipt
approval premium receipt
insurability premium receipt
policy rider
reserves
premiums
unit of coverage
gross premium
cost of benefits
net premium
loading
policy reserve
net amount at risk
personal selling
direct response marketing
underwriting philosophy
underwriting guidelines
Variable Life Insurance Model Regulation
variable life insurance policy
scheduled premium variable life policy
flexible premium variable life policy
benefit base
Universal Life Insurance Model Regulation
universal life insurance policy
interest-indexed policy
industrial life insurance
Industrial Life Insurance Model Bill
facility of payment provision
discount for advance payment of premium provision

ENDNOTES

1. Montana Code Annotated § 49-2-309 (2001).

2. Historically, a distinction existed between a *policy rider*, which provided benefits in addition to those provided in the policy, and a *policy endorsement*, which either limited the benefits payable or clarified the terms of a policy provision. Today, the terms *policy rider* and *endorsement* tend to be used synonymously to include any document that is attached to a life or health policy and that either expands or limits the policy benefits.

3. Definitions adapted from Debra Helwig, "The Missing Link: Extranets and the Evolution of Communication," *Resource* (March 1998): 7–24.

4. For a summary of the UETA, see www.nccusl.org/nccusl.uniformact_summaries/uniformact-s-ueta.asp (24 April 2002).

5. Public Law 106-229 (2000).

6. Available online at www.naic.org/1whatsnew/files/webpost.pdf (24 April 2002).

7. N.Y. U.C.C. Law § 28-3207 (Consol. 1981).

8. 15 U.S.C. §§ 77a *et seq.* (1996).

9. 15 U.S.C. §§ 78a *et seq.* (1996).

10. 15 U.S.C. §§ 80a-1 *et seq.* (1996).

11. 17 C.F.R. § 270.17j-1 (1997).

12. See, for example, N.Y. U.C.C. Law § 28-3201(b)(5) (Consol. 1981).

CHAPTER 2

Life Insurance Advertising and Disclosure Requirements

LEARNING OBJECTIVES

After studying this chapter, you should be able to

- Recognize activities that are considered to be unfair trade practices in the business of insurance

- Identify the types of materials that state insurance regulators consider to be advertisements subject to state insurance advertising requirements

- Identify the regulatory requirements that are imposed on life insurance advertisements

- Recognize the types of information that generally must be included in life insurance sales illustrations and the regulatory requirements insurers must meet as they prepare and use sales illustrations

- Distinguish between the features of the Buyer's Guide provided to prospective purchasers of life insurance and of a policy summary provided to such prospects

- Identify the solicitation disclosure requirements imposed on variable life insurance policies, universal life insurance policies, and pre-need funeral contracts

- Identify situations in which an insurer must provide periodic disclosure reports to life insurance policyowners

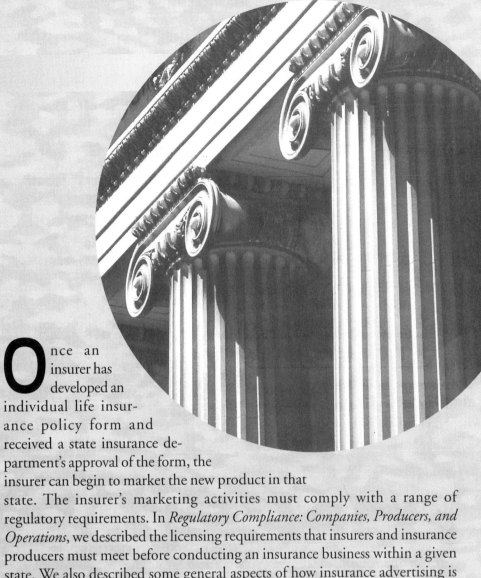

Once an insurer has developed an individual life insurance policy form and received a state insurance department's approval of the form, the insurer can begin to market the new product in that state. The insurer's marketing activities must comply with a range of regulatory requirements. In *Regulatory Compliance: Companies, Producers, and Operations*, we described the licensing requirements that insurers and insurance producers must meet before conducting an insurance business within a given state. We also described some general aspects of how insurance advertising is regulated and the requirements that states impose on how insurance producers conduct their businesses. Figure 2-1 identifies some of the typical requirements the states impose on the conduct of insurance producers.

In this chapter, our goal is to describe how the states regulate the advertising of individual life insurance, including materials used in the sale of life insurance. We also describe the types of information that insurers and insurance producers must disclose to applicants for individual life insurance and the periodic reports that insurers must furnish life insurance policyowners and state insurance departments.

UNFAIR TRADE PRACTICES ACT

Most state insurance codes include a law that defines certain practices as unfair and prohibits those practices if committed (1) flagrantly in conscious disregard

FIGURE 2-1 State Regulation of Insurance Producers.

- State insurance laws prohibit a number of unfair practices that involve misrepresentations of fact by insurance producers.

- All states permit replacements of in-force life insurance and annuity policies, but most states impose requirements that producers and insurers must meet when a transaction involves the replacement of an in-force individual life insurance or annuity policy. These regulatory requirements are designed to make sure that insurers and insurance producers provide consumers with fair and accurate information about policies.

- All but two states have enacted laws to prohibit **rebating**, which is a sales practice in which an insurance producer or insurer offers a prospect an inducement to purchase an insurance policy from the producer or insurer and the inducement is not offered to all applicants in similar situations and is not stated in the policy itself. The goal of these anti-rebating laws is to ensure that all insureds in the same underwriting classification are treated alike.

- A few states require insurers to establish a system to supervise their insurance producers to ensure that producers make product recommendations that are appropriate for their customers' needs. This type of requirement, which often is referred to as a **suitability requirement**, imposes a duty on insurance producers and/or insurers to have reasonable grounds on which to decide that a specific product is suitable for a customer's needs.

Source: Adapted from Harriett E. Jones and Monica R. Maxwell, *Regulatory Compliance: Companies, Producers, and Operations*, 2nd ed. (Atlanta: LOMA, © 2002), 93, 94, 100, 103. Used with permission; all rights reserved.

of the law or (2) so frequently as to indicate a general business practice. Many of those laws are based on the NAIC *Unfair Trade Practices Act*, which identifies a number of general practices that are prohibited as unfair trade practices in the business of insurance. The following are some of the unfair trade practices that life insurers must avoid as they market individual life insurance products:

- **Misrepresentation and false advertising of insurance policies.** The Unfair Trade Practices Act describes the prohibited practice of misrepresentation and false advertising of insurance policies broadly to include making, issuing, circulating, or causing to be made, issued, or circulated any estimate, illustration, circular, statement, sales presentation, omission, or comparison that contains specified types of misrepresentations concerning the benefits, advantages, conditions, or terms of a policy.

- **False information and advertising generally.** Insurers are prohibited from making, publishing, or placing before the public any statement about the business of insurance or any insurer if the statement is untrue, deceptive, or misleading.

- **Defamation.** Insurers may not make, publish, or circulate any oral or written statement that is false or maliciously critical of the financial condition of any insurer and that is calculated to injure that insurer. Insurers also are prohibited from aiding or encouraging another to make such statements.

- **Boycott, coercion, and intimidation.** Entering into an agreement to boycott, coerce, or intimidate other companies resulting in an unreasonable restraint of, or monopoly in, the business of insurance is an unfair trade practice.

- **False statements and entries.** Insurers may not knowingly make any false material statement of fact as to their financial condition. Violations include making such a false statement to a state regulatory official or publishing such a statement to the public. Knowingly making a false entry of material fact in any book, report, or statement of an insurer or knowingly making any false statement to a state insurance department also are unfair trade practices.

- **Unfair discrimination.** The Unfair Trade Practices Act prohibits insurers from making or permitting any unfair discrimination in underwriting and issuing policies, and it lists specific types of unfair discrimination that are prohibited. (See Figure 2-2 for some examples of unfair discrimination.)

- **Failure to maintain marketing and performance records.** An insurer engages in an unfair trade practice if it fails to maintain its books and other business records so that information regarding complaints, claims, rating, underwriting, and marketing are accessible for examination by the state insurance department. The NAIC Unfair Trade Practices Act requires insurers to maintain data for the current calendar year and at least the two preceding years. A number of states require that data be maintained for up to five years or until the date of the insurer's next regulatory examination.

- **Failure to maintain complaint handling procedures.** An insurer engages in an unfair trade practice if it fails to maintain a complete record

FIGURE 2-2. Examples of Unfair Discrimination.

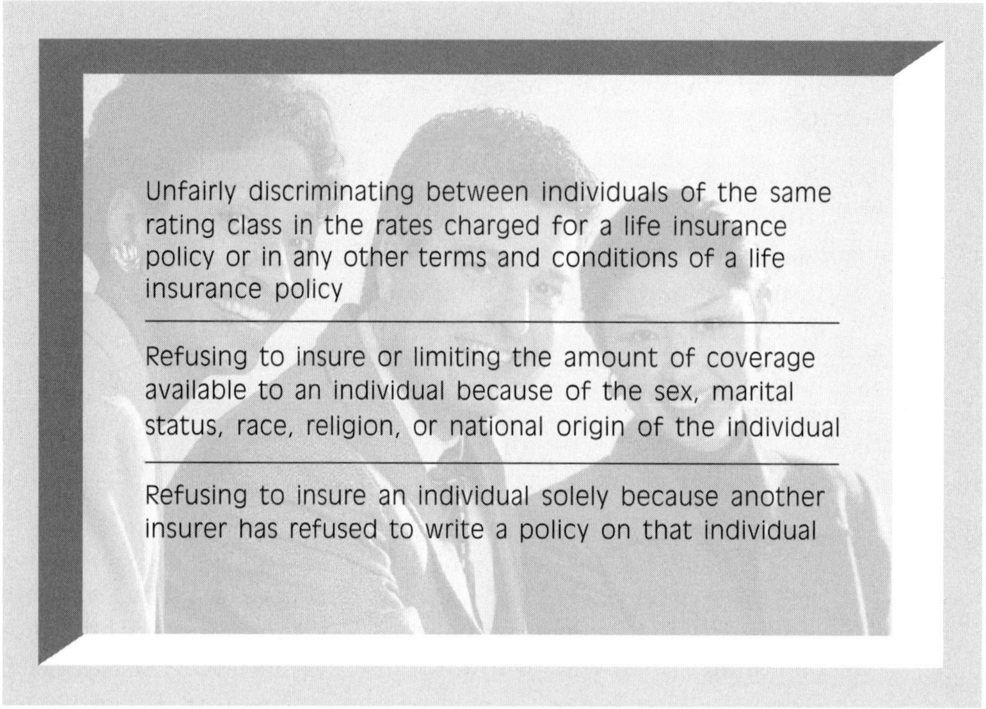

Unfairly discriminating between individuals of the same rating class in the rates charged for a life insurance policy or in any other terms and conditions of a life insurance policy

Refusing to insure or limiting the amount of coverage available to an individual because of the sex, marital status, race, religion, or national origin of the individual

Refusing to insure an individual solely because another insurer has refused to write a policy on that individual

Source: National Association of Insurance Commissioners, *Unfair Trade Practices Act*, 2001.

of all the complaints it receives since the date of its last insurance department examination. For purposes of the Unfair Trade Practices Act, a *complaint* is any written communication primarily expressing a grievance. The complaint record must indicate the total number of complaints, the line of insurance that was the subject of each complaint, the nature of each complaint, the disposition of each complaint, and the time it took to process the complaint.

Note that many of the activities that are unfair trade practices in the business of insurance are also prohibited by other types of state and federal laws. For example, state and federal antitrust laws prohibit boycotts, coercion, and intimidation.

State unfair trade practices acts tend to contain broad prohibitions against specified practices that are unfair and do not identify every activity that is deemed unfair. In many states, additional laws and regulations have been adopted to supplement the unfair trade practices act and to identify more specific practices that are prohibited. We describe some of these more specific requirements in the rest of the chapter.

REGULATION OF LIFE INSURANCE ADVERTISING

Most states have adopted specific regulatory requirements regarding the advertising of life insurance, and advertisements disseminated in such states must comply with the applicable state's requirements. In many states, advertising requirements are based on the NAIC *Advertisements of Life Insurance and Annuities Model Regulation*, which establishes minimum standards that require insurers to disclose to the public all relevant information in their advertisements of life insurance and annuity policies.

In order to determine which advertising materials are subject to a state's advertising requirements, an insurer must refer to the appropriate state's definition of *advertisement*. The Model Regulation defines *advertisement* as any material designed either (1) to create public interest in life insurance or annuities, an insurer, or an insurance producer or (2) to induce the public to purchase, increase, modify, reinstate, borrow on, surrender, replace, or retain a policy. In order to clarify this definition, the Model Regulation lists the following specific materials that are advertisements subject to the Regulation:

- Material used by an insurer or insurance producer in direct mail, newspapers, magazines, radio and television scripts, billboards and similar displays, or the Internet or other mass communication media

- Descriptive literature and sales aids of all kinds issued, distributed, or used by an insurer or insurance producer, including circulars, leaflets, booklets, Web pages, depictions, illustrations, and form letters

- Materials that are used to recruit and train insurance producers and that are designed to be, or are, used to induce the public to purchase, increase, modify, reinstate, borrow on, surrender, replace, or retain a policy

- Sales talks, presentations, and materials prepared for use by insurance producers

Note that advertisements for all types of life insurance products are covered by the Model Regulation. Regardless of who creates an advertisement for an insurer's products, the insurer is ultimately responsible for ensuring that the advertisement complies with applicable regulatory requirements. To enforce this responsibility, the Model Regulation requires the insurer to establish and maintain procedures by which it controls the content, form, and method of dissemination of all advertisements.

Regulatory Requirements

Advertisements for all types of life insurance products must comply with a variety of regulatory requirements. As a general rule, advertisements must not only be truthful, but they also must not be misleading in any respect or have the capacity to mislead. In evaluating whether an advertisement has the capacity to mislead, a state insurance department considers the overall impression that the advertisement may be reasonably expected to create on a person of average intelligence. The following are some of the specific requirements that the Advertisements of Life Insurance and Annuities Model Regulation imposes on advertisements of life insurance:

- An advertisement must prominently describe the type of policy that is being advertised.

- The name or title used to identify the policy being advertised must contain the words *life insurance* or the advertisement must clearly indicate that the policy is life insurance.

- The name of the insurer must be clearly identified.

- Advertisements must be truthful and must not have the capacity to mislead or deceive.

- An advertisement may not contain a recommendation of a commercial rating agency unless the advertisement also clearly defines the scope and extent of the recommendation. *Rating agencies* are organizations, owned independently of any insurer or government body, that evaluate the financial condition of insurers and provide information to potential customers of and investors in insurance companies. After evaluating an insurer, a rating agency assigns the insurer a *quality rating*, which generally is a letter grade or score on a numerical scale representing the rating agency's opinion of the insurer's financial condition. Insight 2-1 describes these rating agencies in more detail. An insurer's ratings may significantly affect consumers' buying decisions. Thus, an acceptable rating enhances customer satisfaction and enhances the security and loyalty of the insurer's sales force.

- An advertisement may not contain statistical information relating to any insurer or policy unless it accurately reflects recent and relevant facts. In addition, the advertisement must identify the source of any statistics.

> **INSIGHT 2-1** **Insurance Company Rating Agencies.**
>
> A number of rating agencies—including A.M. Best Company, Conning & Company, Duff & Phelps, Moody's Investors Service, Standard & Poor's, and Weiss Ratings—now evaluate the financial strength of insurers in the United States. Rating agencies rate an insurer by assigning a grade within their own proprietary system of alphabetical or numerical ratings. Most rating agencies assign a quality rating to insurers according to standards of claims paying ability, credit worthiness, or financial strength.
>
> Each rating agency establishes its own standards, which generally are stricter standards than the minimum solvency standards applied by state regulators. A.M. Best, for example, assigns ratings of financial stability based on a comprehensive quantitative and qualitative analysis of a company's balance sheet strength, operating performance, and business profile.[1]
>
> Each rating agency also decides what types of information it will consider in establishing quality ratings and what sources it will use to obtain that information. Some rating agencies use only information they can obtain from public sources, such as insurers' published financial statements and statutory filings. Some rating agencies obtain information directly from insurers.
>
> Rating agencies typically produce a written report that is provided along with an insurer's rating and that explains the rationale the rating agency used to establish the rating. The report about an insurer is invaluable to an understanding of the given rating.

- An advertisement shall not make unfair or incomplete comparisons of policies, benefits, dividends, or premium rates of other insurers and shall not disparage other insurers, insurance producers, policies, services, or methods of marketing.

As noted, advertisements must clearly identify the name of the insurer. If an application is included as part of an advertisement, the application also must contain the name of the insurer. Advertisements must not include words or symbols that might tend to mislead consumers to believe the solicitation is connected with or endorsed by a governmental program or agency.

In addition to the foregoing rules that apply to all life insurance policy advertisements, some provisions of the Model Regulation pertain to advertisements of specific types of life insurance policies.

- If the policy advertised contains graded or modified benefits, then the advertisement must prominently display any limitation of benefits. If the premium is level and coverage decreases or increases while the policy is in force, then the advertisement must prominently disclose that fact.

- If premiums payable for the advertised policy are not level, then the advertisement must prominently disclose the premium charges.

- An advertisement may not describe a pure endowment benefit as a profit or return of premium rather than as a policy benefit for which a specified premium is paid. A *pure endowment benefit* is a benefit payable if the person insured survives until the end of a specified period.

- If an advertisement describes a policy for which the insurer reserves the right to change the amount of the premium during the policy term, the advertisement must prominently describe this policy feature.

The Advertisements of Life Insurance and Annuities Model Regulation contains a number of provisions that regulate the use of specific words and phrases in life insurance advertisements.

- Advertisements may not use the terms *investment, investment plan, founder's plan, charter plan, deposit, expansion plan, profit, profits, profit sharing, interest plan, savings, savings plan*, or other similar terms in connection with a policy if the advertisement would tend to mislead a consumer to believe she will receive something other than a life insurance policy. (Insight 2-2 addresses the use of such prohibited terms.)

- Advertisements may not use the terms *vanish, vanishing premium*, or similar terms that imply a policy becomes paid up to describe a plan that uses nonguaranteed elements to pay a portion of future premiums.

- Advertisements for policies that are not guaranteed issue may not use terms such as *nonmedical* or *no medical examination required* unless they disclose with equal prominence that the insurer's decision as to whether to issue a policy may depend on the answers to health questions in the application.

INSIGHT 2-2 Terms Prohibited in Life Insurance Advertisements.

Insurers are prohibited from using terms such as *investment* or *savings plan* in advertisements and sales presentations for life insurance products. But if a potential purchaser is looking for a way to accumulate funds for retirement or college tuition and the cash value of a life insurance policy can serve as a means to accumulate such a fund, how is the consumer harmed by the marketing of life insurance as a retirement plan or a college tuition savings plan? Many lawsuits have been filed against insurers by consumers who claim they purchased life insurance thinking they were purchasing an investment vehicle such as a retirement plan. These consumers expected that all the money they "invested" would go into their retirement funds or savings plans. They did not expect their money to be used to pay agents' commissions and other sales and administrative charges or to pay for insurance costs. To avoid charges of misrepresentation, insurers must avoid these terms and clearly identify their products as life insurance.

Advertisements that include a testimonial or endorsement by a third party are subject to additional requirements. An insurer that uses a testimonial in an advertisement is responsible for all statements contained in the advertisement, and all statements must comply with the Model Regulation. Testimonials must be genuine and must represent the current opinion of the individual making the testimonial. An advertisement that includes a testimonial must reproduce the testimonial in such a way that the nature and scope of the testimonial is accurately represented. Finally, the advertisement must prominently disclose any financial interest the individual making the testimonial has in the insurer or any benefit the individual received in exchange for the testimonial.

For example, assume that the Pluto Insurance Company hired a well-known and popular actor to appear in a television commercial advertising a new individual life insurance product. Pluto's market research indicated that the actor's reputation made him an especially believable spokesperson. The actor agreed to appear in the commercial in exchange for a large fee, which included additional compensation if Pluto decided to air the commercial for longer than one year. Because the actor was paid for his testimonial, the advertisement in which he appeared was required to disclose the fact that the actor had been compensated and, thus, had financially benefited from the advertisement. Disclosure protects consumers by informing them of a spokesperson's financial interest so that they may evaluate more fairly the information presented in the advertisement. By contrast, advertisements often feature actors who are not well known and who are paid based on a wage scale negotiated by their actors' union. Consumers are generally aware that the people who appear in advertisements are paid actors and, thus, do not lend particular credence to the information presented by such actors. As a result, the fact that actors are paid scale wages to appear in an advertisement need not be disclosed.

Insurers' Compliance Responsibilities

The Advertisements of Life Insurance and Annuities Model Regulation imposes specific compliance responsibilities on insurers that advertise within a state that has adopted the regulation. As noted earlier, an insurer is ultimately responsible under the law for all of its advertising regardless of who creates the advertising. Each insurer also must maintain at its home office a complete file containing a copy of every printed, published, or prepared advertisement of its individual life insurance policies. Note the breadth of materials the insurer must maintain on file; virtually any advertising material created by or on behalf of the insurer must be included. Each advertisement maintained on file must include a notation that describes how the advertisement has been distributed and the extent of its distribution. The insurer also must note the policy form number of any policy that is advertised. The insurer must maintain records for each advertisement for five years after either its publication or its last use.

Although requirements vary a great deal from state to state, most states do not require insurers to file all life insurance advertisements with the insurance department. However, advertising materials are subject to regulatory filing requirements in some states. The Advertisements of Life Insurance and Annuities Model Regulation gives the state insurance department the authority to require an insurer to file all or part of its advertising materials with the department if the department finds that an advertisement prepared by or on behalf of the insurer is misleading. In addition, each insurer must file with its Annual Statement a certification executed by an authorized officer of the insurer. The certification must state that the advertisements disseminated within the state by or on behalf of the insurer during the period covered by the Annual Statement complied in all respects with the applicable requirements.

LIFE INSURANCE SALES ILLUSTRATIONS

Many permanent life insurance policies contain actuarial values that are fixed and contractually guaranteed when the policies are issued and are guaranteed to remain the same throughout the lives of the policies. A traditional whole life insurance policy, for example, contains a number of such guaranteed actuarial values—it provides a specified amount of insurance in exchange for the payment of a specified premium amount and specifies the amount of the policy's cash value at any given time. By contrast, the amounts of policy dividends payable on participating policies are not guaranteed, but instead vary based on the insurer's experience. Many other types of permanent policies include actuarial values that are not guaranteed by the terms of the policies. These nonguaranteed values include the amount of premium payable, the amount of benefits payable, and the interest rate that will be used to calculate cash surrender values. Universal life insurance policies, for example, are characterized by their flexible premiums, flexible face amounts, and unbundled pricing factors. Variable life insurance policies also contain actuarial values that are not guaranteed.

In marketing individual life insurance policies, insurance producers often use illustrations to demonstrate for consumers how the nonguaranteed elements of a policy might vary over time. Sales illustrations, however, were the focus of a great deal of consumer dissatisfaction during the 1990s. Many consumers sued insurers alleging that insurance producers used illustrations that were misleading. In many of these lawsuits, consumers claimed they purchased policies because insurance producers told them the insurer's experience would be favorable and they would not be required to pay premiums throughout the life of their policies.

Recall that sales illustrations are considered to be advertisements and, thus, must comply with the state advertising requirements described earlier in the chapter. In December 1995, the NAIC revised the *Life Insurance Illustrations Model Regulation* to provide additional rules that insurers and insurance producers must follow when they use illustrations in specific life insurance sales presentations. The goals of the Life Insurance Illustrations Model Regulation are (1) to ensure that illustrations do not mislead purchasers of life insurance and (2) to make illustrations more understandable to consumers. Most states have enacted laws or regulations based on the revised Model Regulation.

The Model Regulation defines *illustration* as a presentation or depiction that includes nonguaranteed values of a life insurance policy. An illustration used in the sale of a life insurance policy may be either a basic illustration or a supplemental illustration. A *basic illustration* is a ledger or proposal that is used in the sale of a life insurance policy and that shows both guaranteed and nonguaranteed policy values. Appendix A contains a sample basic illustration for a whole life insurance policy. A *supplemental illustration* is an illustration that is provided along with a basic illustration and that presents the information in a different format than that used in the basic illustration. Appendix B contains a sample supplemental illustration for that same policy.

The Life Insurance Illustrations Model Regulation applies to individual and group life insurance policies that contain nonguaranteed elements; it does not govern individual or group annuity contracts. The Model Regulation also does not apply to the following types of life insurance policies:

- Variable life insurance
- Credit life insurance
- Policies that provide no illustrated death benefits of more than $10,000 on any individual

Variable life insurance and credit life insurance are subject to separate requirements enacted specifically to regulate those products. We describe the requirements imposed on variable life insurance later in this chapter, and we describe credit life insurance in Chapter 10.

For each policy subject to the Life Insurance Illustrations Model Regulation, an insurer must notify the state insurance department whether the policy form will be marketed with or without an illustration. This notification is generally provided when the insurer files the policy form with the state insurance department for its approval. If the insurer notifies the insurance department that it will use an illustration with a specific policy form, then the insurer must prepare and deliver an illustration with each sales presentation of an individual policy using that form. Alternatively, if the insurer notifies the insurance department that it will *not* use an illustration with a specific policy form, then the insurer is prohibited from using an illustration with any policy using that policy form before the first policy anniversary.

Contents of Basic Sales Illustrations

Basic illustrations used in the sale of life insurance policies must comply with a number of general rules specified in the Life Insurance Illustrations Model Regulation. An illustration must be clearly labeled "life insurance illustration," and it must include the following information:

- The name of the insurer
- The name and business address of the insurance producer, if any
- The name, age, and sex of the proposed insured
- The underwriting or rating classification on which the illustration is based
- Identification of the policy being illustrated, including the generic policy name, the company product name, and the policy form number
- The amount of the initial death benefit provided by the policy
- The dividend option election, if the policy is participating

The Model Regulation also contains a number of specific prohibitions. When using an illustration in the sale of a life insurance policy, an insurer or its insurance producers shall *not*

- Represent the policy as anything other than a life insurance policy
- Use or describe nonguaranteed values in a manner that is misleading
- State or imply that the payment or amount of nonguaranteed values is guaranteed
- Provide an applicant with an incomplete illustration
- Use terms, such as *vanish* or *vanishing premium*, that imply the policy becomes paid up to describe a plan that uses nonguaranteed values to pay a portion of future premiums

In addition to the general rules and prohibitions we have just described, the Life Insurance Illustrations Model Regulation contains standards that all basic illustrations must meet. The following are some of the elements that a basic illustration must contain:

- The illustration must specify the date on which it was prepared.

- The pages contained in an illustration must be numbered and the page numbers must include the total number of pages in the illustration. For example, an illustration that contains a total of five pages must be numbered as "page 1 of 5 pages," "page 2 of 5 pages," and so on. This numbering system makes it easier for the insurer, the insurance producer, and the consumer to be sure that the illustration is complete and all pages are presented.

- The amount of guaranteed death benefit and cash surrender value must be shown and must be clearly labeled *guaranteed*.

- If nonguaranteed values are illustrated, then the Model Regulation places maximum limits on the rates that may be used to illustrate nonguaranteed values. In general, the rates used to illustrate nonguaranteed values may not be more favorable to the policyowner than rates that are reasonably based on the insurer's actual recent experience.

- Guaranteed values must be shown before the corresponding nonguaranteed values. If a page in an illustration shows only nonguaranteed values, then that page must also refer to the corresponding guaranteed values. For example, a statement such as "See page 1 for a description of guaranteed values" must appear on a page that illustrates only nonguaranteed values.

- Illustrations of nonguaranteed values must include a statement that (1) benefits and values are not guaranteed, (2) the assumptions on which benefits and values are based are subject to change by the insurer, and (3) actual results may be more or less favorable than those illustrated.

The Model Regulation requires each basic illustration to include a *narrative summary* that must include the following information:

- A brief description of the policy, including a statement that it is a life insurance policy

- A brief description of the premium payable for the policy

- A brief description of any policy features, riders, or options shown in the basic illustration and a description of how they may affect the policy's benefits and values

- A brief definition of all column headings and key terms used in the basic illustration

- A statement containing the following information: "This illustration assumes that the nonguaranteed elements illustrated will continue unchanged over the period illustrated. This is not likely to occur, and actual results may be more or less favorable than those shown."

Following the narrative summary, a basic illustration must include a *numeric summary* of the death benefits, policy values, and premiums payable, as applicable. This summary must include information for at least policy years 5, 10, and 20, and at the insured's age 70, as applicable; the information must be shown on the basis of (1) policy guarantees, (2) the insurer's illustrated scale, and (3) the insurer's illustrated scale, but with nonguaranteed elements *reduced* according to specified amounts. An ***insurer's illustrated scale*** is a schedule of nonguaranteed elements calculated based on the insurer's recent experience. Note that by including such requirements, the Life Insurance Illustrations Model Regulation places maximum limits on the scale an insurer may use in a sales illustration.

Two statements must be included on the same page as the numeric summary. The first statement must be signed and dated by the applicant or policyowner and should read substantially as follows:

> I have received a copy of this illustration and understand that any nonguaranteed elements illustrated are subject to change and could be either higher or lower. The agent has told me they are not guaranteed.

The second statement must be signed and dated by the insurance producer and should read substantially as follows:

> I certify that this illustration has been presented to the applicant and that I have explained that any nonguaranteed elements illustrated are subject to change. I have made no statements that are inconsistent with the illustration.

If the illustration was provided at a time other than when the application was completed, then an authorized representative of the insurer must sign the foregoing statement.

Note that both the applicant and the insurance producer or other authorized representative of the insurer must sign and date the illustration. These signatures provide evidence of the specific information the insurance producer provided the applicant and help prevent disputes about how the insurance producer described the policy to the applicant.

Contents of Supplemental Illustrations

As noted earlier, the Life Insurance Illustrations Model Regulation permits insurers to provide a supplemental illustration to a prospect for life insurance as long as they provide the supplemental illustration along with a basic illustration that complies with the requirements of Model Regulation. The following additional requirements are imposed on supplemental illustrations:

- The nonguaranteed elements shown in a supplemental illustration may not be more favorable to the policyowner than the corresponding elements in the basic illustration.

- Like basic illustrations, supplemental illustrations of nonguaranteed elements must contain a statement that the policy's benefits and values are not guaranteed.

- A supplemental illustration of a fixed premium policy must be based on the same premium shown in the basic illustration. For flexible premium policies, a supplemental illustration must use the same premium amounts as used in the basic illustration.

- A supplemental illustration, which is not required to illustrate the policy's guaranteed elements, must include a notice that refers the applicant to the basic illustration for explanations of the policy's guaranteed elements and for other important information about the policy.

Review the supplemental illustration included in Appendix B to see the different types of information that are presented. In our sample illustration, the insurer has provided the applicant with the total amount of cumulative premiums expected to be paid through the 65th policy year and with the amount by which the policy cash value is expected to increase each policy year. Note that these amounts are calculated using the policy's current premium as shown in the basic illustration in Appendix A. Insurers that issue variable life policies sometimes use supplemental illustrations to show how a variable policy might perform depending on the investment performance of a specific separate account. In such a case, the supplemental illustration may show how the policy values are expected to increase based on the historical performance of the separate account.

Delivery of Illustrations

Recall that the Life Insurance Illustrations Model Regulation requires insurers to notify the applicable state insurance department as to whether sales illustrations will be used with each policy form. If a policy form is one for which illustrations will be used, then the insurer is responsible for ensuring that the applicant receives an illustration. When an illustration is used in the sale of a life insurance policy and the applicant applies for the policy that was illustrated, then the insurance producer must submit to the insurer along with the application one copy of the signed and dated illustration. The insurance producer must give to the applicant another signed and dated copy.

If the insurer issues a policy other than as applied for, the insurer must send the policyowner a revised basic illustration of the policy as issued. This illustration must be labeled "Revised Illustration" and must be signed and dated by the applicant or policyowner and the insurance producer no later than when the policy is delivered.

If a sales illustration is presented to a customer who decides to apply for a policy other than the one illustrated, then the insurance producer and the applicant must certify that fact on a form provided by the insurer. The applicant also must certify that he understands that, if the insurer issues a policy, he will receive an illustration of that policy no later than when the policy is delivered to him.

In some cases, an illustration is not used in the sale of a life insurance policy for which the insurer has elected to use illustrations. In such cases, the insurance producer must certify on a form provided by the insurer that no illustration was used. On the same form, the applicant for the policy must certify that (1) no illustration was presented and (2) she understands that, if the insurer issues a policy, she will receive an illustration of that policy no later than when the policy is delivered to her. The insurance producer must submit the signed and dated form to the insurer along with the application for insurance.

As we have described, when the insurer issues a policy for which illustrations are to be used, the insurer must be sure that the applicant receives a copy of a basic illustration of the policy as issued. The illustration must be signed by both the applicant and the insurance producer or other representative of the insurer. In addition, the insurer must maintain in its records a copy of the illustration until three years after the policy is no longer in force. The insurer must maintain copies of all certifications that either no illustration was used or the policy applied for was not illustrated. In cases in which the insurer does not issue a policy, then it has no responsibility for maintaining a copy of any illustrations used.

Periodic Reporting Requirements

The Life Insurance Illustrations Model Regulation requires an insurer that has issued a policy designated as one for which illustrations will be used to provide the policyowner with periodic reports concerning the status of the policy; such a report must be provided at least every year. The Model Regulation lists the elements that insurers must include in the annual reports they provide to policyowners. The report for all policies other than universal life insurance policies must include the following information:

- The amount of the current death benefit
- The amount of the annual policy premium
- The amount of the current cash surrender value
- The amount of the current dividend, if any, and the dividend option that is in effect
- The amount of any outstanding policy loan

For universal life insurance policies, the periodic report must include the following information:

- The beginning and ending dates of the current period being reported
- The policy value at the end of the previous report period and the policy value at the end of the current report period
- The total amounts that have been credited or debited to the policy value during the current report period
- The amount of the death benefit at the end of the current report period
- The amount of the policy net cash surrender value at the end of the current report period
- The amount of any outstanding policy loans

If the insurer has changed a nonguaranteed element of the policy since the last report and that change could affect the policy, then the insurer must disclose that fact in the report. The insurer also must prominently display information about the type of change it made. If the policyowner requests it, the insurer is required to provide a current illustration of the policy.

According to the Model Regulation, the insurer's board of directors is required to appoint an ***illustration actuary*** who is an actuary specially qualified in the actuarial standards of practice relating to life insurance sales illustrations.

This appointment must be reported to the state insurance department, and any changes in the actuary who is appointed must also be reported. The illustration actuary is required to certify each year that the illustrations for each policy subject to the Model Regulation comply with the Regulation. This certification must be provided to the insurer's board of directors and the state insurance department. In addition, an officer of the insurer must certify each year that the illustrations comply with the Model Regulation and must provide that certification to the state insurance department.

DISCLOSURE REQUIREMENTS

State regulatory requirements seek to ensure that consumers receive truthful and accurate information that enables them to make informed decisions about life insurance purchases. Insurers that solicit the sale of life insurance from consumers must provide those consumers with specific types of information. Insurers also are required to provide periodic informational statements to the owners of life insurance policies, and in some cases, insurers are required to make periodic filings with state regulators. In this section, we first describe general requirements imposed on most individual life insurance policies. Then we describe the requirements that some specific types of policies must meet.

General Disclosure Requirements

Most states have adopted some version of the NAIC *Life Insurance Disclosure Model Regulation*, which requires insurers to give purchasers of life insurance information that will (1) improve purchasers' ability to select the insurance plan that will best meet the purchasers' needs and (2) improve purchasers' understanding of the life insurance products they buy or consider buying. The Model Regulation's requirements apply to any solicitation, negotiation, or purchase of life insurance within an applicable state, with the following exceptions: (1) credit life insurance, (2) group life insurance, (3) life insurance issued in connection with pension and welfare plans, and (4) variable life insurance under which the amount or duration of life insurance varies based on the investment experience of a separate account. Life insurers subject to requirements based on the Model Regulation must provide specified types of information—including a Buyer's Guide and a policy summary—to prospective purchasers of applicable life insurance products.

Buyer's Guide

According to regulations based on the Life Insurance Disclosure Model Regulation, prospective purchasers of most types of life insurance must receive a

Buyer's Guide. The ***Buyer's Guide*** is a brochure designed to educate consumers about life insurance and enable them to get the most for their money when shopping for life insurance. The Model Regulation sets out the specific language insurers must include in a Buyer's Guide. However, insurers may use different language in their Buyer's Guide if the applicable state insurance department approves the language first. The Buyer's Guide explains to consumers how to determine how much life insurance coverage they need, describes the various types of life insurance policies, and educates consumers about how to compare the costs of similar types of policies.

Policy Summary

In addition to requiring insurers to provide a Buyer's Guide, the Life Insurance Disclosure Model Regulation requires insurers to provide a policy summary to prospective purchasers of a life insurance policy that the insurer has identified as a policy that will be marketed without an illustration. A ***policy summary*** is a written statement that describes specific guaranteed elements of the life insurance policy being considered for purchase. Note that a policy summary may show only guaranteed amounts. In addition, a policy summary must have the title, *Statement of Policy Cost and Benefit Information*, prominently placed on the policy summary. The following are some of the elements that must be included in the policy summary:

- The name and address of the insurance producer, if applicable, or instructions for how the consumer can obtain answers to questions about the policy summary

- The name and address of the insurer

- The generic name of the policy and each rider—the ***generic name*** is a short title that describes the premium and benefit patterns of a policy or rider

- Specific amounts for the first five policy years and representative years thereafter, including (1) the annual premium for the policy and for each rider, (2) the death benefit payable, (3) the cash surrender value, and (4) any endowment amounts payable

- If the policy contains a policy loan provision, the effective annual percentage interest rate charged for policy loans

- The date on which the policy summary was prepared

The insurer must provide an applicant with a Buyer's Guide and policy summary before accepting the applicant's initial premium payment *unless* the policy includes at least a 10-day free-look period. If the policy includes such a free-look provision, then the insurer has until the time it delivers the policy to provide a Buyer's Guide and policy summary. Recall that most states require policies to include at least a 10-day free-look period.

Variable Life Insurance Disclosure Requirements

As we have noted, variable life insurance policies generally are subject to regulatory requirements that are specific to variable life insurance. Many states' requirements are based on the NAIC Variable Life Insurance Model Regulation, which we described in Chapter 1. In these states, insurers that sell variable life insurance policies are subject to a number of disclosure requirements.

Solicitation Disclosure Requirements

An insurer must provide an applicant for a variable life insurance policy with specified information about the provisions and operation of the policy. According to the Variable Life Insurance Model Regulation, the insurer must provide this information before or at the time an applicant completes the application for variable life insurance and must obtain a written acknowledgement that the applicant received the information. The Model Regulation requires an insurer to provide the following information:

- An explanation, in nontechnical terms, of the principal features of the policy

- A statement of the investment policy of the separate account

- A statement of the net investment return of the separate account for each of the last 10 years or a lesser period if the separate account has not been in existence for 10 years

- A statement of the charges levied against the separate account during the previous year

- A summary of the method to be used to value assets held by the separate account

- A summary of the federal income tax aspects of the policy as applied to the policyowner, the insured, and the beneficiary

- Illustrations of benefits payable under the policy

An insurer can satisfy this disclosure requirement by providing the applicant with a prospectus that has been filed with and declared effective by the Securities and Exchange Commission (SEC). Most variable life policies are subject to SEC registration requirements, and insurers usually meet the Model Regulation's requirement by providing a prospectus. (Insight 2-3 describes both the SEC registration requirements and prospectuses.) Some variable life policies—for example, some policies purchased by employers to fund certain employee benefits—are exempt from SEC registration requirements. In such cases, the insurer can satisfy the Model Regulation's disclosure requirement by providing the applicant with information and reports required by the federal Employee Retirement Income Security Act (ERISA).

As noted earlier in the chapter, variable life insurance policies are not subject to the requirements of the Life Insurance Illustrations Model Regulation or the Life Insurance Disclosure Model Regulation. Variable life insurance

---

INSIGHT 2-3 — Federal Regulation of Variable Life Products.

In accordance with the federal **Securities Act of 1933**, the SEC has determined that variable life insurance and variable annuity products are securities that must comply with federal securities laws. The Securities Act requires that each security be registered with the SEC before it is advertised or offered for sale to the public. The issuer of a security—for example, an insurer or an organization affiliated with the insurer that issues variable products—registers the security by filing a registration statement with the SEC and paying a stated fee. The registration statement provides information about the security's issuer and about the security. Upon filing a registration statement, an issuer may begin to advertise the security, but it may not actually offer to sell the security until the registration statement becomes effective; the effective date is typically a stated number of days after its filing.

The SEC reviews each registration statement to determine whether the information it contains is complete and accurate. If the SEC finds that a registration statement is incomplete or inaccurate, the SEC may—after notice to the issuer and an opportunity for a hearing—refuse to permit the statement to become effective until it has been amended.

According to the Securities Act, a **prospectus** is any communication—written or oral—that offers a security for sale. Because of the large amount of information a prospectus must contain, a prospectus is generally a formal, written offer to sell a security. A prospectus must include the following types of information:

- Information about the security's issuer, including its location, the nature of its business, and its financial condition
- Information about the individuals who manage the issuing corporation
- Information about the security, including the terms on which it will be sold, the expenses incurred in its offering, and the proceeds that will be realized from its sale
- Specified financial statements that have been certified by independent public accountants

Source: Adapted from Harriett E. Jones and Monica R. Maxwell, *Regulatory Compliance: Companies, Producers, and Operations*, 2nd ed. (Atlanta: LOMA, © 2002), 305–307. Used with permission; all rights reserved.

policies, however, must comply with requirements based on the Advertisements of Life Insurance and Annuities Model Regulation. In addition, the Variable Life Insurance Model Regulation prohibits an insurer from using any sales material, advertising material, or other materials of any kind in connection with its variable life insurance business in the state if that material is false, misleading, deceptive, or inaccurate.

Periodic Reporting Requirements

The Variable Life Insurance Model Regulation requires insurers to mail two types of periodic reports to variable life insurance policyowners at their last known addresses. The first report is a statement of the policy's cash surrender value, death benefit, any partial withdrawal or policy loan, any interest charge, and any optional payments; each amount reported must be computed as of the policy anniversary date. This report must be provided within 30 days after (1) each policy anniversary or (2) a specified date in each policy year.

The Model Regulation also requires the insurer to mail to each policyowner an annual statement that includes the following information:

- A summary of the financial statement of the separate account based on the last Annual Statement the insurer filed with the state insurance department

- The net investment return of the separate account for the last year and a comparison of that return to the investment return during specified prior years

- A list of investments held by the separate account as of a specified date

- Any charges levied against the separate account during the previous year

- A statement of any change in (1) the investment objective and orientation of the separate account, (2) any investment restriction applicable to the separate account, or (3) the investment adviser of the separate account

Pre-Need Funeral Contracts

Many states impose specific requirements on the sale of ***pre-need funeral contracts***, which are agreements by or on behalf of individuals before their deaths relating to the purchase of funeral or cemetery merchandise or services. When such a contract is funded by life insurance, state insurance laws regulate some aspects of the transaction. As noted earlier, most states have adopted regulations based on the NAIC Life Insurance Disclosure Model Regulation, which imposes various requirements on the sale of pre-need funeral contracts funded by life insurance. The following information must be disclosed at the time of application before acceptance of the initial premium payment:

- The fact that a life insurance policy is being used to fund the prearrangement

- The nature of the relationship among the insurance producer, the provider of the funeral or cemetery merchandise or services, the administrator of the plan, and any other party to the transaction

- The relationship of the life insurance policy to the funding of the prearrangement

- The existence and nature of any guarantees relating to the prearrangement

- A list of the merchandise and services that are contracted for in the prearrangement and all relevant information concerning the price of the funeral services, including an indication that the purchase price is either guaranteed at the time of purchase or to be determined at the time of need

If a sales commission or other compensation is to be paid for the sale of the pre-need funeral contract, then that fact must be disclosed to the applicant. Also, the applicant must be told which individual or entity will receive the commission or compensation.

Emerging Market Conduct Issues

At any given time, state insurance departments are investigating various aspects of the market conduct operations of insurance companies in an effort to identify activities that may be unfairly affecting the public. During 2000 and 2001, the NAIC and various state insurance departments were examining two issues related to the market conduct operations of life insurers. First, a number of state insurance departments have identified insurers operating within their jurisdictions that used race as a factor in setting life insurance premium rates. The state insurance departments in most states have surveyed companies about their practices and are continuing to investigate such practices.

State insurance departments also have found that many companies have in-force policies with relatively small face amounts that have been in force for such a long time that the total amount of premiums paid far exceeds the face amounts of the policies. As a result, state insurance regulators are concerned that policyowners may not understand the actual costs of their policies. In order to protect purchasers of small face amount policies, the NAIC is in the process of developing the *Disclosure for Small Face Amount Life Insurance Policies Model Act*. This proposed model law will require insurers to provide a specified notice to policyowners who purchase a small face amount policy if at any time during the term of the policy the total amount of premiums paid will be more than the policy face amount. The proposed model defines *small face amount policy* as a life insurance policy with an initial face amount of $15,000 or less. The required notice must be delivered to the policyowner no later than when the policy is delivered. It informs the policyowner that the cost over time may exceed the amount of the coverage and points out the policy's free-look period during which the policyowner can return the policy and receive a full refund of premiums paid.

KEY TERMS AND CONCEPTS

rebating
suitability requirement
Unfair Trade Practices Act
complaint
Advertisements of Life Insurance and Annuities Model Regulation
advertisement
rating agencies
quality rating
Life Insurance Illustrations Model Regulation

illustration
basic illustration
supplemental illustration
insurer's illustrated scale
illustration actuary
Life Insurance Disclosure Model Regulation
Buyer's Guide
policy summary
generic name
pre-need funeral contract

ENDNOTE

1. *Best's Insurance Reports: Life-Health U.S.,* 2001 ed. (Oldwick, NJ: A.M. Best Company, 2001), x.

CHAPTER 3

Regulation of Individual Health Insurance Products

LEARNING OBJECTIVES

After studying this chapter, you should be able to

- Identify the provisions that state insurance laws require individual health insurance policies to contain and the provisions that such policies are permitted to contain

- List the types of minimum standards the states impose on individual health insurance products

- Identify the types of limitations and exclusions that individual health insurance policies are permitted to contain

- Recognize types of benefits the states require individual health insurance policies to provide

- Identify the types of guaranteed renewability and guaranteed availability requirements the federal Health Insurance Portability and Accountability Act (HIPAA) imposes on issuers of individual health insurance policies

A wide range of health insurance products provide consumers with protection against the risk of financial loss resulting from an insured person's sickness, accidental injury, or disability. Some of these health insurance products provide various types of *medical expense coverage* to pay for the treatment of an insured's illnesses and injuries. Others of these health insurance products provide *disability income benefits* to an insured who is unable to work because of a covered sickness or injury. State insurance laws and regulations use various terms to refer to health insurance, including *accident and health insurance* and *accident and sickness insurance*. These differences in terminology are historical in nature. Industry terminology has changed dramatically since the regulatory requirements were developed. In this text, we use the term *health insurance* to include both medical expense coverages and disability income coverages.

The next four chapters describe the regulatory requirements imposed on health insurance. In this chapter, we look at the compliance issues that an insurer faces in the process of developing individual health insurance products. Chapter 4 describes the regulatory requirements imposed on the advertising and sale of health insurance. Chapter 5 describes the regulatory requirements imposed on some specific types of health insurance products—Medicare supplement insurance and long-term care (LTC) insurance. Chapter 6 describes state requirements imposed on managed care systems that provide medical expense coverage, including health maintenance organizations (HMOs) and preferred provider arrangements (PPAs).

Although our focus in this chapter is on traditional indemnity insurance products, the requirements we describe also are generally imposed on newer forms of health insurance products including Medicare supplement insurance, long-term care insurance, and health benefit plans that include a preferred provider arrangement. By contrast, most states have enacted specific laws to regulate HMOs, and in those states, the requirements described in this chapter do not apply to HMOs. Group health insurance plans also are governed by separate state regulations, which we describe in Chapter 8.

HEALTH INSURANCE PRODUCT DEVELOPMENT

An insurer developing an individual health insurance product typically follows the same general product development process we described in Chapter 1 with reference to life insurance. In developing a health insurance policy form and the underwriting guidelines for that form, the health insurer must consider many of the same compliance issues that life insurers consider in the technical development of life insurance products.

Policy Form Development

Most states require health insurers to file a new policy form with, and receive approval from, the state insurance department before the form is delivered or issued for delivery within the state. In this section, we describe the types of regulatory requirements that individual health insurance policy forms must meet in order to receive state insurance department approval.

Readability Requirements

As noted in Chapter 1, most states require individual life and health insurance policies to comply with the NAIC *Life and Health Insurance Policy Language Simplification Model Act*. If an individual health insurance policy must receive at least a specified score on a readability test, then the policy form filing submission package must include a certification stating that the policy form achieved the minimum score.

Policy Face Page Requirements

Regulatory requirements concerning the information that must appear on the face page of an individual health insurance policy vary from state to state and vary depending on the type of coverage provided by the policy. Many states require the face page to contain specified information about the conditions under which the policy may be renewed. Most states require policies to provide at least a 10-day free-look period, and many of those states require the policy face page to include a description of the free-look provision. The length of the required free-look period ranges from 10 to 30 days, depending on the state and the type of policy. For example, about half of the states require Medicare supplement policies and long-term care policies to provide a 30-day free-look period.

Other requirements tend to vary depending on the type of coverage provided by the policy. A number of states require policies that provide limited coverages—such as policies that provide benefits only for losses resulting from a specific disease such as cancer—to include on the policy face page a notice that the policy provides limited benefits. Some states require policies that provide coverage only for losses resulting from accident to include a prominent statement that the policy is an accident-only policy and does not pay benefits for losses resulting from sickness.

Required Policy Provisions

Most states have adopted the NAIC *Uniform Individual Accident and Sickness Policy Provision Law (Uniform Policy Provision Law or UPPL)*, which specifies the provisions that individual health policies must contain. An insurer that delivers or issues individual health policies for delivery in a state that has adopted the UPPL must comply with the Uniform Law. Note that in states that have enacted specific HMO legislation, the UPPL applies to all individual health policies other than contracts issued by an HMO.

The UPPL imposes the following general requirements on individual health insurance policy forms:

- The policy must specify the amount of the required premium.

- The policy must specify the time at which coverage begins and ends.

- Usually, the policy must insure only one person. The exception is for *family coverage*, which must be issued to an adult member of a family, known as the *policyholder*, and may cover any two or more eligible family members, including husband, wife, dependent children or children under a specified age, and any other person dependent upon the policyholder.

- The style, arrangement, and overall appearance of the policy form must not give undue prominence to any portion of the text.

Insurers also are required to include specified provisions in policies subject to the UPPL. Those provisions usually must be worded in the statutory language but may be worded in alternative language if the change does not make the provision less favorable to the insured or beneficiary *and* the state insurance department approves the change. In addition, the NAIC has adopted a *Restatement of UPPL in Simplified Language*, which revises most of the required policy provisions into simplified language.

The UPPL requires policies to include the following provisions in the same order as listed here with the captions listed unless the state insurance department approves a change. In the following sections, we describe the information that each provision must contain. Figure 3-1 provides a comparison of types of policy provisions that are included in both individual life and individual health insurance policies.

Entire contract provision. The *entire contract provision* specifies the documents that constitute the insurance contract. With the exception of open contracts issued by fraternal insurers, the entire contract must consist of the policy and any endorsements and other documents attached to the policy, including the application for insurance and policy riders. The entire contract provision also must state that the policy terms may not be changed unless an officer of the insurer approves the change and notes that approval on the policy or on an attachment to the policy before the policy is issued. Thus, insurance producers are not authorized to change the terms of a policy form.

Time limit on certain defenses provision. The *time limit on certain defenses provision* is a required provision that limits the time during which the insurer may contest the validity of the contract on the ground of misrepresentation or may reduce or deny a claim on the ground that it results from a preexisting condition. The provision must state a maximum time following the date of policy issue during which the insurer has the right to contest the policy or to deny a claim only on the ground of fraudulent misstatements in the application. The provision also must state that the insurer may not reduce or deny a claim incurred after the specified time limit on the ground that a disease or physical condition that is not specifically excluded from coverage by the policy had existed prior to the effective date of coverage. According to the Uniform Policy Provision Law, the time limit on certain defenses provision may include a maximum time limit of three years. Most states, however, have modified this requirement and allow a maximum limitation period of two years following policy issue.

Grace period provision. Individual health insurance policies must include a *grace period provision*, and the UPPL requires a specified minimum grace period following a renewal premium due date during which coverage continues

FIGURE 3-1 A Comparison of Provisions Contained in Individual Life Policies and Provisions Contained in Individual Health Policies.

The following provisions are found in both individual life and individual health insurance policies:

- The **entire contract provision** defines the documents that constitute the contractual agreement between the insurer and the policyowner.

- The **grace period provision** grants the policyowner a specified period following a renewal premium due date within which to pay the premium. The length of the grace period provided by a life insurance policy generally is at least 31 days. The length of the grace period provided by a health insurance policy varies depending on the frequency of premium payments.

- The **misstatement of age provision** describes how policy benefits will be adjusted if the insured's age has been misstated. Both individual life and individual health insurance policies provide that benefits will be paid based on the coverage the premiums actually paid would have provided if the insured's age had been stated correctly. Although individual life insurance policies are required to include a misstatement of age provision, individual health insurance policies are permitted but not required to include such a provision.

- The **reinstatement provision** gives the policyowner the right to meet specified requirements and reinstate a policy that has lapsed for nonpayment of premium. Although both individual life and individual health insurance policies are required to include a reinstatement provision, the conditions under which an insurer must reinstate a policy vary depending on whether the policy provides life or health coverage.

- All individual life insurance policies include a **beneficiary provision** that identifies the party or parties who are to receive the policy proceeds following the insured's death. Individual health policies sometimes include a death benefit, and these policies also must include a beneficiary provision identifying who is entitled to receive any death benefit payable under the policy.

- Individual life insurance policies are required to include an **incontestability provision** that limits the time in which the insurer may contest the validity of the contract based on misrepresentations in the application for insurance. Individual health insurance policies are required to include a similar provision known as the **time limit on certain defenses provision**, which limits the time during which the insurer may (1) contest the validity of the contract on the ground of misrepresentations in the application or (2) reduce or deny a claim on the ground it results from a preexisting condition.

even if the premium is unpaid. The length of the required grace period varies depending on the frequency of premium payments. Weekly premium policies must provide a grace period of at least 7 days; monthly premium policies must have a grace period of at least 10 days; and all other policies must have a grace period of at least 31 days.

Renewal provision. The *renewal provision* included in an individual health insurance policy describes the conditions under which the insurer has the right to cancel or refuse to renew the coverage, and it describes the insurer's right to increase the policy's premium rate at the time of a renewal. If the insurer reserves the right to refuse to renew the policy other than for nonpayment of premium, then it may not exercise that right before the renewal date on or following the policy anniversary date. Any refusal to renew the policy will not affect any claim that occurred while the policy was in force. We describe additional aspects of the renewal provision later in the chapter.

Reinstatement provision. The *reinstatement provision* states that the insurer will reinstate a policy that has lapsed for nonpayment of premiums if certain conditions are met. The insurer's acceptance of a renewal premium payment after the end of the grace period without requiring an application for reinstatement will automatically reinstate the policy. An insurer's receipt of a premium payment does not constitute acceptance of that payment. The insurer's actions following receipt of a payment determine whether it accepted the payment. If, for example, the insurer deposits the funds into its bank account along with other premium payments it received, then the insurer probably will be deemed to have accepted the payment. By contrast, the insurer can refuse to accept a payment by returning the payment to the policyowner and providing the policyowner with information on how to reinstate the policy.

The reinstatement provision must state that if the insurer requires an application for reinstatement along with payment of the renewal premium, then the insurer will issue a conditional premium receipt in exchange for the premium. If the application is approved, the policy is reinstated as of the approval date. Unless the insurer has notified the insured in writing that the application is disapproved, the policy will be reinstated on the 45th day after the date of the conditional receipt.

In most cases, the reinstated policy is required to cover only losses that result from either an injury sustained after the date of reinstatement or a sickness that starts more than 10 days after reinstatement. In all other respects, the risk of the insured and the insurer will remain the same as stated in the original policy, subject to any provisions noted on or attached to the reinstated policy.

Notice of claim provision. The *notice of claim provision* states that written notice of a claim must be given to the insurer within 20 days after the occurrence or commencement of a covered loss or as soon thereafter as is reasonably possible. Although individual claimants may provide separate written notices to an insurer, most claims are submitted to the insurer by physicians and other providers using computerized claim administration systems. Insight 3-1 describes how electronic data interchange (EDI) enables insurers, customers, and providers to conduct many types of transactions.

Claim forms provision. The *claim forms provision* states that the insurer will furnish the claimant with forms for filing proofs of loss when it receives notice of a claim.

Proofs of loss provision. The *proofs of loss provision* specifies the time limits within which claimants must provide the insurer with proof of a covered loss. If the policy provides for periodic payments for a continuing loss, written proof of loss must be given to the insurer within 90 days after the end of each period for which the insurer is liable. For any other loss, written proof must be given within 90 days after such loss. If written proof cannot be provided within the time required, the insurer may not reduce or deny the claim if the proof is filed as soon as reasonably possible. In any event, the proof required must be given no later than one year from the date of loss unless the claimant was legally incapacitated.

Time of payment of claims provision. The *time of payment of claims provision* states that after receiving written proof of loss for which the policy provides periodic benefit payments, the insurer will pay those benefits as

---

INSIGHT 3-1 — Technology in Claim Administration.

Many insurers now reap advantages that result from the use of new technology. One of the most important applications of technology to claim administration is the use of **electronic data interchange (EDI)**, which is a computer-to-computer information exchange that uses a standardized format for electronic movement of data so that various companies and individuals can exchange information easily. Through the use of EDI, claimants can submit life and health insurance claims electronically. Claimants can also track a submitted claim to learn the date a claim was received by an insurer, the current status of the claim, the payment amount for the claim, or if applicable, the denial date of the claim.

Claim analysts also use EDI to automatically notify claimants that submitted claims contain errors. Analysts can send information electronically to policyowners, agents, providers, vendors, and others. Finally, providers, such as physicians, can use EDI to submit a patient's claim to an insurer using a voice response system that recognizes a specified person's voice.

Source: Adapted from Jane Brown, Jennifer W. Herrod, and Monica R. Maxwell, *Claim Administration: Principles and Practices*, 3rd ed. (International Claim Association, © 2001), 7. Used with permission; all rights reserved.

described in the policy. Upon receiving written proof of any other covered loss, the insurer will immediately pay the policy benefits.

Payment of claims provision. The *payment of claims provision* states that claims for loss of life will be payable to the named beneficiary. All other claims will be payable to the insured.

Physical examinations and autopsy provision. Under the *physical examinations and autopsy provision*, the insurer has the right to conduct a medical examination of the insured at its own expense when reasonably necessary while a claim is pending. If the insured dies, the insurer also has the right to an autopsy unless otherwise forbidden by law.

Legal actions provision. The *legal actions provision* states that a claimant may not file a legal action to recover under the policy until at least 60 days after furnishing the insurer with written proof of loss. In addition, such an action may not be filed more than three years after proof of loss is required. A number of states limit the time in which an action may be filed to two years after proof of loss is required.

Change of beneficiary provision. Health insurance policies sometimes provide a benefit payable following the insured's death, and these policies must identify the party or parties to whom this death benefit is payable. These policies are required to include a *change of beneficiary provision*, which states that, unless the policyowner makes an irrevocable beneficiary designation, the policyowner has the right to change the designation and to surrender or assign the policy without the beneficiary's consent.

Optional Policy Provisions

The insurer has the option of including certain other provisions in individual health insurance policies, including medical expense and disability income policies, if those provisions conform to the provisions specified in the Uniform Policy Provision Law. The following optional provisions are permitted by the Uniform Law.

Change of occupation provision. A *change of occupation provision* specifies how benefits or premiums will be adjusted if the insured changes to a more or less hazardous occupation. If a covered loss occurs after the insured has changed occupations to one the insurer classifies as more hazardous than the prior occupation, the policy benefit will be limited to the amount that the premium paid would have provided at the prior less hazardous occupation. Note that the insurer is authorized to reduce the benefit level only if a covered loss occurs after a change in occupation. If the insured notifies the insurer that she has changed occupations to one the insurer classifies as less hazardous, then the insurer will reduce the premium rate accordingly; the amount of benefits payable will remain the same as stated in the policy.

Misstatement of age provision. According to the *misstatement of age provision*, if the age of the insured has been misstated, any benefit payable under the policy will be equal to the benefit that the premium paid would have purchased at the insured's correct age, according to the insurer's published premium rates at the time of policy issue.

Overinsurance provision. An *overinsurance provision* defines the insurer's liability to pay policy benefits for covered losses that are insured by more than one policy regardless of whether the same insurer issued all of those policies. The purpose of the provision is to prevent an insured from receiving more in policy benefits than she incurred in covered losses, and virtually all individual health insurance policies contain an overinsurance provision.

Various types of overinsurance provisions may be included in health insurance policies at the option of the insurer. State insurance laws allow all types of health policies to provide that if the insured has more than one policy with the same insurer, only one policy, chosen by the insured, will be effective. Insurers' underwriting guidelines are designed to prevent such a situation from occurring; however, if it should occur, the insurer will refund all premiums paid for all the other policies.

Policies that provide medical expense benefits also may include an overinsurance provision that addresses situations in which an insured has overlapping coverage provided by policies issued by different insurers. Such an overinsurance provision limits the insurer's liability for paying policy benefits if total benefits payable exceed the amount of covered expenses incurred.

Unpaid premiums provision. The *unpaid premiums provision* states that when a claim is paid, any premium due and unpaid may be deducted from the claim payment.

Conformity with state statutes provision. The *conformity with state statutes provision* states that any policy provision that is in conflict with the laws of the state in which the insured resides is amended to conform to the minimum requirements of such laws.

Illegal occupation provision. According to the *illegal occupation provision*, the insurer will not be liable for any loss that results from the insured's committing or attempting to commit a felony or from the insured's engaging in an illegal occupation. For example, an insured who is injured while committing armed robbery or while engaged in illegal drug sales or prostitution is not eligible to receive policy benefits for the treatment of that injury.

Intoxicants and narcotics provision. The *intoxicants and narcotics provision* states that the insurer will not be liable for any loss resulting from the insured's being under the influence of alcohol or any narcotic unless taken on the advice of a physician.

Minimum Policy Standards

More than one-half of the states impose minimum standards on individual health insurance policies delivered or issued for delivery within the states. Most such requirements are based on the NAIC *Accident and Sickness Insurance Minimum Standards Model Act (Minimum Standards Act)*, which establishes certain standards for all individual health policies other than Medicare supplement policies and for certain group supplemental health insurance policies. The Minimum Standards Act requires the state insurance commissioner to adopt regulations to define such standards and requirements. Most state insurance departments have adopted regulations based on the NAIC *Model Regulation to Implement the Accident and Sickness Insurance Minimum Standards Model Act (Minimum Standards Model Regulation)*. The Minimum Standards Act and Model Regulation are designed to standardize and simplify the terms of health policies, to facilitate public understanding of health policies, and to provide full disclosure in the sale of such policies. These regulatory requirements include (1) definitions of terms often included in health policies, (2) minimum benefit standards, (3) required policy provisions, (4) prohibited policy provisions, and (5) disclosure requirements. In this section, we describe the first four types of regulatory requirements; we describe disclosure requirements in the next chapter.

According to the Model Regulation, the following types of individual policies are exempt from its requirements:

- Policies issued to individuals who exercise a conversion privilege granted by a group or individual contract that contains provisions inconsistent with the requirements of the Model Regulation. (We describe the conversion provision included in group health insurance policies in Chapter 8.)

- Policies issued to employees or members as additions to franchise plans that were in existence when the Model Regulation was adopted. Note that such policies issued after a state has adopted the Model Regulation must comply with the Regulation. A *franchise plan* is individual coverage that is issued to specified members of an employer-employee or other type of group.

- Medicare supplement policies subject to the Medicare Supplement Insurance Minimum Standards Model Act, which we describe in Chapter 5.

- Long-term care insurance policies subject to the Long-Term Care Insurance Model Act, which we describe in Chapter 5. Long-term care policies, however, are subject to the Accident and Sickness Insurance Minimum Standards Model Act.

- *Civilian Health and Medical Program of the Uniformed Services (CHAMPUS)* supplement insurance policies. CHAMPUS is a federal program that provides health insurance coverage to the families of military personnel, including military retirees, military spouses, and dependents of military personnel.

Policy definitions. Health insurance policies are often complex documents that include a range of provisions to define the benefits the policies provide. In order to standardize the terminology used in health insurance policies, the Minimum Standards Model Regulation defines a number of terms that are often used in health insurance policies and prohibits an insurer from issuing a policy that defines any of those terms more restrictively than the specified definition. This requirement, thus, imposes minimum standards on the policy definitions of the specified terms, which are listed in Figure 3-2.

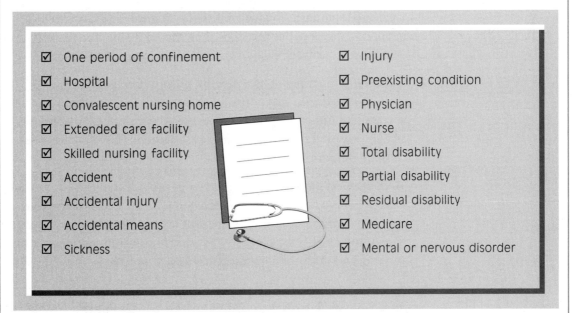

FIGURE 3-2 Policy Terms Defined in the Minimum Standards Model Regulation.

- ☑ One period of confinement
- ☑ Hospital
- ☑ Convalescent nursing home
- ☑ Extended care facility
- ☑ Skilled nursing facility
- ☑ Accident
- ☑ Accidental injury
- ☑ Accidental means
- ☑ Sickness
- ☑ Injury
- ☑ Preexisting condition
- ☑ Physician
- ☑ Nurse
- ☑ Total disability
- ☑ Partial disability
- ☑ Residual disability
- ☑ Medicare
- ☑ Mental or nervous disorder

Source: National Association of Insurance Commissioners, *Model Regulation to Implement the Accident and Sickness Insurance Minimum Standards Model Act* § 5, 1999.

Minimum benefit standards. The Model Regulation specifies minimum benefit standards that policies subject to the Regulation must provide. Many of these benefit standards refer to terms such as coinsurance, copayments, and deductibles. These terms are defined in Figure 3-3.

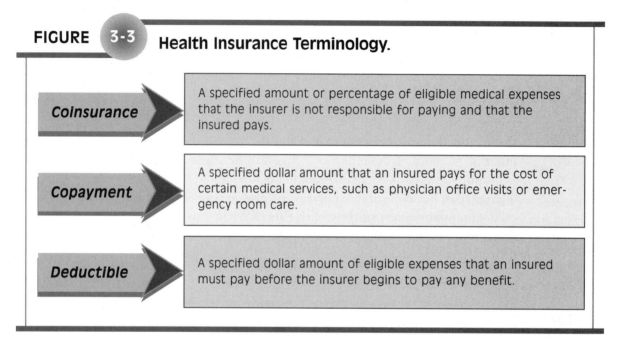

FIGURE 3-3 **Health Insurance Terminology.**

Coinsurance — A specified amount or percentage of eligible medical expenses that the insurer is not responsible for paying and that the insured pays.

Copayment — A specified dollar amount that an insured pays for the cost of certain medical services, such as physician office visits or emergency room care.

Deductible — A specified dollar amount of eligible expenses that an insured must pay before the insurer begins to pay any benefit.

The required standards, which are listed in Figure 3-4, vary depending on the types of coverage a policy provides. The Model Regulation includes minimum benefit standards for each of the following types of coverage:

- *Basic hospital expense coverage* provides coverage for a period of at least 31 days during any continuous hospital confinement for each person insured under the policy. Coverage consists of benefits for the costs of daily hospital room and board, miscellaneous hospital expenses, and hospital outpatient services.

- *Basic medical-surgical expense coverage* provides coverage for expenses each person insured under the policy incurs for necessary services rendered by a physician for treatment of an injury or sickness. Coverage consists of benefits for expenses incurred for surgical services, anesthesia services, and in-hospital medical services.

- *Hospital confinement indemnity coverage* provides a daily benefit of at least $40 per day for a period of at least 31 days during any hospital confinement.

- *Major medical expense coverage* provides comprehensive hospital, medical, and surgical expense coverage, including benefits for daily hospital room and board, miscellaneous hospital services, surgical services, anesthesia services, in-hospital medical services, and out-of-hospital care. Benefits may be subject to an aggregate maximum of not less than $500,000 per year. Coinsurance may not exceed 50 percent of covered charges per year, provided that, after deductibles, the coinsurance out-of-pocket maximum does not exceed $10,000 per year. Deductibles imposed may not exceed 5 percent of the aggregate maximum benefit.

- *Basic medical expense coverage* provides comprehensive hospital, medical, and surgical expense coverage, including benefits for daily hospital room and board, miscellaneous hospital services, surgical services, anesthesia services, in-hospital medical services, and out-of-hospital care. Benefits may be subject to an aggregate maximum of not less than $250,000 per year. Coinsurance may not exceed 50 percent of covered charges per year, provided that, after deductibles, the coinsurance out-of-pocket maximum does not exceed $25,000 per year. Deductibles imposed may not exceed 10 percent of the aggregate maximum benefit.

- *Disability income protection coverage* provides periodic payments, either weekly or monthly, for a specified period during the continuance of a disability.

- *Accident only coverage* provides coverage for death, dismemberment, disability, and/or hospital and medical care caused by accident. Accidental death and double dismemberment benefits under the policy must be at least $1,000, and single dismemberment benefits must be at least $500.

- *Specified disease coverage* pays benefits for the diagnosis and treatment of a specifically named disease or diseases. Such coverage is sometimes referred to as *dread disease coverage*.

- *Specified accident coverage* provides benefits for death or dismemberment resulting from a specifically identified type of accident.

- *Limited benefit health coverage* provides benefits that are less than the minimum benefit standards required for any of the foregoing medical expense coverages.

Note that long-term care coverage is not included in this categorization because that coverage was developed after the states adopted minimum benefit standards regulations.

FIGURE 3-4 Minimum Benefit Standards for Individual Health Insurance Policies.

Basic hospital expense coverage:

Daily hospital room and board: Minimum benefit payable must be at least 80% of the cost for a semiprivate room or $100 a day. Benefit payment period must be at least 31 days.

Miscellaneous hospital expenses: Minimum benefit payable must be at least 80% of the incurred expenses up to a maximum of $3,000 or 10 times the daily hospital room and board benefit.

Hospital outpatient services consisting of (a) hospital services on the day outpatient surgery is performed, (b) hospital services rendered within 72 hours after injury in an amount of at least $150, and (c) x-ray and laboratory tests if benefits for the services would have been less than $100 if they had been rendered to an in-patient of the hospital.

The daily hospital room and board and miscellaneous hospital expenses benefits may be subject to a combined deductible of no more than $100.

Basic medical-surgical expense coverage:

Surgical services: Minimum benefit payable must be at least (a) amounts listed in a specified surgical fee schedule up to a maximum of $1,000 for each surgical procedure or (b) 80% of the reasonable charges.

Anesthesia services: Minimum benefit payable must be at least 80% of the reasonable charges or 15% of the amount of the surgical services benefit.

In-hospital medical services: Minimum benefit payable must be at least 80% of the reasonable charges or $50 per day for at least 21 days during one period of confinement.

Hospital confinement indemnity coverage:

Minimum benefit payable of at least $40 per day for at least 31 days during one period of confinement.

Major medical expense coverage:

Aggregate maximum benefit must be at least $500,000. Coinsurance may not exceed 50% of covered charges. Deductible may not exceed 5% of the aggregate maximum benefit; if the policy complements underlying hospital and medical insurance, then the deductible may be increased as specified in the Model Regulation.

Disability income protection coverage:

Elimination period may not exceed 90 days if benefits are payable for 1 year or less, 180 days if benefits are payable for at least 1 but not more than 2 years, or 365 days for all other benefits.

Benefits must be payable for a period of at least 6 months except when the policy covers disability arising out of pregnancy, childbirth, or miscarriage in which case the benefit period must be at least 1 month.

If periodic benefit payments are reduced because the insured is age 62 or older, then the reduced benefit must be at least 50% of the original benefit amount payable before age 62.

Figure 3-4. Minimum Benefit Standards for Individual Health Insurance Policies, *continued*.

Accident only coverage:

Accidental death benefit and double dismemberment benefit must each be at least $1,000. Benefit payable for a single dismemberment must be at least $500.

Specified disease coverage:

Noncancer coverages:

(1) Deductible of no more than $250. Overall aggregate benefit limit must be at least $10,000. Benefit period must be at least two years. Specific expenses must be covered, including hospital room and board, treatment by a legally qualified physician, private duty services of a registered nurse, drugs and medicines prescribed by a physician, and any other expenses necessarily incurred in treating the disease.

(2) No deductible. Overall aggregate benefit limit of at least $25,000 payable at the rate of at least $50 a day while confined in a hospital. Benefit period may not be less than 500 days.

Lump-sum indemnity coverage of any specified disease:

Benefit payable as a fixed, one-time payment made within 30 days of submission to the insurer of proof of diagnosis of the specified disease. Dollar benefits may be offered for sale only in even increments of $1,000.

Cancer coverages payable on an expense incurred basis:

Deductible of no more than $250. Overall aggregate benefit limit of at least $10,000. Benefit period of at least 3 years. Specified expenses must be covered, including home health care and nursing home care that meet requirements specified in the Model Regulation.

Cancer coverages payable on a per diem indemnity basis:

(1) A fixed payment of at least $100 per day of hospital confinement. Benefit period of at least 365 days.

(2) A fixed payment equal to one-half the hospital inpatient benefit for each day of hospital or nonhospital outpatient surgery, chemotherapy, and radiation therapy. Benefit period of at least 365 days of treatment.

(3) A fixed payment of at least $50 per day for blood and plasma. Benefit period of at least 365 days of treatment.

Policies may provide benefits tied to confinement in a skilled nursing home or to receipt of home health care. Such benefits must meet requirements specified in the Model Regulation.

Specified accident coverage:

Accidental death benefit and double dismemberment benefit each must be at least $1,000. Benefit payable for a single dismemberment must be at least $500.

Limited benefit health coverage:

Must meet the minimum benefit requirements imposed on specified disease coverage.

Source: Adapted from NAIC, *Model Regulation to Implement the Accident and Sickness Insurance Minimum Standards Model Act* § 7, 1999. Reprinted with permission from the National Association of Insurance Commissioners.

The Minimum Standards Model Regulation imposes additional standards on specific types of coverages provided by individual health insurance policies.

- Family policies typically provide coverage for dependent children until they reach a specified age. Family policies must provide for the continuation of coverage for any dependent child who is incapable of self-sustaining employment due to mental or physical incapacity on the date that child's coverage would otherwise terminate. If a family policy provides accidental death and dismemberment coverage, the insured must have the option of obtaining such coverage for all insureds and not just the principal insured.

- Family policies that include accidental death and dismemberment coverage may not limit such coverage to only the principal insured but must give the principal insured the option of including all other insureds under the coverage.

- Policies that have a military service exclusion that suspends an insured's coverage during military service must, upon written receipt, provide a refund of premiums applicable to that insured on a pro rata basis.

- Policies that provide pregnancy benefits and that may be cancelled or renewed at the option of the insurer must provide that, if the insurer cancels or does not renew the policy, any covered pregnancy commencing while the policy was in force will continue to be covered.

- Policies that provide convalescent or extended care benefits following hospitalization often impose a condition on the payment of such benefits—that is, the insured must be admitted to a convalescent or extended care facility within a specified time after being discharged from the hospital. Policies may not impose such a time period requirement of less than 14 days after discharge from the hospital.

- Policies that provide coverage for the recipient in a transplant operation also must provide reimbursement of any medical expenses incurred by a live donor. Such expenses must be covered only to the extent that benefits remain available after payment of the insured's covered expenses.

- A policy cannot require that a recurrent disability be separated by more than six months from the date that an original disability ends. A *recurrent disability* is a disability that results from the same cause as an original disability and that reappears after the original disability ends and after the insured returns to work. A recurrent disability is considered a continuation of the original disability.

- Accidental death and dismemberment benefits must be payable if the covered loss occurs within 90 days from the date of the accident.

- Accident policies that provide disability income benefits may impose a time limitation within which disability must commence following the accident. Such policies, however, may not impose a time limitation of less than 30 days after the date of the accident.

A number of requirements are imposed on specified disease policies, which must provide benefits not only for the specified disease but also for any other conditions or diseases directly caused or aggravated by the specified disease or treatment of the specified disease. These policies also must be guaranteed renewable or noncancellable and guaranteed renewable, and they may not contain a probationary period of more than 30 days. The application for specified disease coverage must contain a statement above the applicant's signature verifying that the person to be provided specified disease coverage is not covered by any Medicaid program.

Required policy provisions. The Minimum Standards Model Regulation requires health insurance policies to include a renewal provision that is consistent with the type of policy. The renewal provision must be appropriately captioned and must appear on the policy face page. If the policyowner's right to renew the coverage is limited to a specified time, then the renewal provision must specify that time.

If the terms *noncancellable* or *guaranteed renewable* are included, then the meaning of those terms must be clearly explained. For medical expense policies, the term *noncancellable* may be used only if the policyowner has the right to continue the coverage until the insured reaches age 65 or becomes eligible for Medicare. In the case of disability income policies, the term may be used if the policyowner has a right to continue coverage until the insured attains an age specified in the policy. Until that time, the insurer may not change any provision in the policy. The same requirements are imposed on policies that use the term *guaranteed renewable* except that the insurer may retain the right to change the premium rate charged for a guaranteed renewable policy if it does so for a class of policies.

Termination of a policy does not affect the insurer's obligation to pay claims for covered losses that occurred or commenced while the policy was in force. As we describe later in the chapter, the federal Health Insurance Portability and Accountability Act (HIPAA) imposes requirements on the renewability of individual health policies. As a general rule, if a state's requirements are more favorable to policyowners than are HIPAA's requirements, then the state's requirements apply.

Prohibited policy provisions. The Minimum Standards Model Regulation also lists a number of policy provisions that insurers are prohibited from including in individual health insurance policies. The Model Regulation contains a general prohibition against a policy's limiting or excluding coverage based on the type of illness, accident, treatment, or medical condition an insured suffers. This general prohibition, however, is subject to a number of exceptions. The Model Regulation allows an individual policy to contain the following limitations or exclusions:

- Coverage may be limited or excluded for treatment of mental or emotional disorders, alcoholism, and drug addiction. As we describe later in the chapter, however, many states mandate that policies provide coverage of such conditions.

- Coverage may be limited or excluded for conditions arising out of war or act of war; participation in a felony, riot, or insurrection; service in the armed forces; suicide (whether sane or insane); attempted suicide or intentionally self-inflicted injury; and aviation.

- A policy may limit or exclude coverage for cosmetic surgery.

- Policies are not required to cover foot care in connection with corns, calluses, flat feet, fallen arches, weak feet, chronic foot strain, or other such complaints relating to the feet.

- Policies are not required to cover treatment provided in a government hospital or to duplicate benefits provided by governmental programs, including Medicare, Medicaid, and workers' compensation programs.

- Policies may limit or exclude coverage of dental care, eyeglasses, hearing aids, custodial care, transportation, and routine physical examinations.

Accident policies are prohibited from including a *probationary period* or *waiting period*, which is a period following the policy's effective date during which no benefits are payable. As a result, policies are required to provide immediate coverage for losses resulting from accidents. We noted earlier that specified disease policies may not impose a probationary period of more than 30 days. The Minimum Standards Model Regulation also limits situations in which other types of health insurance policies may include a probationary period. The following are the only cases in which an individual health insurance policy may impose a probationary period:

- A policy generally may define the term *sickness* as sickness or disease that is diagnosed or treated by a physician after the policy's effective date and while the policy is in force. Policies also may impose a probationary period of no more than 30 days during which losses resulting from sickness are not covered.

- Policies may impose a probationary period of no more than six months during which specific diseases or conditions—hernia, disorder of reproduction organs, varicose veins, adenoids, appendix, and tonsils—are not covered. However, benefits must be payable without regard to a probationary period requirement if such a disease or condition is treated on an emergency basis.

The Minimum Standards Model Regulation contains standards concerning *preexisting conditions policy provisions* that exclude preexisting conditions from coverage for a specified period following the effective date of coverage. These policy provisions must meet requirements concerning (1) how they define the term *preexisting condition* and (2) the length of time they may exclude preexisting conditions from coverage. We describe requirements imposed by HIPAA later in the chapter.

According to the Model Regulation, a *preexisting condition* may not be defined more restrictively than the following:

> . . . the existence of symptoms which would cause an ordinarily prudent person to seek diagnosis, care, or treatment within a five-year period preceding the effective date of the coverage of the insured person or a condition for which medical advice or treatment was recommended by a physician or received from a physician within a five-year period preceding the effective date of the coverage of the insured person.

In the case of family policies, congenital anomalies of a covered dependent child born while the policy is in force may not be excluded from coverage as a preexisting condition.

The Model Regulation generally permits policies to exclude coverage for any losses resulting from preexisting conditions for a period of up to 12 months following policy issue. A longer exclusion period may be imposed on a preexisting condition if

- The application for insurance included questions about the proposed insured's health or prior medical treatment *and*

- The terms of the policy specifically exclude coverage for that named preexisting condition.

As noted earlier, in most states, the required time limit on certain defenses provision limits to a period of two years the time during which the insurer may reduce or deny a claim on the ground that the loss resulted from a preexisting condition that is not specifically excluded from coverage.

Mandated Benefits

Many federal and state laws specify that all individual health insurance policies must provide certain benefits in addition to those we have already described. When applying federal standards to health insurance policies, states are free to impose more stringent standards that favor the insured. The federal laws we describe here apply in those states that have not enacted more stringent standards.

Federal Mandated Benefits

The federal *Women's Health and Cancer Rights Act of 1998 (WHCRA)* provides protections to patients who choose to have breast reconstruction in connection with a mastectomy.[1] Although this federal law does not require health plans or insurers to pay for mastectomies, if a health plan or health insurance issuer chooses to cover mastectomies, then the plan or issuer is generally subject to WHCRA requirements. The WHCRA requires that health plans and health insurers that cover mastectomies provide the following benefits:

- Reconstruction of the breast on which the mastectomy has been performed
- Surgery and reconstruction of the other breast to produce a symmetrical appearance
- Prostheses (e.g., breast implant)
- Treatment for physical complications of the mastectomy

The federal *Newborns' and Mothers' Health Protection Act of 1996 (NMHPA)* affects the amount of time women and their newborn children are covered for a hospital stay following childbirth.[2] As a general rule, health plans and health insurance carriers that are subject to the NMHPA may not restrict benefits for a hospital stay in connection with childbirth to less than 48 hours following a vaginal delivery or 96 hours following a delivery by cesarean section. The NMHPA does not require health plans and health insurance issuers to provide coverage for hospital stays following childbirth. Policies may impose deductibles, coinsurance, and other cost-sharing requirements on hospital expenses incurred after childbirth so long as those expenses are no greater than those charged preceding childbirth.

State Mandated Benefits

The specific benefits that individual health insurance policies are required to provide vary a great deal from state to state. In this section, we describe some of the specific benefits that states require all individual health insurance policies to provide.

Maternity benefits. States impose a number of requirements on coverages for pregnancy and complications of pregnancy. Many states require medical expense policies to provide the same coverages for complications of pregnancy as are provided for any other sickness. A few states require major medical policies to provide maternity benefits, and several states require insurers to offer maternity benefits in individual health insurance policies if they offer those benefits in family health insurance policies. A few states also require all health policies that provide pregnancy-related benefits to provide coverage for in vitro fertilization procedures. A number of states also prohibit insurers from restricting the availability of maternity benefits based on an insured's marital status. Several states require disability income policies to provide disability income benefits for at least one month for pregnancy, childbirth, and miscarriage.

Alcoholism and substance abuse. A few states require individual medical expense policies to provide coverage for treatment of alcoholism and substance abuse. Some states require policies that cover treatment for such conditions to provide benefits whether treatment is received in a general hospital or a psychiatric hospital; some states require coverage for treatment received in a licensed treatment center.

Allied medical practitioners. Many states impose requirements concerning coverage for services performed by *allied medical practitioners* who are licensed health care providers other than licensed medical doctors. The specific allied medical practitioners covered by these requirements vary from state to state and include practitioners such as chiropractors, osteopaths, nurse anesthetists, podiatrists, psychologists, optometrists, and nurse midwives. Although regulatory requirements vary from state to state, they generally require that any policy providing payment for medical expense benefits or procedures shall be construed to include payment to a specific type of allied practitioner who provides the covered medical service benefits or procedures within the scope of that practitioner's license. For example, when a policy provides coverage for a medical expense benefit or procedure that a chiropractor is licensed to provide, then the policy must provide benefits for those services provided by a chiropractor.

Newborn children. Most states have adopted laws based on the NAIC *Model Newborn Children Bill*, which requires that policies providing coverage for a family member of the insured must provide coverage for a newly born child of the insured from the moment of birth. A newborn child must be provided coverage for injury or sickness including the necessary care and treatment of medically diagnosed congenital defects and birth abnormalities. Policies, however, are not required to provide newborn children with routine well-baby care services. If an additional premium amount is required to provide coverage for a child, then the policy may require the insured to notify the insurer of the child's birth and pay the required premium within 31 days after the birth in order for coverage to continue beyond the 31-day period.

Availability and Renewability of Health Insurance

Public concern over the availability and renewability of health insurance has led to the adoption of both federal and state legislation addressing these issues. The federal *Health Insurance Portability and Accountability Act (HIPAA)* imposes a number of requirements on employer-sponsored group health insurance plans, health insurance companies, and health maintenance organizations.[3] HIPAA's provisions amend three federal laws—the Employee Retirement Income Security Act (ERISA), the Internal Revenue Code, and the Public Health Service Act. Figure 3-5 describes these Acts and the Internal Revenue Code in more detail.

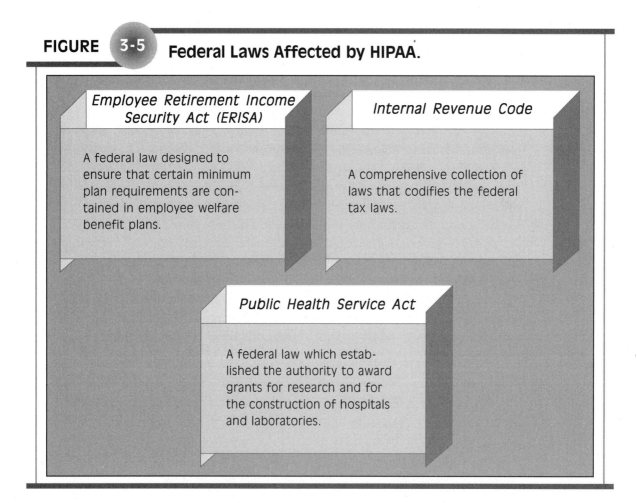

FIGURE 3-5. Federal Laws Affected by HIPAA.

In this section, we describe HIPAA's provisions that amend provisions of the federal Public Health Service Act affecting individual medical expense insurance coverages. First, we describe HIPAA's requirements concerning the guaranteed renewability of individual health policies. Then, we describe the guaranteed availability requirements imposed on individual health insurance policies by HIPAA and by state insurance laws. (We describe how HIPAA affects group health insurance plans in Chapter 9.) HIPAA does not preempt state insurance laws that are more favorable to insureds than the minimum requirements imposed by HIPAA.

Guaranteed renewability requirements. HIPAA imposes a general requirement that insurers must renew or continue an individual health insurance policy in force at the option of the policyowner. Insurers, however, have the right to discontinue or not renew coverage of an individual under any of the following conditions:

- Nonpayment of premium

- The individual has committed fraud or made an intentional misrepresentation of material fact under the terms of the coverage

- The insurer ceases to offer the coverage in accordance with statutory requirements we describe later in the section

- Coverage is offered under a network health care plan; the insured no longer resides, lives, or works in the network's service area; and the insurer terminates such coverage uniformly without regard to any factor related to the health of covered individuals. A *network plan* is a health care plan that provides health care through a network of preferred health care providers.

- Coverage is available only through one or more associations, the insured is no longer an association member, and the insurer terminates such coverage uniformly without regard to any factor related to the health of covered individuals

HIPAA permits an insurer to discontinue offering a particular type of individual health insurance coverage within a state if it (1) notifies all insureds 90 days before the termination of their coverage and (2) offers each insured the option to purchase any other individual health insurance policy the insurer is then offering in the state. In such cases, the insurer must act uniformly without regard to any factor relating to the health of insured individuals.

An insurer also may discontinue offering all individual health insurance in a state if it notifies both the state insurance department and all insureds at least 180 days before coverage terminates. The insurer then must discontinue all such coverage and may not issue any individual health insurance in the state for a period of five years.

HIPAA gives insurers the right to modify the coverage provided by an individual policy form if the insurer complies with all applicable state regulatory requirements and the modification is effective on a uniform basis for all policies using that form.

Guaranteed availability requirements. HIPAA requires the guaranteed availability of individual health insurance coverage to certain individuals who have had group health insurance coverage. For purposes of these requirements, an *eligible individual* is someone who meets the following requirements:

- The individual is not eligible for coverage under a group health plan, Medicare, or Medicaid.

- The individual has at least 18 months of *creditable coverage*—that is, coverage under any of a number of specified types of health plans without a lapse of 63 days or more. The types of plans specified include individual and group health insurance, as well as Medicare, Medicaid, and other governmental benefit plans. We describe these requirements in detail in Chapter 9.

- The individual's most recent creditable coverage must have been provided by a group health plan, governmental plan, or church plan.

- The individual's most recent coverage was not terminated because of fraud or nonpayment of premium.

- The individual has no other health coverage and has exhausted the benefits to which he was entitled under the federal *Consolidated Omnibus Budget Reconciliation Act (COBRA)*. COBRA requires that individuals whose group health insurance coverage terminates for specified reasons have the option of continuing their group health insurance coverage for a specified period. We describe COBRA's requirements in detail in Chapter 9.

HIPAA prohibits an insurer from declining to cover an eligible individual or imposing any preexisting condition exclusion on the coverage of an eligible individual. Health insurers, however, are exempt from this requirement if the state in which they conduct business implements an acceptable alternative mechanism by which such eligible individuals may obtain coverage. An *acceptable alternative mechanism* is a state-approved plan that meets the following requirements:

1. All eligible individuals are given a choice of health insurance coverage.

2. The coverage does not impose any preexisting condition exclusions.

3. The choice of coverage includes at least one policy form that provides coverage comparable either to comprehensive health coverage offered in the individual health insurance market or to standard coverage available under the state's group or individual health insurance laws.

As of this writing, 48 states have implemented an acceptable alternative mechanism. As mentioned earlier, the states also have adopted laws designed to improve the availability of health insurance coverage. We describe these state requirements in the rest of this section.

About one-half of the states have adopted legislation based on the NAIC *Small Employer and Individual Health Insurance Availability Model Act*. The purpose of this Model Act is to increase the availability of health insurance coverage to small employers and to individuals not covered by or eligible for group health insurance or other state-required health benefits. Provisions of the Model Act that affect small employers will be discussed in Chapter 8. In this chapter, we discuss how the Model Act affects insurers that issue individual health insurance policies.

The Small Employer and Individual Health Insurance Availability Model Act requires insurers to offer any individual health insurance plan that they actively market in a state to all eligible individuals of the state. The Model Act requires that the insurer offer at least one basic health benefit plan and one standard health benefit plan. According to the Model Act, a *basic health benefit plan* is a low-cost health benefit plan. A *standard health benefit plan* is a more expensive health benefit plan that may contain more extensive benefits than a basic health benefit plan.

The Model Act requires insurers to develop individual health insurance rates based on an *adjusted community rate*, which is a rate that reflects the medical and hospital costs to all insureds in a particular community. This rate can vary based only on geographic area, an enrollee's family composition, and the age of an enrollee. For example, when issuing coverage to an enrollee who is a minor child, an insurer can charge the lowest allowable rate that it would charge an adult.

Under the Small Employer and Individual Health Insurance Availability Model Act, states may adopt one of two enrollment methods for issuing individual health coverage:

- An insurer can allow enrollment 365 days per year.
- An insurer can allow a 30-day open enrollment period each year.

If an insurer imposes a preexisting condition policy provision, the provision can be enforced for no longer than a 12-month period. The insurer must waive the waiting period related to the preexisting condition for the period of time the individual was covered by creditable coverage, provided that the creditable coverage did not terminate more than 90 days prior to the commencement of new coverage.

The Small Employer and Individual Health Insurance Availability Model Act specifies that individual health benefit plans must be renewable for all individuals and dependents at the option of the enrollee. An insurer can, however, decline to renew coverage under the following circumstances:

- An individual fails to pay premiums.
- An individual commits an act of fraud or makes a material misrepresentation concerning terms of the coverage.
- The insurer ceases offering all health insurance in the state.

An insurer is not required to issue an individual health insurance policy to an individual under the following conditions:

- The individual is enrolled or is eligible to be enrolled in an employer-sponsored health insurance plan.
- The individual is covered or eligible to be covered under a health insurance plan of the individual's spouse, parent, or guardian.
- The individual has coverage under an individual health insurance plan.
- The individual is covered or is eligible to be covered under any private or public health program, including Medicare or Medicare supplement programs.
- The individual is covered or is eligible to be covered through group health coverage under the Internal Revenue Code, ERISA, the Public Health Service Act, or any state-required group coverage.

A few states have adopted laws based on the *Individual Health Insurance Portability Model Act,* which is an NAIC model law designed to increase access to individual health insurance coverage. The Individual Health Insurance Portability Model Act contains provisions similar to the Small Employer and Individual Health Insurance Availability Model Act concerning rating guidelines, availability of coverage, and renewability of coverage. A notable difference between the two model acts is that under the Individual Health Insurance Portability Model Act, an insurer is not required to issue individual health insurance coverage to any individual who:

- Fails to apply for coverage within 31 days after becoming ineligible under previous health insurance coverage, including coverage provided by another individual health insurance plan, a group health insurance plan, Medicare, Medicaid, CHAMPUS, or a state-required plan for uninsurable individuals

- Fails to apply for coverage within 31 days of attaining the age of majority

- Fails to apply for coverage within 31 days of a loss of dependent status under previous coverage

A few states have adopted laws based on the *Model Health Plan for Uninsurable Individuals Act*, which is an NAIC model law that provides for the establishment of a state health insurance plan that offers medical expense insurance coverage to uninsurable individuals who meet certain criteria. An *uninsurable individual* is an individual who represents a risk of loss that is too great for an insurer to cover at all or at standard risk rates. Under the Model Health Plan for Uninsurable Individuals Act, the following individuals are eligible for coverage:

- An individual who has been rejected for coverage by an insurer for health reasons.

- An individual who can receive insurance only at rates that exceed maximum standard rates offered by other health plans.

- Specified individuals who have not experienced a significant break in coverage and who continue to be a resident of the state. A *significant break in coverage* is a period of 63 consecutive days during which an individual does not have creditable coverage.

As a general rule, risk rates for uninsurable individuals are necessarily higher than standard risk rates for insurable individuals. While the Model Act does not prohibit higher rates for uninsurable individuals, it establishes that risk rates for these individuals may not exceed 200 percent of the maximum standard risk rate allowed for insurable individuals in a state.

ACTUARIAL CONSIDERATIONS

The actuarial considerations that arise in the process of developing any type of health insurance product are the same general considerations we described in Chapter 1 concerning life insurance products. The fundamental principles underlying the pricing of health insurance are the same as those underlying life insurance pricing. That is, health insurance premiums must be adequate to provide the promised benefits and must be equitable to all policyowners. We describe some basics of health insurance pricing in Insight 3-2.

INSIGHT 3-2   Some Basics of Health Insurance Pricing.

Premium rates for traditional indemnity health insurance products are established in a process similar to that used to price life insurance. (See Insight 1-1.) The premium charged for an individual health insurance product is calculated as a **gross premium** that is composed of two elements: the net premium and the loading.

The **net premium** is the amount the insurer expects to pay in benefits for the product. Net premium calculations are based on actuarial assumptions regarding **morbidity rates**, which measure the incidences of sickness and accidents among a given group of insureds. The insurer uses these actuarial assumptions to project the amount of its claim costs for each type of benefit provided by the product. In calculating health insurance net premiums, actuaries must consider several factors that are not present in life insurance net premium calculations. Because medical care costs are increasing all the time, medical expense insurance claim costs are affected by inflation. Also, medical care costs vary from geographic area to geographic area, and premium rates for medical expense coverages must reflect such variations.

The **loading** is an amount sufficient to cover the insurer's expenses of doing business and includes an amount for unforeseen contingencies. Because the risk is more uncertain for health insurance than for life insurance, insurers usually include in their loading for health insurance premiums a greater amount for unforeseen contingencies than they include for life insurance premiums.

Health insurance premium rates generally are calculated on an annual basis. If premiums are payable more frequently than annually, then the insurer will add a small amount to the gross annual premium to cover the additional expenses incurred in collecting the larger number of premiums.

Minimum Reserve Standards

State insurance codes include minimum reserve requirements for health insurance policies, and about one-half of the states have based their requirements on the NAIC *Health Insurance Reserve Model Regulation*. These reserve standards apply to all types of individual and group health insurance products except Medicare supplement and long-term care policies that are subject to the specific types of regulatory requirements described in Chapter 5. The NAIC Minimum Reserve Standards establish minimum reserve standards for three types of health insurance reserves:

1. *Contract reserves* are required for all level premium health insurance policies except those that cannot be continued after one year from issue.

2. *Claim reserves* are required for all incurred but unpaid health insurance claims. Because of the frequency and sometimes long-term nature of health claims, claim reserves are a particularly significant portion of an insurer's health insurance reserves.

3. *Unearned premium reserves* are required for all health insurance contracts for which premiums, other than premiums paid in advance, have been paid beyond the date of valuation for the reserves.

Premium Rate Filing Requirements

Health insurance premium rates are more directly regulated than are life insurance premium rates. States typically require insurers to file and obtain approval of premium rates for individual and group health insurance policies. Regulators evaluate a health insurance product's premium rates to ensure that the benefits provided by the product are reasonable in relation to the premiums charged.

Premium rates must be filed as part of the policy form submission package and must be accompanied by an actuarial memorandum that describes the basis on which rates were determined and the calculation of the policy's expected loss ratio. The *loss ratio* measures the percentage of premiums paid out in policy benefits and can be expressed as

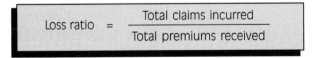

$$\text{Loss ratio} = \frac{\text{Total claims incurred}}{\text{Total premiums received}}$$

Most states require the loss ratio for a health insurance policy to equal at least a minimum stated percentage; specific requirements vary from state to state and policy to policy. The premium rate filing also must include a certification by a qualified actuary stating that to the best of the actuary's knowledge and judgment the rate filing complies with the applicable laws and regulations of the state to which it is submitted and that the benefits are reasonable in relation to premiums.

KEY TERMS AND CONCEPTS

Uniform Individual Accident and Sickness Policy Provision Law (UPPL)
time limit on certain defenses provision
notice of claim provision
claim forms provision
proofs of loss provision
time of payment of claims provision
payment of claims provision
physical examinations and autopsy provision
legal actions provision
change of beneficiary provision
change of occupation provision
overinsurance provision
unpaid premiums provision
conformity with state statutes provision
illegal occupation provision
intoxicants and narcotics provision
Accident and Sickness Insurance Minimum Standards Model Act
Model Regulation to Implement the Accident and Sickness Insurance Minimum Standards Model Act
franchise plan
Civilian Health and Medical Program of the Uniformed Services (CHAMPUS)
coinsurance
copayment
deductible
basic hospital expense coverage
basic medical-surgical expense coverage
hospital confinement indemnity coverage
major medical expense coverage
basic medical expense coverage
disability income protection coverage
accident only coverage
specified disease coverage
specified accident coverage
limited benefit health coverage
recurrent disability
noncancellable policy
guaranteed renewable policy
probationary period
preexisting conditions policy provision
preexisting condition
Women's Health and Cancer Rights Act of 1998 (WHCRA)
Newborns' and Mothers' Health Protection Act of 1996 (NMHPA)
allied medical practitioner
Model Newborn Children Bill
Health Insurance Portability and Accountability Act (HIPAA)
Employee Retirement Income Security Act (ERISA)
Internal Revenue Code
Public Health Service Act
network plan
eligible individual
creditable coverage
acceptable alternative mechanism
Small Employer and Individual Health Insurance Availability Model Act
basic health benefit plan
standard health benefit plan
adjusted community rate
Individual Health Insurance Portability Model Act
Model Health Plan for Uninsurable Individuals Act
uninsurable individual
significant break in coverage
Health Insurance Reserves Model Regulation
loss ratio

ENDNOTES

1. Public Law 105-277 (October 21, 1998).

2. 42 U.S.C. § 300gg-4 (1999).

3. Public Law 104-101 (August 21, 1996).

CHAPTER 4

Health Insurance Advertising and Solicitation Disclosure Requirements

LEARNING OBJECTIVES

After studying this chapter, you should be able to

- Identify the types of health insurance materials that state insurance regulators consider to be advertisements subject to state insurance advertising regulation

- Identify regulatory requirements imposed on health insurance advertisements

- Distinguish between an institutional advertisement, an invitation to inquire, and an invitation to contract, and identify regulatory requirements imposed on each type of advertisement

- Recognize situations in which an insurer must provide an applicant or insured with an outline of coverage

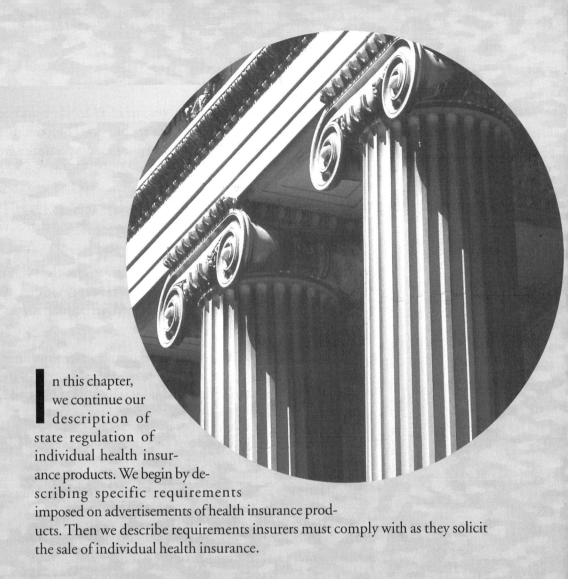

In this chapter, we continue our description of state regulation of individual health insurance products. We begin by describing specific requirements imposed on advertisements of health insurance products. Then we describe requirements insurers must comply with as they solicit the sale of individual health insurance.

REGULATION OF HEALTH INSURANCE ADVERTISING

State regulation of health insurance advertising is fairly uniform because almost all of the state insurance departments have adopted regulatory requirements based on the NAIC *Advertisements of Accident and Sickness Insurance Model Regulation.* This Model Regulation, which we refer to as the Health Insurance Advertising Model Regulation, is designed to protect prospective purchasers by establishing minimum criteria that health insurance advertisements must meet in order to ensure they properly and accurately describe the products they advertise. The guidelines and standards contained in the Model Regulation are intended to prevent unfair, deceptive, and misleading advertising, and they apply to all health advertisements, including advertisements of both individual and group health insurance plans.

The Health Insurance Advertising Model Regulation regulates advertisements of all types of health insurance benefits. Although the Model Regulation refers to *health insurance*, it governs advertisements of all accident and sickness benefits regardless of whether those benefits are provided by a traditional indemnity insurance plan or a managed care plan offered by a health maintenance organization (HMO). For purposes of the Model Regulation, an *insurer* includes an individual, corporation, association, fraternal benefit society, HMO, hospital service corporation, medical service corporation, or prepaid health plan that is defined as an insurer in the state insurance code and that advertises itself or a health insurance policy.

As with other state insurance advertising regulations, the Health Insurance Advertising Model Regulation applies to a wide range of materials that the Model Regulation defines as *advertisements*. Materials that are subject to the Model Regulation include

- Printed material, audiovisual material, and descriptive literature of an insurer used in direct mail, newspapers, magazines, radio scripts, television scripts, Web sites and other Internet displays, billboards and similar displays

- Descriptive literature and sales aids of all kinds issued by an insurer or insurance producer for presentation to the public

- Prepared sales presentations and materials for use by insurance producers regardless of who prepared the materials

The following types of materials are specifically excluded from the definition of *advertisement* for purposes of the Model Regulation:

- Material that is used only for training an insurer's employees and agents

- Material used in-house by insurers

- Internal communications not intended for distribution to the public

- Communications of a personal nature between an insurer and a current policyholder other than materials that urge policyholders to expand or increase coverage

- Communications between an insurer and a prospective group policyholder during the course of contract negotiations

- Court-ordered and approved material that is disseminated to policyholders

- A general announcement by a group policyholder to eligible employees explaining that a health insurance program or contract has been arranged, provided that the announcement does not describe specific benefits

The specific requirements imposed on an advertisement depend on the type of advertisement. The Health Insurance Advertising Model Regulation identifies three types of insurance advertisements. An *institutional advertisement* is an advertisement that is designed to promote the consumer's interest in the concept of insurance or the insurer as a seller of insurance. An *invitation to inquire* is an advertisement that is designed to induce the audience to inquire further about a specific policy and that contains only a brief description of the coverage being advertised. The Model Regulation states that an invitation to inquire about health insurance may not refer to cost. For purposes of the Model Regulation, all other types of insurance advertisements are defined as *invitations to contract*. As we describe throughout this section, the Model Regulation imposes additional requirements on invitations to contract beyond those imposed on the other two types of advertisements.

Advertising Requirements

The Health Insurance Advertising Model Regulation contains a number of broad requirements that all health insurance advertisements must meet. Both the content and format of an advertisement must be clear and complete and must avoid deception or the capacity to mislead. According to the Model Regulation, the format of an advertisement is the arrangement of the text and the captions. Advertisements are prohibited from omitting information or including words or phrases that have the capacity or tendency to mislead prospects as to the nature or extent of any policy benefit payable, loss covered, or premium payable.

The Model Regulation includes several examples of words and phrases that are prohibited from being used in advertisements. Figure 4-1 lists some of these examples.

The state insurance department is authorized to evaluate whether an advertisement has the capacity to mislead; such a determination is based on the overall impression the advertisement may reasonably be expected to create upon a person of average education or intelligence, within the segment of the public to which the advertisement is directed. Insurance terminology that the audience is not likely to be familiar with must be avoided. The Model Regulation makes it clear that insurers must create distinctly different advertisements for general circulation publications and scholarly, technical, or business publications. Thus, the amount of information an advertisement includes in order to explain insurance terminology varies depending on the expected audience for an advertisement. The Health Insurance Advertising Model

FIGURE 4-1 Examples of Prohibited Words, Phrases, and Statements in Health Insurance Advertisements.

➤ An advertisement may not use terms such as "liberal" or "generous" when describing claim settlements.

➤ An advertisement may not contain statements such as "anyone can apply," or "anyone can join," except with respect to a guaranteed issue product for which administrative procedures exist to ensure the policy is issued within a reasonable time after the insurer receives an application.

➤ An advertisement may not state or imply that a policy will provide immediate coverage unless administrative procedures exist to ensure the policy is issued within 15 working days after the insurer receives an application.

➤ An advertisement may not use devices designed to create undue fear or anxiety in the minds of the audience. For example, an advertisement should not use phrases such as "cancer kills somebody every two minutes" unless it also describes the total population from which such statistics are taken.

➤ An advertisement may not use the word *plan* without identifying it as an accident and sickness insurance policy.

➤ An advertisement may not imply in any way that the prospective insured may realize a profit from obtaining hospital, medical, or surgical insurance coverage.

➤ An advertisement that does not require the premium to accompany the application must not overemphasize that fact and must make the effective date of that coverage clear.

➤ An advertisement must not exaggerate the effects of statutorily required benefits or required policy provisions and must not imply that such provisions are unique to the advertised policy. For example, the phrase "Money Back Guarantee" is an exaggerated description of the required free-look provision and is unacceptable.

➤ An advertisement may not directly or indirectly make unfair or incomplete comparisons of policies of other insurers.

➤ An advertisement may not refer to special awards, such as "safe drivers' awards."

➤ An advertisement may not contain statements such as "no red tape" or "here is all you do to receive benefits."

➤ An advertisement shall not state that prospective insureds will become group members or quasi-group members covered under a group contract, unless that is the fact.

Source: Excerpted and adapted from NAIC, *Advertisements of Accident and Sickness Insurance Model Regulation*, 2001. Reprinted with permission from the National Association of Insurance Commissioners.

Regulation also requires health insurance advertisements to identify the product being advertised as a health insurance policy or health benefits product.

Any information required in an advertisement must be set out conspicuously so that the information is prominent, is presented in an unambiguous fashion, and is placed so that it is not confusing or misleading. This requirement can be met in one of two ways. First, required information can be presented "in close conjunction with" the statements to which such information relates. Alternatively, required information can be presented under appropriate captions that accurately describe the information and that are prominent enough so as to be easily noticed and understood by the audience. In addition, when an advertisement consists of more than one piece of material, each piece must comply with the requirements of the Model Regulation.

In general, health insurance advertisements must be truthful and may not attempt to mislead the consumer in any manner. For example, advertisements containing introductory or special offers must accurately state the terms of the offer. Advertisements stating that applicants will receive substantial advantages that will not be available at a later time, that a limited number of policies will be sold, or that a policy will stop being sold at a specified date must be true and accurate. In addition, advertisements containing statistical information, such as the number of people insured or the dollar amount of claims paid, must accurately reflect current facts. These advertisements also must reveal the source of the statistics.

Identity of the Insurer

The Health Insurance Advertising Model Regulation requires advertisements to include the name of the insurer marketing the product. In addition, the Model Regulation imposes a number of specific requirements concerning identification of the insurer. The goal of these requirements is to ensure that the reader of an advertisement is not deceived about the actual identity of the insurer or the purpose of the advertisement. For example, advertisements may not use words, phrases, or symbols that would tend to confuse or mislead consumers to believe that the solicitation is connected somehow with a governmental agency or that the consumer may lose a governmental benefit if he does not respond to the advertisement. If an advertisement is mailed to a prospective insured, then the stationery and envelope used in the mailing also are considered advertising materials subject to the Model Regulation. Such stationery and envelopes may not use words, slogans, or symbols to imply that the insurer or the product advertised is connected with a governmental agency, such as the Social Security Administration.

Exceptions, Limitations, and Reductions

Health insurance policies usually include provisions that restrict or limit the coverage provided. The Health Insurance Advertising Model Regulation identifies three types of such provisions. An *exception* is a provision that entirely eliminates coverage for a specific hazard. A *reduction* is a provision that reduces the amount of the benefit payable. A *limitation* is any other type of provision that restricts coverage. (Figure 4-2 provides an illustrative exception, reduction, and limitation.) Advertisements for policies that contain exceptions, reductions, or limitations must comply with the following regulatory requirements:

- An invitation to contract must disclose all exceptions, reductions, and limitations that affect the basic provisions of the policy being advertised.

- An advertisement may not describe policy exceptions, reductions, or limitations in a positive manner to imply that they are benefits. For example, an advertisement stating that "even preexisting conditions are covered after two years" is unacceptable. Descriptions of exceptions, reductions, and limitations must fairly and accurately disclose their negative features.

- Advertisements may not use words such as "only," "just," "merely," "minimum," or "necessary" to describe the applicability of any exceptions, reductions, or limitations. The following statement, for example, is un-

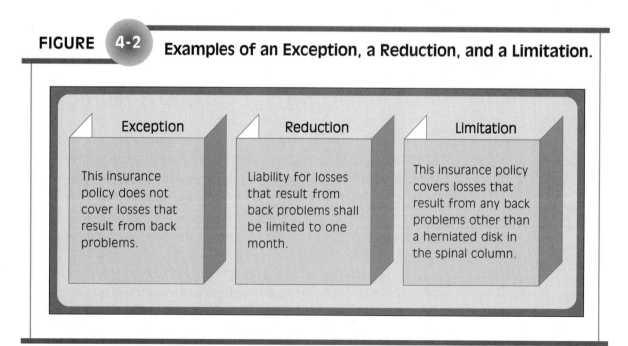

FIGURE 4-2 Examples of an Exception, a Reduction, and a Limitation.

Exception	Reduction	Limitation
This insurance policy does not cover losses that result from back problems.	Liability for losses that result from back problems shall be limited to one month.	This insurance policy covers losses that result from any back problems other than a herniated disk in the spinal column.

acceptable: "This policy is subject to the following minimum exceptions and reductions."

- An advertisement that refers to "hospitalization for injury" must disclose that the policy does not cover some injuries or sicknesses if the policy in question excludes certain injuries or sicknesses.

- An advertisement must disclose that the definition of *hospital* does not include facilities such as nursing homes, convalescent homes, or other extended care facilities when a policy excludes these facilities in the definition of hospital.

- Advertisements that contain the term *confining sickness* must explain the term so as not to be misleading. The following statement, for example, is acceptable: "Benefits are payable for total disability due to a confining sickness only as long as the insured is necessarily confined indoors."

- An advertisement must disclose any waiting period or elimination period.

- An advertisement that describes benefits that vary by age must disclose that benefits vary by age.

- An advertisement for a policy providing benefits for specified illnesses only must clearly and conspicuously state the limited nature of the policy. Language similar to the following statement is acceptable: "THIS IS A LIMITED POLICY."

Invitations to Contract

The Health Insurance Advertising Model Regulation imposes the following requirements on advertisements that are invitations to contract. These requirements are not imposed on the other two types of advertisements.

- In addition to containing the name of the insurer, an invitation to contract must include the policy form number of the product being advertised.

- If the insurer requires a medical examination for a specified policy, then an invitation to contract must disclose that such an examination is required.

- An invitation to contract must disclose any applicable deductible or coinsurance percentage.

- An invitation to contract must disclose in negative terms the extent to which a loss caused by a preexisting condition is not covered by the advertised policy. The term *preexisting condition* may not be used in the advertisement unless it is defined.

- An invitation to contract must disclose policy provisions relating to renewability, cancellability, and termination or modification of benefits, losses covered, or premiums payable.

- When an invitation to contract refers to a choice of benefit levels, the advertisement must disclose that the amount of benefits provided depends on the plan selected and that the premium will vary with the amount of benefits selected.

- When an invitation to contract refers to various benefits that may be contained in two or more policies, the advertisement must disclose that the benefits are available only through a combination of policies.

Testimonials

Advertisements sometimes include a testimonial or endorsement of a product or advertiser by a third party. A testimonial, for example, might feature a statement by a well-known individual about the value of a specific insurance product. The Model Regulation requires any such testimonial or endorsement used in a health insurance advertisement to be genuine, to represent the current opinion of the author, to apply to the policy advertised, and to be accurately reproduced. When a testimonial or an endorsement is used more than one year after it was originally given, the insurer must confirm that the endorsement continues to represent the author's opinion.

The Model Regulation contains specific rules regarding advertisements that include a testimonial made by a spokesperson. A *spokesperson* may include:

- A person who makes a testimonial or endorsement and who has a financial interest in the insurer

- A person who is in a policy-making position and is affiliated with the insurer

- A person who is in any way directly or indirectly compensated for making the testimonial or endorsement

- A person who speaks on behalf of an entity formed or controlled by the insurer

The fact that a spokesperson has a financial interest in the insurer must be disclosed in the advertisement. For example, if an advertisement includes a testimonial for which the spokesperson was compensated, then the advertisement must contain a disclosure such as "Paid Endorsement." Television and radio advertisements are not required to include this disclosure if the only compensation the spokesperson received was the payment of union scale wages for such an advertisement.

When an advertisement contains a testimonial or an endorsement by an individual, group of individuals, society, or association that is involved in a proprietary relationship with the insurer, the advertisement must reveal the proprietary relationship. When a testimonial refers to benefits received under a policy, the insurer must maintain a file of specific data regarding the claim to which the testimonial referred for a period of four years or until the insurer's next regulatory examination.

Insurer's Compliance Responsibilities

All advertisements of a health insurer's products are the responsibility of the insurer, regardless of who created and distributed those advertisements. In order to carry out this responsibility, each insurer is required to establish and maintain a system by which it can control the content, form, and method of distribution of advertisements for its health insurance policies. An insurer has a responsibility to ensure that all advertisements comply with state regulations. Insight 4-1 discusses some compliance problems with advertisements distributed through fax machines.

An insurer must maintain at its home office or principal office a complete file containing every printed, published, or prepared advertisement of its individual health insurance policies. The file should contain all advertisements distributed in any state, and the insurer should attach to each advertisement a notation as to the manner and extent to which it was distributed and the form number of any policy advertised. Each advertisement must be maintained in the advertising file for either four years or until the insurer's next regulatory examination.

Many states require that advertisements of specific health insurance products be filed with and approved by the state insurance department before being used. Also, when an insurer subject to the Accident and Health Insurance Advertising Model Regulation files its Annual Statement with the state insurance department, the insurer must file a certification executed by an authorized officer of the insurer. This certification must state that to the best of the officer's knowledge, information, and belief, the advertisements used by the insurer during the preceding year complied with state insurance laws and regulations.

INSIGHT 4-1: Agency Cracks Down on Insurance Faxes.

Got a fax machine? Odds are decent you've been the unwanted recipient of advertising trying to sell you some insurance.

The [Arizona] Department of Insurance can't halt those unsolicited messages. That relief may lie elsewhere. But the agency is cracking down on the agents who are sending the faxes—a move that, if it doesn't result in fewer faxes, at least will result in more informative ones.

Erin Klug, special assistant to the [Arizona] state insurance director, said the problem was brought to her agency's attention in a most direct way: The fax machine in the office began spitting out ads from companies selling insurance.

"It seems like there was a real rash of this stuff," she said.

Sending out ads by fax isn't necessarily illegal, said Insurance Director Charles Cohen. But what is illegal is sending ads that don't comply with the state Insurance Code.

Cohen, in a written warning to agents, said all types of insurance advertising must be "truthful and not misleading in fact or implication." But Cohen said his staffers have found two types of situations where agents aren't complying with those requirements.

In the first case, he said, a fax ad either doesn't identify which insurance company's policy is being sold—or lists multiple insurers, each of which may not offer all of the benefits being touted.

Cohen said state regulations require the identity of insurers to be "made clear in all advertisements."

"Even where only one insurer's product is described in the advertisement, the insurer must still be named and cannot be referred to in vague terms such as 'All plans issued by an A-rated company,' " Cohen said.

Where the agent is offering policies from multiple insurance companies, the problem is different. Cohen said it is illegally misleading if each of the companies being touted does not offer all of the products or benefits being touted in the ad.

Cohen said some of the ads do not even list the name of the insurance agency sending the fax, instead providing only a phone number. He said while the law does not contain such a requirement, he said it would be "beneficial" to consumers.

The other major problem Cohen said his staffers found is that the fax ads highlight some features of the policies offered without bothering to disclose the various exceptions and limitations.

"While it is a natural inclination to tout the most compelling features of a policy, that does not always tell the whole story," he said. For example Cohen said his agency has seen ads with phrases such as "best deals, lower cost—save 30 percent or more," "prescription card: included," and "chiropractic care: covered." What isn't told, he said, is the conditions.

"Advertisements for insurance are not the same as advertisements for home appliances or mattresses," he said.

Cohen said regulations require that the "particulars" of a policy be disclosed "so that the consumer has complete and detailed information upon which to make a decision."

Source: Excerpted from Howard Fischer, "Agency Cracks Down on Insurance Faxes," Capitol Media Services (2 August 2001). Used with permission.

SOLICITATION DISCLOSURE REQUIREMENTS

As noted in the previous chapter, the NAIC Accident and Sickness Insurance Minimum Standards Model Act and the Model Regulation to Implement the Accident and Sickness Insurance Minimum Standards Model Act impose a number of disclosure requirements on the sale of individual health insurance. According to the Model Regulation, an insurer cannot deliver or issue for delivery in the state an individual health policy unless the insurer completes an appropriate *outline of coverage* that briefly describes the coverage provided by the policy and delivers that outline either to the policyowner when the policy is delivered or to the applicant when the application is completed. If the outline is provided at the time of application, the applicant must acknowledge or certify receipt of the outline and that acknowledgement must be provided to the insurer. If the insurer issues a policy other than as applied for on a basis that would require revising the outline of coverage, then the insurer must provide a substitute outline of coverage when it delivers the policy. The substitute outline must contain the following statement in no less than 12-point type immediately above the insurance company's name:

> NOTICE: Read this outline of coverage carefully. It is not identical to the outline of coverage provided upon application, and the coverage originally applied for has not been issued.

The Model Regulation contains sample forms for insurers to follow in developing an outline of coverage for each type of accident and health insurance coverage, including (1) basic hospital expense coverage, (2) basic medical-surgical expense coverage, (3) basic hospital and medical-surgical expense coverage, (4) hospital confinement indemnity coverage, (5) individual major medical expense coverage, (6) individual basic medical expense coverage, (7) disability income protection coverage, (8) accident-only coverage, (9) specified disease or specified accident coverage, and (10) limited benefit health coverage. (The benefits provided by each of these coverages were identified in Chapter 3.) Figure 4-3 contains the outline of coverage required for policies that provide individual major medical expense coverage.

FIGURE 4-3 **Outline of Coverage Required for Individual Major Medical Expense Coverage Policy.**

[COMPANY NAME]
INDIVIDUAL MAJOR MEDICAL EXPENSE COVERAGE
OUTLINE OF COVERAGE

1. Read Your Policy Carefully—This outline of coverage provides a very brief description of the important features of your policy. This is not the insurance contract and only the actual policy provisions will control. The policy itself sets forth in detail the rights and obligations of both you and your insurance company. It is, therefore, important that you READ YOUR POLICY CAREFULLY.

2. Individual major medical expense coverage is designed to provide, to persons insured, comprehensive coverage for major hospital, medical, and surgical expenses incurred as a result of a covered accident or sickness. Coverage is provided for daily hospital room and board, miscellaneous hospital services, surgical services, anesthesia services, in-hospital medical services, and out-of-hospital care, subject to any deductibles, copayment provisions, or other limitations which may be set forth in the policy. Basic hospital or basic medical insurance coverage is not provided.

3. [A brief specific description of the benefits, including dollar amounts, contained in this policy, in the following order:

    Daily hospital room and board;

    Miscellaneous hospital services;

    Surgical services;

    Anesthesia services;

    In-hospital medical services;

    Out-of-hospital care;

    Maximum dollar amount for covered charges; and

    Other benefits, if any.]

4. [A description of any policy provisions which exclude, eliminate, restrict, reduce, limit, delay or in any other manner operate to qualify payment of the benefits described in (3) above.]

5. [A description of policy provisions respecting renewability or continuation of coverage, including age restrictions or any reservation of right to change premiums.]

Source: Excerpted from NAIC, *Model Regulation to Implement the Accident and Sickness Insurance Minimum Standards Model Act* § 8, 1999. Reprinted with permission from the National Association of Insurance Commissioners.

Key Terms and Concepts

Advertisements of Accident and Sickness Insurance Model Regulation
institutional advertisement
invitation to inquire
invitation to contract
exception
reduction
limitation
spokesperson
outline of coverage

CHAPTER 5

Regulation of Specific Health Insurance Products

LEARNING OBJECTIVES

After studying this chapter, you should be able to

- Recognize the general types of benefit standards that are imposed on Medicare supplement insurance policies

- Identify the marketing and disclosure requirements that are imposed on insurers that sell Medicare supplement insurance and the requirements imposed on insurers that sell other health coverages to individuals eligible for Medicare coverage

- Recognize the provisions and features that long-term care (LTC) insurance policies generally are required to include

- Identify the marketing and disclosure requirements imposed on insurers that market long-term care insurance

Insurers that market some specific types of health insurance products must comply with regulatory requirements in addition to those described in the previous two chapters. Most of the general regulatory requirements described in Chapters 3 and 4 apply to all types of health insurance products. In addition, however, Medicare supplement policies and long-term care policies are subject to additional requirements that the states enacted specifically to regulate these products. This chapter describes these specific regulatory requirements that the states impose on Medicare supplement policies and long-term care policies.

MEDICARE SUPPLEMENT INSURANCE

Medicare is a federal program that provides hospital and medical expense coverage for persons age 65 and older, disabled individuals, and specified others. Medicare covers only specified medical care expenses, and individuals generally must pay a portion of the cost of their medical care.

Total medical expenses incurred	−	Total expenses covered by Medicare	=	Total financial responsibility of the individual

Individuals can meet their financial responsibility for the costs not covered by Medicare by purchasing Medicare supplement coverage. *Medicare supplement insurance policies*, sometimes referred to as *Medigap policies*, are policies advertised, marketed, or designed primarily to cover the gap between the amount of hospital, medical, and surgical expenses incurred by an individual eligible for Medicare and the amount of those expenses that Medicare covers.

All states impose specific requirements on the marketing and sale of Medicare supplement policies, and most states' requirements are based on the NAIC *Medicare Supplement Insurance Minimum Standards Model Act (Medicare Supplement Model Act)*. This Model Act imposes specified minimum standards on Medicare supplement policies and group certificates and requires state insurance departments to adopt regulations that impose additional standards. Note that these requirements apply to both individual and group Medicare supplement policies and group Medicare supplement certificates.

All states have adopted regulations based on the NAIC *Model Regulation to Implement the NAIC Medicare Supplement Insurance Minimum Standards Model Act (Medicare Supplement Model Regulation)*. This Model Regulation contains extensive requirements designed to standardize the coverages provided by individual and group Medicare supplement policies, to facilitate public understanding of such policies, and to ensure full disclosure in the sale of such policies.

The Model Act requires all Medicare supplement policies and group certificates to be filed with and approved by the state insurance department before they are delivered or issued for delivery within the state. Insurers also must file and receive approval of the premium rates charged for Medicare supplement policies.

Required Policy Provisions

As noted earlier, individual Medicare supplement policies must comply with state insurance laws governing all individual health insurance policies. The Uniform Individual Accident and Sickness Policy Provision Law (UPPL) specifies a number of provisions that individual Medicare supplement policies must contain. These required provisions, which we described in Chapter 3, are listed in Figure 5-1. Note that the UPPL also requires these provisions to be included in individual long-term care policies, which we describe later in this chapter. (We describe requirements imposed on group health insurance policies, including group Medicare supplement policies, in Chapter 8.) State requirements for Medicare supplement policies impose two specific requirements.

FIGURE 5-1 Provisions That Individual Medicare Supplement Policies and Long-Term Care Policies Must Include.

- ☑ Entire contract provision
- ☑ Time limit on certain defenses provision
- ☑ Grace period provision
- ☑ Renewal provision
- ☑ Reinstatement provision
- ☑ Notice of claim provision
- ☑ Claim forms provision
- ☑ Proofs of loss provision
- ☑ Time of payment of claims provision
- ☑ Payment of claims provision
- ☑ Physical examination and autopsy provision
- ☑ Legal actions provision

- The UPPL requires all individual health policies to include a renewal provision. The Medicare Supplement Model Regulation requires the renewal provision in a Medicare supplement policy to provide that the policy is guaranteed renewable. The insurer may not cancel or refuse to renew a policy for any reason other than nonpayment of premium. This provision must appear on the policy face page.

- States generally require individual health insurance policies to include a free-look provision. The Medicare Supplement Model Act requires Medicare supplement policies to provide at least a 30-day free-look period and to include the free-look provision on the policy face page.

Benefit Standards

The Medicare Supplement Model Act and Model Regulation impose minimum benefit standards on any Medicare supplement policy that is advertised, solicited, delivered, or issued for delivery within a state that has adopted these models. The following are some of the general benefit standards all Medicare supplement policies and group certificates must meet:

- Medicare supplements may not provide benefits that duplicate benefits provided by Medicare.

- Policies may not exclude or limit benefits for losses incurred more than six months following the effective date of coverage because a loss involved a preexisting condition. In addition, a policy's definition of preexisting condition must be limited to conditions occurring no more than six months before the effective date of coverage.

- Policies must cover losses resulting from sickness on the same basis as they cover losses resulting from accidents.

- Policies must provide that benefits designed to cover cost sharing amounts under Medicare will be changed automatically to coincide with any changes in the applicable Medicare deductible amount and copayment percentage factors. Premiums may be modified to correspond with such changes.

Standard Benefit Plans

The Medicare Supplement Model Regulation identifies 10 standard benefit plans that insurers are permitted to market. Each plan consists of a specific set of benefits. Under the Model Regulation, insurers must give every prospect for Medicare supplement insurance the right to purchase a policy that provides certain basic benefits. This basic benefit plan insurers must offer is referred to as *plan A* and includes benefits such as coverage of Medicare Part A expenses for hospitalization to the extent not covered by Medicare.[1] The other benefit plans, which insurers are permitted but not required to offer, are referred to as plans B through J. (Figure 5-2 lists these standard benefit plans and identifies the benefits included in each plan.) The benefit plans that insurers are required and permitted to offer vary somewhat from state to state.

The Model Regulation requires insurers to provide an open enrollment period in which individuals who become eligible for Medicare may purchase Medicare supplement insurance on a guaranteed issue basis. Insurers may not refuse to issue coverage and may not charge different premium amounts to any applicant prior to or for six months following the first day of the first month the applicant is both 65 years of age or older *and* is enrolled for benefits under Medicare Part B.

Chapter 5: Regulation of Specific Health Insurance Products

FIGURE 5-2 Outline of Medicare Supplement Coverage.

[Company Name]
Outline of Medicare Supplement Coverage-Cover Page:
Benefit Plans _____ [insert letters of plan being offered]

Medicare supplement insurance can be sold in only ten standard plans plus two high deductible plans. This chart shows the benefits included in each plan. Every company must make available Plan "A". Some plans may not be available in your state.

Basic Benefits: Included in All Plans.
Hospitalization: Part A coinsurance plus coverage for 365 additional days after Medicare benefits end.
Medical Expenses: Part B coinsurance (generally 20% of Medicare-approved expenses) or, in the case of hospital outpatient department services under a prospective payment system, applicable copayments.
Blood: First three pints of blood each year.

A	B	C	D	E	F	F*	G	H	I	J	J*
Basic Benefits	Basic Benefits	Basic Benefits	Basic Benefits	Basic Benefits	Basic Benefits	Basic Benefits	Basic Benefits	Basic Benefits	Basic Benefits	Basic Benefits	Basic Benefits
		Skilled Nursing Co-Insurance	Skilled Nursing Co-Insurance	Skilled Nursing Co-Insurance	Skilled Nursing Co-Insurance	Skilled Nursing Co-Insurance	Skilled Nursing Co-Insurance	Skilled Nursing Co-Insurance	Skilled Nursing Co-Insurance	Skilled Nursing Co-Insurance	Skilled Nursing Co-Insurance
	Part A Deductible	Part A Deductible	Part A Deductible	Part A Deductible	Part A Deductible	Part A Deductible	Part A Deductible	Part A Deductible	Part A Deductible	Part A Deductible	Part A Deductible
		Part B Deductible			Part B Deductible	Part B Deductible				Part B Deductible	Part B Deductible
						Part B Excess (100%)	Part B Excess (80%)		Part B Excess (100%)	Part B Excess (100%)	
		Foreign Travel Emergency	Foreign Travel Emergency	Foreign Travel Emergency	Foreign Travel Emergency	Foreign Travel Emergency	Foreign Travel Emergency	Foreign Travel Emergency	Foreign Travel Emergency	Foreign Travel Emergency	Foreign Travel Emergency
			At-Home Recovery				At-Home Recovery		At-Home Recovery	At-Home Recovery	
								Basic Drugs ($1,250 Limit)	Basic Drugs ($1,250 Limit)	Extended Drugs ($3,000 Limit)	
				Preventive Care							Preventive Care

*Plans F and J also have an option called a high deductible plan F and a high deductible plan J. These high deductible plans pay the same or offer the same benefits as Plans F and J after one has paid a calendar year [$1530] deductible. Benefits from high deductible plans F and J will not begin until out-of-pocket expenses are [$1530]. Out-of-pocket expenses for this deductible are expenses that would ordinarily be paid by the policy. These expenses include the Medicare deductibles for Part A and Part B, but does not include, in plan J, the plan's separate prescription drug deductible or, in Plans F and J, the plan's separate foreign travel emergency deductible.

Source: Excerpted from NAIC, *Model Regulation to Implement the NAIC Medicare Supplement Insurance Minimum Standards Model Act* § 17, 2001. Reprinted with permission from the National Association of Insurance Commissioners.

Advertising Requirements

In most states, the advertising of Medicare supplement insurance must comply with regulations based on the Advertisements of Accident and Sickness Insurance Model Regulation, which we described in Chapter 4. A few states, however, have adopted rules based on the *NAIC Model Rules Governing Advertisements of Medicare Supplement Insurance*, which specifically address advertising of Medicare supplement coverages. These Model Rules impose substantially similar requirements as those imposed by the Advertisements of Accident and Sickness Insurance Model Regulation.

Marketing Standards

The Medicare Supplement Model Regulation defines marketing standards for Medicare supplement policies and group certificates and requires insurers to establish procedures for verifying their compliance. According to these standards, an insurer must establish marketing procedures to ensure that any policy comparisons used by its insurance producers are fair and accurate. The insurer also must establish marketing procedures to ensure that it does not issue excessive insurance coverage to any insureds. In implementing these procedures, an insurer must make every reasonable effort to identify whether a prospective applicant already has health insurance and the types and amounts of any such insurance. The following notice must prominently appear on the first page of each Medicare supplement policy:

> Notice to buyer: This policy may not cover all of your medical expenses.

In recommending that a consumer purchase or replace a Medicare supplement policy, an insurance producer must make reasonable efforts to determine whether the purchase or replacement is appropriate for the consumer. Any sale of Medicare supplement coverage that will provide an individual with more than one such policy is prohibited.

In addition to the prohibitions contained in the applicable state's Unfair Trade Practices Act, the Medicare Supplement Model Regulation prohibits the following marketing practices:

- **Twisting.** Knowingly making any misleading representation or incomplete or fraudulent comparison of any policies or insurers for the purpose of inducing a person to lapse, surrender, retain, assign, borrow on, or convert an insurance policy.

- **High pressure tactics.** Employing any marketing method that tends to induce the purchase of insurance through force, fear, threat, or undue pressure.

- **Cold lead advertising.** Using any marketing method that fails to disclose in a conspicuous manner that its purpose is for solicitation of insurance and that an insurance producer or insurer will contact the consumer. Although the Model Regulation entitles this prohibition "cold lead advertising," the use of cold lead advertising is not prohibited. *Cold lead advertising* is any advertising disseminated to a prospect with whom the insurer or insurance producer has had no prior contact. An insurance producer, for example, is permitted to mail letters to any number of consumers as a method of generating sales leads. Such letters, however, must disclose that their purpose is to solicit sales of insurance.

Disclosure Requirements

The Medicare Supplement Insurance Minimum Standards Model Act and the Model Regulation contain a number of requirements designed to ensure that consumers who are eligible for Medicare have adequate information about their insurance needs and the coverages available to meet those needs. Adequate disclosure prevents consumers from purchasing duplicate coverages that they do not need. The Medicare Supplement Model Act prohibits the delivery of a Medicare supplement policy unless the applicant received an outline of coverage when he completed the application for insurance. For Medicare supplement policies, an *outline of coverage* provides information about the benefits provided by all ten standard benefit plans, identifies the benefit plans offered by the insurer, and specifies the premium amounts payable for each benefit plan offered by the insurer. Figure 5-2 illustrates the format and types of information that insurers must provide on the cover page of the Medicare supplement outline of coverage, including a description of the benefits provided by each of the 10 standard benefit plans described earlier in the chapter. If the policy is marketed through a personal selling system rather than a direct response system, then the applicant must sign a form acknowledging that he received the outline of coverage at the time of the application.

Applications for Medicare supplement insurance policies also must contain the following statements:

- You do not need more than one Medicare supplement policy.

- If you purchase this policy, you may want to evaluate your existing health coverage and decide if you need multiple coverages.

- You may be eligible for benefits under Medicaid and may not need a Medicare supplement policy.

- The benefits and premiums under your Medicare supplement policy can be suspended, if requested, for 24 months during your entitlement to benefits under Medicaid. You must request this suspension within 90 days of becoming eligible for Medicaid. If you are no longer entitled to Medicaid, your policy will be reinstituted if requested within 90 days of losing Medicaid eligibility.

- Counseling services may be available in your state to provide advice concerning your purchase of Medicare supplement insurance and concerning medical assistance through the state Medicaid program.

Applications must contain questions designed to elicit information as to whether the applicant has other Medicare supplement or health insurance coverages. If a sale will involve replacement of Medicare supplement coverage, then the insurer must provide the applicant with a notice regarding replacement, which is illustrated in Figure 5-3. The notice must be signed by the insurance producer, if applicable, and the applicant for a Medicare supplement policy.

The Medicare Supplement Model Regulation also requires insurers to provide specified notices to owners of Medicare supplement policies. We noted earlier that Medicare supplement policies must allow the insurer to modify the benefits payable to ensure the policies reflect changes to Medicare benefits. When such changes occur, insurers must notify their policyowners of any such modifications made to Medicare supplement policies. The notice must describe the changes made in the Medicare program and the modifications made to the coverage provided by the applicable policy. The notice also must specify when any resulting premium change will become effective. These required notices may not include, or be accompanied by, any solicitations.

Additional Requirements

The Medicare Supplement Insurance Model Regulation imposes other requirements on insurers that market Medicare supplement policies. These requirements include standards for claim payments and minimum loss ratio standards. The Model Regulation also imposes limits on the compensation that may be paid to insurance producers who sell Medicare supplement policies. These limits are designed to prevent marketing abuses that sometimes result when producers earn high first-year commissions on product sales.

FIGURE 5-3 Notice to Applicant Regarding Replacement of Medicare Supplement Insurance.

NOTICE TO APPLICANT REGARDING REPLACEMENT OF MEDICARE SUPPLEMENT INSURANCE
[Insurance company's name and address]

SAVE THIS NOTICE! IT MAY BE IMPORTANT TO YOU IN THE FUTURE

According to [your application] [information you have furnished], you intend to terminate existing Medicare supplement insurance and replace it with a policy to be issued by [Company Name] Insurance Company. Your new policy will provide thirty (30) days within which you may decide without cost whether you desire to keep the policy.

You should review this new coverage carefully. Compare it with all accident and sickness coverage you now have. If, after due consideration, you find that purchase of this Medicare supplement coverage is a wise decision, you should terminate your present Medicare supplement coverage. You should evaluate the need for other accident and sickness coverage you have that may duplicate this policy.

STATEMENT TO APPLICANT BY ISSUER, AGENT [BROKER OR OTHER REPRESENTATIVE]:

I have reviewed your current medical or health insurance coverage. To the best of my knowledge, this Medicare supplement policy will not duplicate your existing Medicare supplement coverage because you intend to terminate your existing Medicare supplement coverage. The replacement policy is being purchased for the following reason (check one):

_____ Additional benefits.

_____ No change in benefits, but lower premiums.

_____ Fewer benefits and lower premiums.

_____ Other. (please specify)

_____

1. Health conditions which you may presently have (preexisting conditions) may not be immediately or fully covered under the new policy. This could result in denial or delay of a claim for benefits under the new policy, whereas a similar claim might have been payable under your present policy.

2. State law provides that your replacement policy or certificate may not contain new preexisting conditions, waiting periods, elimination periods or probationary periods. The insurer will waive any time periods applicable to preexisting conditions, waiting periods, elimination periods, or probationary periods in the new policy (or coverage) for similar benefits to the extent such time was spent (depleted) under the original policy.

Figure 5-3. Notice to Applicant Regarding Replacement of Medicare Supplement Insurance, *continued*.

3. If you still wish to terminate your present policy and replace it with new coverage, be certain to truthfully and completely answer all questions on the application concerning your medical and health history. Failure to include all material medical information on an application may provide a basis for the company to deny any future claims and to refund your premium as though your policy had never been in force. After the application has been completed and before you sign it, review it carefully to be certain that all information has been properly recorded. [If the policy or certificate is guaranteed issue, this paragraph need not appear.]

Do not cancel your present policy until you have received your new policy and are sure that you want to keep it.

_____

(Signature of Agent, Broker or Other Representative)*

[Typed Name and Address of Issuer, Agent or Broker]

_____

(Applicant's Signature)

_____

(Date)

*Signature not required for direct response sales.

Source: Excerpted from NAIC, *Model Regulation to Implement the NAIC Medicare Supplement Insurance Minimum Standards Model Act* § 18, 2001. Reprinted with permission from the National Association of Insurance Commissioners.

Health Insurers' Compliance Responsibilities

In addition to imposing requirements on insurers that market Medicare supplement insurance policies, the Medicare Supplement Model Regulation imposes requirements on insurers that market health insurance other than Medicare supplement policies to individuals who are eligible for Medicare. At the time of application, insurers that use personal selling techniques to market such hospital or medical expense coverage to people who are eligible for Medicare must provide applicants with a document known as a *Guide to Health Insurance for People with Medicare* and must obtain a signed acknowledgement from the applicants. This document was developed by the

NAIC and the federal Centers for Medicare and Medicaid Services (CMS) to provide consumers with information to help them make informed purchase decisions.[2] Direct response insurers must deliver a copy of the Guide to each individual who is eligible for Medicare and who applies for health insurance other than Medicare supplement insurance no later than when a policy is delivered to that applicant.

Insurers marketing health coverages other than Medicare supplement coverage to individuals who are eligible for Medicare also must notify applicants that the policies being marketed are not Medicare supplement policies. This notice must appear on the face page of each non-Medicare supplement policy issued to an individual who is eligible for Medicare. Applications for such a policy must contain specified information about the extent to which the policy provides coverages that duplicate Medicare benefits.

The Medicare Supplement Model Regulation imposes reporting requirements on insurers that market Medicare supplement insurance. Each year, such an insurer must report to the state insurance department certain information about every individual who resides in the state and who is insured by more than one Medicare supplement policy issued by the insurer. The insurer must report (1) the policy number and (2) the date of policy issue for each such individual. Insurers also must annually file with the state insurance department their premium rates, rating schedules, and supporting documentation including loss ratio information.

LONG-TERM CARE INSURANCE

For regulatory purposes, *long-term care insurance* is a policy or rider advertised, marketed, offered, or designed to provide coverage for not less than 12 consecutive months for medically necessary care an insured receives in a setting other than a hospital, such as in the insured's home or a nursing home facility. Care provided under a long-term care policy may include diagnostic, preventive, therapeutic, rehabilitative, maintenance, or personal care services. Long-term care benefits generally are payable if an insured has a cognitive impairment or loses his physical functional capacity. As noted, long-term care coverage can be provided by a long-term care policy or by a long-term care rider attached to a life insurance policy. When a rider is attached to a life insurance policy, long-term care benefits are provided as an accelerated benefit—that is, the payment of long-term care benefits reduces the amount of the death benefit payable under the life insurance policy.

Although long-term care insurance makes up a relatively small portion of the health care market, long-term care policies are becoming more attractive to purchasers as prices are becoming more affordable. Sales of long-term care insurance are expected to increase dramatically within the next decade, as the population ages. In order to encourage taxpayers to purchase long-term care insurance, Congress amended the federal income tax laws in 1996 to provide favorable treatment for *qualified long-term care insurance policies* that meet specified requirements. Insight 5-1 describes qualified long-term care plans.

INSIGHT 5-1 **Federal Income Tax Incentives for the Purchase of Long-Term Care Insurance.**

The enactment of the federal Health Insurance Portability and Accountability Act resulted in changes to several federal laws, including the federal income tax laws. A number of these changes affect the federal income tax treatment of premiums paid for and benefits received under qualified long-term care insurance products after 1996. A qualified long-term care insurance policy is a long-term care policy that meets requirements specified in the federal tax code and thus qualifies for favorable federal income tax treatment. For example, a qualified long-term care policy must be guaranteed renewable and must contain specific provisions designed to protect policyowners and insureds.

Premiums an individual taxpayer pays for a qualified long-term care insurance policy now are deductible as a medical expense. Note, however, that individuals are permitted to deduct the cost of their unreimbursed medical expenses—including insurance premiums—only if the total cost is at least 7½ percent of their adjusted gross incomes. Benefits received under a qualified long-term care policy are not taxable income to the recipients.

Employers that provide qualified group long-term care insurance plans for employees are allowed to deduct as a business expense the amount of long-term care premiums they pay. In addition, long-term care coverage provided to employees by an employer is not treated as taxable income to the employees.

Source: Internal Revenue Code § 77028 (1999).

Almost all of the states have adopted insurance laws and regulations based on the NAIC *Long-Term Care Insurance Model Act* and the NAIC *Long-Term Care Insurance Model Regulation*. The Model Act establishes standards for both group and individual long-term care insurance and is designed to protect the public and, at the same time, promote the availability of long-term care coverage and flexibility in the design of such coverage. The Model Regulation implements provisions of the Model Act and establishes additional standards for long-term care insurance policies.

Policy Provisions

Most states require insurers to file long-term care policies with the state insurance department and receive the department's approval of those policies before delivering or issuing policies for delivery within the state. As noted earlier in the chapter, the UPPL specifies provisions that individual health insurance policies—including long-term care policies and Medicare supplement policies—must include. These provisions are listed in Figure 5-1. In addition, long-term care policies must contain provisions required by the Long-Term Care Insurance Model Act. Laws based on the Model Act require all individual and group long-term care insurance policies to comply with the following requirements:

- Coverage may not be cancelled or terminated by the insurer because of an insured's age or mental or physical condition.

- Policies may not limit coverage to skilled nursing care or provide reduced benefits for care other than skilled nursing care.

- Long-term care policies may include a preexisting conditions provision, but such a provision must comply with specific requirements. The policy definition of a preexisting condition must be limited to conditions occurring within six months preceding the effective date of coverage, and policies may include a maximum waiting period of six months following the effective date of coverage during which preexisting conditions are not covered. A policy may not exclude, limit, or reduce coverage for specifically named preexisting conditions for more than six months following the effective date of coverage.

- Long-term care policies must provide at least a 30-day free look period. The face page of an individual long-term care policy must contain a prominent notice of the policyowner's right to return the policy within 30 days following policy delivery and receive a premium refund. Each group certificate also must contain such a notice of the certificateholder's right to return the certificate and receive a refund.

The Long-Term Care Insurance Model Regulation requires individual long-term care policies to contain a renewal provision, which must be included on the policy face page. The following two types of renewal provisions are permitted:

- A policy that is *noncancellable* is one that the insured may continue in force by making required premium payments and for which the insurer has no right to change any policy provision or the policy premium rate.

- A policy that is *guaranteed renewable* is one that the insured may continue in force by making required premium payments and for which the insurer may not change policy provisions, but may change the premium rate if it does so for a class of policies.

Long-term care policies often include a time limit on certain defenses provision. The Model Act, however, limits the time within which an insurer may rescind a long-term care policy or group certificate. For six months following delivery of the policy or group certificate, an insurer may rescind the policy or certificate or deny an otherwise valid claim only if the application contains a misrepresentation that was material to the insurer's acceptance of the risk. After six months but before a policy has been in force for two years, the insurer may rescind the policy or group certificate or deny an otherwise valid claim only if the application contains a misrepresentation that (1) was material to the insurer's acceptance of the risk *and* (2) relates to the condition for which benefits are sought. After a policy or group certificate has been in force for two years, the insurer may rescind the policy or certificate or deny an otherwise valid claim only if the insurer obtains evidence that the insured knowingly and intentionally misrepresented relevant facts related to her health. Once an insurer has paid policy benefits, it may not recover those benefits even if the policy is later rescinded.

Laws based on the Long-Term Care Model Act prohibit an insurer from issuing or issuing for delivery in the state a long-term care insurance policy unless the insurer offers the policyowner the option of purchasing a policy that includes nonforfeiture benefits. Specific requirements for such nonforfeiture benefits are stated in the Long-Term Care Insurance Model Regulation. According to these requirements, nonforfeiture benefits must be provided in the form of paid-up long-term care coverage following lapse of a policy; the length of the paid-up coverage varies depending on the amount of the nonforfeiture value. The Model Regulation specifies how insurers must calculate nonforfeiture benefits; requirements are the same for both individual and group long-term care policies.

State insurance laws and regulations govern the types of exclusions and limitations that individual and group long-term care policies may include. Laws based on the Long-Term Care Model Regulation generally prohibit long-term care policies from limiting or excluding coverage on the basis of illness, treatment, medical condition, or accident. This general prohibition, however, is subject to a number of exceptions. A policy exclusion or limitation may be based on any of the following conditions:

- Preexisting conditions (as discussed earlier in the chapter)

- Mental or nervous disorders, except that benefits must be provided for Alzheimer's disease

- Alcoholism and drug addiction

- Illness, treatment, or medical condition arising out of war or act of war whether declared or undeclared; participation in a felony, riot, or insurrection; service in the armed forces; suicide while sane or insane, attempted suicide, or intentionally self-inflicted injury; or aviation in the case of non-farepaying passengers

- Treatment provided in a government facility; services for which benefits are available under a governmental program; services provided by a member of the covered person's immediate family; and services for which no charge is normally made in the absence of insurance

The Model Regulation lists a number of terms and prohibits individual and group long-term care policies from using the terms unless the terms are defined in the policy and the definitions are those specified in the Model Regulation. Some of these terms are listed and defined in Figure 5-4.

The Model Regulation requires insurers that offer long-term care policies to offer an inflation protection option that provides for benefit levels to increase over time in order to account for reasonably anticipated increases in the costs of covered long-term care services. Such an inflation protection feature may include reasonable benefit maximums and must conform to minimum requirements specified in the Model Regulation. A prospective applicant for long-term care insurance must be provided a graphic comparison of the benefit levels of a policy with an inflation protection feature to the benefit levels of a policy without such a feature; this comparison must show benefit levels over a period of at least 20 years. An insurer must include an inflation protection feature in each long-term care policy unless it obtains a signed rejection of such coverage from the policyowner. A signed rejection is considered a part of the application for insurance and, thus, a part of the contractual agreement between the insurer and the policyowner.

Standards for Benefit Triggers

States that have adopted the Long-Term Care Insurance Model Regulation require insurers to comply with specified standards for evaluating whether an insured is eligible to receive long-term care benefits. According to the Model Regulation, insurers must condition the payment of benefits on a determination of the insured's ability to perform *activities of daily living* and on *cognitive impairment*. Eligibility for benefits may not be more restrictive than requiring either that the insured be unable to perform three activities of daily living or that the insured suffer from cognitive impairment. (See Figure 5-4 for definitions of these terms.) Assessments of an insured's ability to perform activities

> **FIGURE 5-4 Policy Definitions Required in Long-Term Care Policies.**
>
> **Activities of daily living** means at least bathing, continence, dressing, eating, toileting, and transferring. Long-term care policies typically provide that benefits are payable when an insured becomes unable to perform a stated number of activities of daily living or becomes cognitively impaired.
>
> - **Bathing** means washing oneself by sponge bath or in either a tub or shower, including the task of getting into or out of the tub or shower.
>
> - **Continence** means the ability to maintain control of bowel and bladder function or, when unable to maintain control of bowel or bladder function, the ability to perform associated personal hygiene (including caring for catheter or colostomy bag).
>
> - **Dressing** means putting on and taking off all items of clothing and any necessary braces, fasteners, or artificial limbs.
>
> - **Eating** means feeding oneself by getting food into the body from a receptacle (such as a plate, cup, or table) or by a feeding tube or intravenously.
>
> - **Toileting** means getting to and from the toilet, getting on and off the toilet, and performing associated personal hygiene.
>
> - **Transferring** means moving into or out of a bed, chair, or wheelchair.
>
> - **Cognitive impairment** means a deficiency in a person's short- or long-term memory; orientation as to person, place, and time; deductive or abstract reasoning; or judgment as it relates to safety awareness.
>
> **Source:** Excerpted and adapted from NAIC, *Long-Term Care Insurance Model Regulation* § 5, 2000. Reprinted with permission from the National Association of Insurance Commissioners.

of daily living or of an insured's cognitive impairment must be performed by licensed or certified professionals, such as physicians, nurses, or social workers.

Requirements for Application Forms

Except in the case of guaranteed issue coverages, applications for individual and group long-term care insurance must contain clear and unambiguous questions that are designed to enable the insurer to ascertain the applicant's health condition. The Model Regulation requires applications for such policies to include the following notice set out conspicuously and in close conjunction with the applicant's signature:

> Caution: If your answers on this application are incorrect or untrue, [the insurer] has the right to deny benefits or rescind your policy.

A similar notice also must appear on long-term care policies other than guaranteed issue policies.

The Model Regulation requires application forms to contain specified questions designed to elicit information as to whether the applicant intends to replace an in-force long-term care insurance policy or group certificate. When an insurer determines that a sale will involve the replacement of a long-term care policy, the insurer must provide the applicant with a notice regarding replacement of accident and sickness or long-term care coverage. With one exception, this notice of replacement must be provided before the insurer issues the policy, and the insurer must maintain a copy of the notice that has been signed by the applicant. In the case of direct response solicitations, the insurer must provide the notice of replacement when it issues the policy.

Advertising Requirements

Like the advertising of Medicare supplement insurance, the advertising of long-term care insurance in most states is subject to regulations based on the Advertisements of Accident and Sickness Insurance Model Regulation, which we discussed in Chapter 4. In addition, the Long-Term Care Insurance Model Regulation specifically requires insurers to file advertising materials with the state insurance department for review and approval as required by state law. Insurers also must maintain all advertisements of long-term care insurance for at least three years from the date the advertisement was first used.

Marketing Standards

Insurers that market long-term care policies must comply with provisions of the Long-Term Care Model Regulation that establish marketing standards for those policies, and insurers must establish procedures for verifying their compliance. According to the Model Regulation standards, insurers must establish marketing procedures to ensure that any policy comparisons used by their sales producers are fair and accurate. Insurers also must establish marketing procedures to ensure that they do not issue excessive insurance coverages to insureds. These procedures must include making every reasonable effort to identify whether a prospective applicant already has health insurance and the types and amounts of any such insurance. The following notice must appear on the first page of each long-term care policy:

> Notice to buyer: This policy may not cover all of the costs associated with long-term care incurred by the buyer during the period of coverage. The buyer is advised to review carefully all policy limitations.

Insurers must establish procedures for verifying their own compliance with the foregoing requirements. Also, if the state in which a long-term care policy is to be delivered has a senior insurance counseling program approved by the state insurance department, then insurers must provide prospective applicants with written notice that such a program is available. Insurers also must provide prospects with the name, address, and telephone number of the counseling program. Insight 5-2 describes two such senior insurance counseling programs.

Like the Medicare Supplement Model Regulation described earlier in the chapter, the Long-Term Care Model Regulation prohibits certain marketing practices in the sale of long-term care insurance. Prohibited practices include twisting, misrepresentation, high pressure tactics, and cold lead advertising that fails to conspicuously disclose that the purpose of the advertisement is the solicitation of insurance.

INSIGHT 5-2 Senior Health Insurance Counseling Programs.

State insurance departments have established a variety of programs to provide assistance to insurance consumers. A number of states have established programs specifically designed to provide senior citizens with assistance with their health insurance needs and questions. In 1986, the State of Idaho established such a program known as the Senior Health Insurance Benefits Advisors (SHIBA) Program. Illinois established its Senior Health Insurance Program (SHIP) in 1988. Volunteers throughout both states agree to provide free information, counseling, and assistance to seniors in their geographic areas.

These programs provide information concerning the benefits provided by Medicare and Medicaid, as well as information about the types of private health insurance coverages that are available to seniors. Counseling services help seniors evaluate their insurance needs and decide on what type of insurance coverages are suitable for them. Program volunteers also help seniors resolve problems connected with their insurance coverages.

Source: Idaho Department of Insurance, "SHIBA Program," http://www.doi.state.id.us/shwelcome.htm (24 April 2002), and Illinois Department of Insurance, "Senior Health Insurance Program (SHIP): Fact Sheet," http://www.state.il.us/ins/Ship/shipfacts.htm (24 April 2002).

Solicitation Disclosure Requirements

The Long-Term Care Insurance Model Act and Model Regulation impose a number of disclosure requirements on insurers and insurance producers who market long-term care coverage. Insurers are required to make specific disclosures to applicants at the time of application for a policy for which premiums may increase. If the application method does not allow for delivery of the required disclosures, the insurer must deliver them no later than when it delivers the policy. The required disclosures provide applicants with information about the insurer's rating practices. The following are examples of the information an insurer must provide:

- A statement that the policy may be subject to future premium rate increases
- The current premium rate or rate schedules that apply to the applicant
- An explanation of potential future premium rate revisions and the policyowner's options in the event of a rate revision
- A general explanation of how the insurer will make premium rate revisions, including a description of when adjustments will be effective
- Information about actual premium rate increases for the product over the previous 10 years

An applicant for long-term care coverage must sign an acknowledgement that the insurer made the required disclosures. The remaining disclosure requirements vary depending on whether coverage is provided by a long-term care policy or a life insurance policy that provides long-term care coverage by means of an accelerated benefit provision or rider.

Long-Term Care Policies

Insurers that market long-term care policies must provide every prospective applicant with an *outline of coverage* at the time of an initial solicitation. According to the Model Act, an outline of coverage for a long-term care policy must include the following information:

- A description of the principal benefits and coverage provided by the policy
- A statement of the principal exclusions, limitations, and reductions contained in the policy

- A statement of the terms under which the policy may be continued in force, including any reservation in the policy of the right to change the premium payable

- A statement that the outline of coverage is a summary only and is not an insurance contract

- A description of the terms under which the policy may be returned in exchange for a premium refund

- A brief description of the relationship between cost of care and benefits provided by the policy

- A statement disclosing whether the policy is a qualified long-term care insurance policy under federal tax laws

The Model Regulation contains additional requirements as to the format and content of an outline of coverage. According to these requirements, an outline of coverage must be a separate document printed in at least a specified minimum type size. The outline may not contain any advertising material and must be printed in a standard format that is contained in the Model Regulation.

Prospective applicants for a long-term care insurance policy must receive a copy of a publication entitled *Shopper's Guide to Long-Term Care Insurance*. The NAIC has developed this publication to provide consumers with information about the long-term care insurance coverages that are available and to help consumers make informed purchase decisions. Insurance producers must provide the Shopper's Guide to a prospect before presenting an application form for a long-term care policy. In the case of direct response solicitations, the insurer must provide the Shopper's Guide in conjunction with the application.

Life Insurance Policies with Accelerated Benefits

Long-term care coverage is generally provided by long-term care insurance policies designed specifically to provide such coverage. In addition, life insurance policies may provide long-term care coverage by means of an accelerated benefit provision or rider. Sales of such life insurance policies are subject to several specific disclosure requirements contained in the Long-Term Care Insurance Model Act. When soliciting the sale of a life insurance policy that contains such an accelerated benefit provision or rider, an insurer is required to provide prospects with the Shopper's Guide to Long-Term Care Insurance. In addition, at the time of policy delivery, the insurer must deliver a *policy summary* that contains the following information:

- An explanation of how the long-term care benefit interacts with other components of the policy, including deductions from death benefits

- An illustration of the amount of benefits, the length of the benefit period, and the guaranteed lifetime benefits if any, for each covered person

- Any exclusions, reductions, and limitations on benefits for long-term care

- If applicable, a description of how the long-term care benefits are affected by the exercise of other policy rights, guarantees related to the cost of insurance, and current and projected maximum lifetime benefits

At the time of application for such a life insurance policy, the applicant must be provided with a disclosure statement that accelerated benefits may be considered taxable income and that tax advice should be sought. Note that tax consequences could arise at the federal, state, and local levels. This disclosure statement also must appear on the face page of the policy or rider. Any life insurance policy or rider that is advertised or offered as long-term care insurance is subject to all other requirements of the Long-Term Care Model Act and Model Regulation.

Suitability Standards

The Long-Term Care Insurance Model Regulation requires insurers that market long-term care coverage—except coverage provided as an accelerated benefit under a life insurance policy—to establish suitability standards to determine whether the purchase or replacement of long-term care coverage is appropriate for the needs of applicants. Insurers must use these standards in evaluating applications for long-term care coverage and must train their insurance producers in how to use these suitability standards. Insurance producers must use these standards to market long-term care coverage. An insurer's suitability standards must include procedures that require the insurer and insurance producers to consider the following factors:

- The applicant's ability to pay for the proposed coverage and other pertinent financial information related to the purchase of the coverage

- The applicant's goals or needs for long-term care and the advantages and disadvantages of meeting those needs through insurance

- The values, benefits, and costs of the applicant's existing insurance, if any, compared to the values, benefits, and costs of the recommended long-term care coverage

Insurers and insurance producers must make reasonable efforts to obtain the required information from applicants, and these efforts must include providing two documents to applicants at or before the time of completing an application for long-term care coverage:

- The applicant must receive a *Long-Term Care Insurance Personal Worksheet*, which includes questions for the applicant to answer. The completed worksheet must be returned to the insurer along with the application for insurance.

- The applicant also must receive a disclosure form entitled *Things You Should Know Before You Buy Long-Term Care Insurance*, which must be in the format contained in Figure 5-5 and must be printed in at least 12-point type.

FIGURE 5-5 NAIC Long-Term Care Insurance Disclosure Form.

Things You Should Know Before You Buy Long-Term Care Insurance	
Long-Term Care Insurance	A long-term care insurance policy may pay most of the costs for your care in a nursing home. Many policies also pay for care at home or other community settings. Since policies can vary in coverage, you should read this policy and make sure you understand what it covers before you buy it.
	[You should **not** buy this insurance policy unless you can afford to pay the premiums every year.] [Remember that the company can increase premiums in the future.] [**Drafting Note:** For single premium policies, delete this bullet; for noncancellable policies, delete the second sentence only.]
	The personal worksheet includes questions designed to help you and the company determine whether this policy is suitable for your needs.
Medicare	Medicare does **not** pay for most long-term care.
Medicaid	Medicaid will generally pay for long-term care if you have very little income and few assets. You probably should **not** buy this policy if you are now eligible for Medicaid.
	Many people become eligible for Medicaid after they have used up their own financial resources by paying for long-term care services.

Figure 5-5. NAIC Long-Term Care Insurance Disclosure Form, *continued.*

Medicaid, *continued*	When Medicaid pays your spouse's nursing home bills, you are allowed to keep your house and furniture, a living allowance, and some of your joint assets.
	Your choice of long-term care services may be limited if you are receiving Medicaid. To learn more about Medicaid, contact your local or state Medicaid agency.
Shopper's Guide	Make sure the insurance company or agent gives you a copy of a book called the National Association of Insurance Commissioners' "Shopper's Guide to Long-Term Care Insurance." Read it carefully. If you have decided to apply for long-term care insurance, you have the right to return the policy within 30 days and get back any premium you have paid if you are dissatisfied for any reason or choose not to purchase the policy.
Counseling	Free counseling and additional information about long-term care insurance are available through your state's insurance counseling program. Contact your state insurance department or department on aging for more information about the senior health insurance counseling program in your state.

Source: Excerpted from NAIC, *Long-Term Care Insurance Model Regulation,* Appendix C, 2000. Reprinted with permission from the National Association of Insurance Commissioners.

Additional Requirements

The Long-Term Care Insurance Model Regulation imposes other requirements on insurers that market long-term care policies. These requirements specify how insurers must calculate reserves for long-term care policies, and they establish minimum loss ratio standards for long-term care products. The Model Regulation contains an optional provision that limits the amount of the first-year commission that insurance producers are permitted to receive for the sale of long-term care policies. (Recall that similar limits are placed on the compensation that producers may receive for the sale of Medicare supplement insurance.) The states are encouraged to adopt this optional provision if they think that large first-year commissions are resulting in marketing abuses in the sale of long-term care insurance.

Insurers' Compliance Responsibilities

In addition to requirements we have already described, the Long-Term Care Insurance Model Regulation imposes a number of compliance responsibilities on insurers that market long-term care coverages. In states that have adopted the Long-Term Care Model Regulation, at least 30 days before an insurer issues a long-term care policy in the state, the insurer must file the following information with the state insurance department:

- A copy of the required disclosure document that provides applicants with information about the insurer's premium rating practices

- An actuarial certification that includes specified statements about the adequacy and equitability of the policy's premium rates

The Model Regulation also requires that, at least 30 days before an insurer notifies its policyowners of a premium rate increase, the insurer must notify the state insurance department of the increase. Along with the notification of a pending increase, the insurer must provide the insurance department with specified information, including an actuarial certification and an actuarial memorandum justifying the rate schedule change.

Insurers also must take a series of actions designed to protect insureds against unintentionally allowing their long-term care coverage to lapse. Before issuing a long-term care policy or group certificate, an insurer must obtain one of the following documents from the applicant:

- A written designation of at least one person other than the applicant who is to receive notice of lapse or termination of the policy

- A signed waiver by an applicant who elects not to designate another person to receive such notices

When another person is designated to receive notices of lapse or policy termination, the insurer must notify the insured at least every two years that she has the right to change the designation. A long-term care policy may not be lapsed for nonpayment of premium unless the insurer notifies the insured—and any other person designated by the insured—at least 30 days before such lapse. Long-term care policies and group certificates also must include a reinstatement provision that provides for reinstatement following lapse for nonpayment if the insurer receives proof that the insured had a cognitive impairment or had lost physical functional capacity before the expiration of the policy grace period. The insured must be given a five-month period following lapse in which to request such a reinstatement.

The Long-Term Care Insurance Model Regulation imposes various recordkeeping and reporting requirements on an insurer that markets long-term care coverage. The insurer must maintain records for each long-term care insurance producer of (1) the amount of the producer's replacement sales as a percent of the producer's total annual sales and (2) the amount of lapses of long-term care insurance policies sold by the producer as a percent of the producer's total annual sales. The insurer must report the following types of information each year to the state insurance department:

- The 10 percent of the insurer's producers with the greatest percentages of replacements and lapses

- The number of the insurer's lapsed long-term care policies as a percent of its total annual sales and as a percent of its total number of policies in force at the end of the preceding calendar year

- The number of replacement policies the insurer sold as a percent of its total annual sales and as a percent of its total number of policies in force at the end of the preceding calendar year

- The number of long-term care claims the insurer denied for each class of business, expressed as a percentage of claims denied

KEY TERMS AND CONCEPTS

Medicare
Medicare supplement insurance policy
Medicare Supplement Insurance Minimum Standards Model Act
Model Regulation to Implement the NAIC Medicare Supplement Insurance Minimum Standards Model Act
NAIC Model Rules Governing Advertisements of Medicare Supplement Insurance

Guide to Health Insurance for People with Medicare
long-term care insurance
qualified long-term care insurance policy
Long-Term Care Insurance Model Act
Long-Term Care Insurance Model Regulation
Shopper's Guide to Long-Term Care Insurance

ENDNOTES

1. *Medicare Part A* provides basic hospital insurance coverage to all eligible individuals. Individuals eligible for Medicare Part A benefits have the option of purchasing coverage under *Medicare Part B*, which provides supplementary medical insurance including coverage of physician's services, medical supplies, outpatient services, diagnostic tests, and other services necessary for the diagnosis or treatment of an illness or injury.

2. The federal Centers for Medicare and Medicaid Services (CMS) was formerly known as the Health Care Financing Administration (HCFA). The CMS is the federal agency responsible for administering the federal Medicare and Medicaid programs.

CHAPTER 6

Regulation of Managed Care Plans

LEARNING OBJECTIVES

After studying this chapter, you should be able to

- Identify the types of medical expense plans that are subject to specific regulatory requirements imposed on managed care plans

- Recognize the types of federal regulatory requirements that are imposed on health maintenance organizations (HMOs)

- Recognize the types of state regulatory requirements that are imposed on managed care plans

- Recognize the types of regulatory requirements that are imposed on preferred provider arrangements (PPAs)

Medical expense insurance traditionally has been provided by insurance companies through insurance policies designed to reimburse insureds for covered expenses they incurred. These insurance plans, referred to as *indemnity plans*, allow insureds to select their own medical care providers and typically include cost-containment features such as deductible and coinsurance requirements. Today, many people are insured by health benefit plans, known as *managed care plans*, that integrate both the financing and the delivery of health care within a system that seeks to manage the cost, accessibility, and quality of care. NAIC model laws define a *managed care plan* as a health benefit plan that either requires insureds to use health care providers managed, owned, under contract with, or employed by the health carrier or creates incentives for insureds to use such providers. Insight 6-1 compares features of some types of managed care plans to illustrate how traditional medical expense insurance differs from pure managed care plans.

State insurance laws have been modified over the years to facilitate the organization and operation of managed care plans. In this chapter, we describe federal regulation of health maintenance organizations (HMOs) under the Health Maintenance Organization (HMO) Act of 1973. Then, we describe various state regulatory requirements that are placed on HMOs, as well as other managed care plans. Finally, we discuss some of the regulatory requirements that are imposed on preferred provider arrangements (PPAs).

INSIGHT 6-1 The Managed Care Continuum.

Medical expense insurance traditionally has been provided by means of indemnity insurance plans under which an insured is reimbursed—or indemnified—for the covered medical expenses the insured incurs. Indemnity plans typically include cost-sharing features that require an insured to pay an annual deductible amount and impose coinsurance requirements under which the insured pays a percentage, such as 20 percent, of covered expenses. The insured is free to select any qualified medical care provider and is responsible for paying the provider's fees. The insurance risk is shared between the insured person and the insurer. The more often a given insured needs medical care, the more expensive it is for the insured and the insurer. The medical care provider, however, benefits financially the more an insured receives medical care services.

Managed care plans broaden the financial risk sharing to include health care providers. The theory is that when health care providers share in the financial risk of medical expense insurance, providers are encouraged to deliver the necessary care in a more cost-effective way than if they had no risk. Managed care plans achieve risk sharing by negotiating fee arrangements with providers and making other contractual agreements that encourage cost-effective care. The nature of the specific arrangements depends on the type of managed care plan.

Because of the variety of managed care plans, it is not always possible to classify a plan as a traditional indemnity plan or a managed care plan. The health insurance continuum illustrated below illustrates this point. On the far left side of the continuum are traditional indemnity insurance plans; on the far right are pure managed care plans. Various types of managed care systems are positioned in between. The further right a plan is located on the continuum, the more elements of a managed care plan it contains.

HMOs contain the most features of managed care plans by providing or arranging for the delivery of specified health care services in exchange for a prepaid fee. HMO enrollees must choose their medical care providers from within a network of providers who contract with the HMO. HMOs typically do not impose deductible or coinsurance requirements; however, members are usually required to make a small copayment whenever they receive specified medical services. HMOs use many managed care techniques that enable them to reduce the costs of providing health care to enrollees.

Point of service (POS) plans are hybrid plans that combine features of traditional indemnity coverage with managed care coverage. POS members choose, at the time they need medical services, whether to go to a network or out-of-network provider. POS plans encourage the use of network services by offering a greater amount of coverage for services provided within the network and by requiring members to pay higher deductibles and coinsurance amounts for out-of-network services than they pay for network services.

Preferred provider organization (PPO) plans are much more like traditional indemnity plans than managed care plans. PPOs are organizations that negotiate contracts between health care providers and health care purchasers, such as employers, third party administrators (TPAs), insurance companies, and unions. Like HMOs, PPOs use a network of health care providers. But unlike HMOs, PPO plans do offer some coverage for insureds who choose to use the services of non-network—or out-of-network—providers. To encourage insureds to see the preferred providers in the PPO network, PPOs pay a higher portion of those medical expenses incurred with PPO providers than they pay for services provided by out-of-network providers.

| Traditional Indemnity Plans | PPOs | POSs | HMOs | Pure Managed Care Plans |

Regulation of HMOs

Managed care plans originally took the form of HMOs that combine the financing and delivery of health care to provide comprehensive health care services for subscribing members in a particular geographic area. Individuals insured by an HMO are often referred to as *enrollees*. An HMO is both an insurer and a provider of health care services and may be organized in a variety of ways. (See Insight 6-2 for descriptions of various types of HMOs.)

INSIGHT 6-2   Types of HMOs.

HMOs can be classified in a number of ways, and new types of HMOs are continuing to evolve. HMOs can be classified by the fee structures they use to compensate physicians who provide services to HMO enrollees. Following are some examples of fee structures:

- Under a **capitation** arrangement, the provider is paid the same amount each month for an enrollee regardless of how often the enrollee receives medical attention or of the cost of that medical attention.

- Some HMOs compensate physicians with a predetermined **salary**.

- Under a **discounted fee-for-service** arrangement, physicians are paid a specified percentage of their normal fees.

- A **fee schedule payment structure** allows the HMO to place caps or limits on the dollar amounts that it will reimburse physicians for covered medical procedures and services.

In addition, we can broadly classify an HMO as either an *open panel HMO* or a *closed panel HMO* depending on how it contracts with medical care providers. An **open panel HMO** is an HMO that can contract with any physician or provider who meets the HMO's specific standards to provide services to enrollees. Open panel HMOs include the following arrangements:

- Arrangements in which an HMO contracts with an **individual practice association (IPA)**, which is an association of physicians that agrees to provide services to HMO enrollees

- **Direct contract HMO** arrangements in which an HMO contracts directly with individual physicians to provide medical services for HMO enrollees

A **closed panel HMO** is an HMO that limits the physicians with whom it contracts by using one of the following two models:

- In a **staff model HMO**, physicians are employees of the HMO and generally operate out of offices in the HMO's facilities.

- A **group model HMO** functions much as a staff model HMO, except that the physicians are employees of a physicians' group practice, rather than employees of the HMO. The physicians in such a group practice generally share office space, support staff, and medical equipment at a common health center or clinic. A group model HMO that contracts with more than one group practice of physicians is called a **network model HMO**.

As noted earlier, new types of HMOs continue to evolve, and many HMOs do not fit neatly into the classifications we describe here. Some HMOs, for example, combine characteristics of two or more of the HMOs we describe and are known as **mixed model HMOs**.

The federal *Health Maintenance Organization Act of 1973* served to encourage the growth of HMOs during the late 1970s and 1980s by providing funds to HMOs that met specified requirements and requiring employers in certain situations to provide employees with the option of participating in either a federally qualified HMO or the employers' traditional group medical expense insurance plans.

At about the same time, states began enacting insurance laws to regulate HMOs, and most such state laws are based on the NAIC *Health Maintenance Organization (HMO) Model Act*. The HMO Model Act regulates all aspects of the organization and operation of HMOs conducting business in a state that has enacted such a law. These regulatory requirements are very similar to requirements imposed on health insurance companies but are adapted to fit the features unique to HMOs. For example, because HMOs undertake to provide or arrange for medical care services for enrollees, HMOs perform functions that traditionally have been regulated by state public health laws. HMOs subject to the HMO Model Act are specifically exempt from regulation by other state insurance laws and by laws that regulate the practice of medicine. In states that have enacted laws based on the Model Act, therefore, unless another state insurance law specifies that it applies to HMOs, the law does not apply.

According to the HMO Model Act, a *health maintenance organization* is a person, partnership, association, trust, or corporation that undertakes to provide or arrange for the delivery of basic health care services to enrollees on a prepaid basis, but that leaves enrollees responsible for paying copayments and deductibles. Note that, unlike insurers, which must be organized as corporations, an HMO may be an individual or one of many types of business entities. *Basic health care services* are defined as the following medically necessary services:

- Preventive care
- Emergency care
- Inpatient and outpatient hospital and physician care
- Diagnostic laboratory services
- Diagnostic and therapeutic radiological services

Basic services do *not* include mental health services, services for alcohol or drug abuse, dental or vision services, or long-term rehabilitation treatment. HMOs are permitted but not required to provide such services in addition to basic health care services.

Licensing of HMOs

In states that have adopted the HMO Model Act, a party must obtain from the state insurance department a certificate of authority before establishing and operating an HMO within the state. A *certificate of authority* is a document issued by a state insurance department granting an insurer the right to conduct an insurance business in the state. The process of obtaining such a certificate of authority is quite similar to the process by which life and health insurers are licensed to conduct business. An applicant must complete an application form and file the form, along with specified types of information, with the state insurance department. The filing must include the following:

- Organizational documents such as partnership agreements, trust agreements, or articles of incorporation and bylaws, depending on the organizational form under which the applicant operates

- Biographical information about the individuals who will be responsible for the HMO's day-to-day operations and copies of all contract forms the HMO will use for agreements with those individuals

- Contract forms the HMO will use for agreements with other parties, such as health care providers and third party administrators

- Copies of the coverage forms the HMO will issue to enrollees

- Information about the HMO's financial condition and a financial feasibility plan including specified information

- A description of the geographic area in which the HMO will operate

- The names, addresses, and license numbers of the health care providers who have entered into agreements with the HMO

The HMO also must submit a description of a proposed quality assurance program that complies with requirements contained in the Model Act. A *quality assurance program* establishes procedures to ensure that health care services provided to enrollees are rendered under reasonable standards of quality of care consistent with prevailing professionally recognized standards of medical practice. The procedures must include mechanisms to ensure availability, accessibility, and continuity of care.

The HMO also must file a description of the internal grievance procedures it will use to investigate and resolve enrollee complaints and grievances. The Model Act requires HMOs to establish and maintain a grievance procedure that has been approved by the state insurance department. HMOs also must maintain records regarding grievances received.

Solvency Requirements

As noted earlier, HMOs subject to the HMO Model Act generally are exempt from complying with other state insurance laws, including the solvency requirements imposed on health insurance companies. In many states, for example, HMOs are not required to belong to the state life and health insurance guaranty association. Instead, the HMO Model Act contains solvency requirements that HMOs must meet.

According to the Model Act, an HMO must have a net worth at least equal to a specified dollar amount in order to receive a certificate of authority from the state insurance department. Thereafter, the HMO must maintain a specified minimum net worth, which varies depending on the amount of the HMO's health care expenditures. An HMO's *net worth* is equal to its total admitted assets minus its total liabilities, and the Model Act specifies which assets and liabilities must be included in this calculation.

An HMO must deposit in trust with the state insurance department cash and/or securities that at all times have a specified minimum value. The deposit is used to protect the interests of enrollees of the HMO in case it becomes financially impaired. As in the case of required deposits by foreign and alien insurers, an HMO sometimes may meet this requirement by making such a deposit with a state official of its domiciliary state. The amount deposited is treated as an admitted asset for purposes of determining the amount of the HMO's net worth.

In addition to the deposit that each HMO must make, an HMO is required to make an additional deposit if its uncovered expenditures exceed ten percent of its total health care expenditures. *Uncovered expenditures* are the costs to the HMO for health care services that are the obligation of the HMO *and* for which an enrollee may also be liable if the HMO is insolvent. These expenditures, for example, do not include costs for services when the provider of those services has agreed not to bill the enrollee if the HMO fails to pay the costs; the Model Act requires that contracts between an HMO and health care providers include such an agreement. This deposit, known as an *uncovered expenditures insolvency deposit*, is held in trust and, if the HMO becomes insolvent, may be used by the state insurance commissioner on behalf of enrollees in the state to pay claims for uncovered expenditures. For purposes of determining the HMO's net worth, the amount of such an additional deposit is treated as an admitted asset.

The HMO Model Act requires each HMO to have a plan for handling insolvency. If the HMO becomes insolvent, this plan must allow the HMO to continue benefits (1) for contract periods for which it has received premium payments and (2) for enrollees who are confined in an inpatient facility on the date of insolvency. The following are types of features the state insurance department may require such a plan to include:

- Insurance to cover the expenses to be paid for continued benefits
- Stipulations in provider contracts requiring health care providers to render services the HMO is obligated to provide following an insolvency
- Insolvency reserves
- Acceptable *letters of credit*, which are documents issued by a bank guaranteeing the payment of a customer's bank drafts up to a stated amount for a specified period

The Model Act also prescribes regulatory actions the state insurance department must take in the event an HMO becomes financially impaired or insolvent. These actions are similar to regulatory actions undertaken when an insurer becomes impaired or insolvent, including placing the HMO under administrative supervision or placing it in rehabilitation or liquidation.

Enrollee Contracts

HMOs are required to provide each group and individual contract holder with a contract that specifies the benefits and services available to enrollees. The contract must clearly state the following information:

- The name and address of the HMO
- Eligibility requirements that enrollees must meet
- Covered benefits and services within the service area
- Emergency care benefits and services
- Out-of-area benefits and services, if any
- Copayments, deductibles, or other out-of-pocket expenses
- Limitations and exclusions
- Enrollee termination
- Enrollee reinstatement, if any
- Claims procedures
- Enrollee grievance procedures

- Continuation of coverage provision
- Conversion provision
- Extension of benefits, if any
- Coordination of benefits, if applicable
- Description of the service area
- Entire contract provision
- Term of coverage
- Cancellation provision
- Renewal provision
- Grace period provision
- Conformity with state law provision

The foregoing information also must be included in the *evidence of coverage,* which is a written statement that outlines the essential features and services of an HMO and that is provided to individuals enrolled under group HMO contracts.

Individual HMO contracts also must provide for a ten-day period in which the enrollee may examine and return the contract in exchange for a full premium refund. If an enrollee receives services during the ten-day period and returns the contract for a premium refund, then the enrollee must pay for all services received.

Filing and Reporting Requirements

Most states prohibit HMOs from delivering or issuing for delivery within the state an individual or group contract form providing health care coverage unless the HMO has filed the contract form with, and received the approval of, the state insurance department. Group HMOs also must file and receive approval of evidence of coverage forms before using the forms. Filing requirements are similar to requirements imposed on other health insurance policy forms.

HMOs must file an annual report with the state insurance department. This annual report must be filed on a form approved by the state insurance department and must be verified by at least two of the HMO's principal officers. HMOs also must file the following information with the state insurance department each year:

- Audited financial statements
- A list of the health care providers who have executed a contract agreeing to provide services to HMO enrollees
- A description of the HMO's grievance procedures, the total number of grievances handled, a compilation of the causes underlying those grievances, and a summary of the final disposition of the grievances

Disclosure Requirements

The HMO Model Act requires HMOs to provide enrollees with specified information. Upon enrollment in an HMO, an enrollee must be provided with a list of the HMO's health care providers. Any material change in the operation of an HMO affecting enrollees must be reported to enrollees within 30 days of the change. For example, a major change in the provider network is considered a material change that must be reported to enrollees. By contrast, the termination of one medical care provider from the provider network would not qualify as a material change unless that provider is a primary care provider. When a primary care physician is terminated from the network, the HMO must notify all enrollees who received primary care from the terminated physician of the termination and must help those enrollees to transfer to another primary care provider. The HMO also must provide enrollees with information on how HMO services may be obtained and where additional information on access to services can be obtained. Enrollees also must be provided with a toll-free telephone number where they can contact the HMO.

Regulatory Supervision and Enforcement

HMOs are subject to the same types of supervision by the state insurance department as other health insurers. The HMO Model Act requires the state insurance department to conduct an examination of an HMO's operations at least every three years. The state insurance department is authorized to suspend or revoke an HMO's certificate of authority in specified situations. Violations of the Act also may subject an HMO to the payment of penalties.

STATE REGULATION OF MANAGED CARE PLANS

Requirements imposed on managed care plans vary a great deal among states. State insurance laws addressing the regulation of managed care plans often attempt to ensure that covered individuals have reasonable access to quality health care services. In this section, we discuss regulatory requirements that focus on accessibility of service, quality of service, and grievance procedures.

The NAIC *Managed Care Plan Network Adequacy Model Act* requires that managed care plans meet specified requirements in contractual arrangements with providers. The Model Act requires managed care plans to meet specified adequacy and accessibility requirements that include:

- Maintaining an adequate number and adequate types of providers in a network plan

- Establishing provider selection standards and making those standards available to all health care professionals

Under the Managed Care Plan Network Adequacy Model Act, managed care plans and providers must hold a covered individual harmless against provider collections—that is, a provider cannot seek compensation from covered individuals if the managed care plan fails to compensate a provider. The Model Act also requires that managed care plans give providers who participate in the plan a 60-day written notice before terminating a provider contract without cause and give patients who receive care from those providers a 15-day notice that the provider contract has been terminated.

To improve the quality as well as the accessibility of health care, a few states have adopted the NAIC *Health Care Professional Credentialing Verification Model Act*, which requires a managed care plan to establish a credential verification program that serves to verify the credentials of all participating health care professionals who participate in the plan. A managed care plan must verify such information at least every 3 years.

A managed care plan must verify the following information about a health care professional who applies for participation in the managed care plan:

- Current license

- License history in all states

- Current level of professional liability coverage

- Current hospital privileges (if applicable)

- Specialty board certification status (if applicable)

- Drug Enforcement Agency (DEA) registration certificate (if applicable)

- Evidence of graduation from health care professional school

- Evidence of post graduate training (if applicable)
- Practice history
- Malpractice history

Health care professionals have a right to review and correct any information obtained by a managed care plan during the credential verification process. Managed care plans must establish written credential verification procedures that they disclose upon written request to any health care professional who applies to the plan.

Other states have adopted laws based on the NAIC *Quality Assessment and Improvement Model Act*. The Model Act requires a managed care plan to develop a *quality assessment program*, which is a program that measures and evaluates the quality of health care services rendered by health care professionals who participate in the plan. A managed care plan must submit a written description of this program to the state insurance commissioner. If a plan detects that a participating provider has delivered persistent problematic care, the plan must report the provider to the proper licensing authority.

Many states have adopted laws based on the NAIC *Health Carrier Grievance Procedure Model Act* to ensure that covered individuals have an opportunity to resolve their grievances concerning health care decisions rendered by managed care plans. The Model Act specifies that managed care plans must establish a second-level grievance review for covered individuals who are dissatisfied with first-level grievance review decisions. This second-level grievance review panel must be composed of persons who were not previously involved in the grievance. A covered individual may attend a second-level review and present her case to the review panel. The individual can submit material in support of her case to the review panel and have legal representation present if she so desires.

Under the Grievance Procedure Model Act, the review panel must schedule and hold a second-level review within 45 days of receiving a request for the meeting. The review panel must notify the covered individual of the meeting at least 15 working days prior to holding the review. If the plan elects to have legal representation present during the review, it must include this information in the notification to the covered individual. The review panel must issue a written decision to the covered individual within five days of completing the second-level review. The Model Act also specifies that managed care plans must develop written procedures for the expedited review of any grievance where the normal time for such a review would jeopardize the life or health of a covered individual.

REGULATION OF PREFERRED PROVIDER ARRANGEMENTS

For regulatory purposes, a *preferred provider arrangement (PPA)* is a contract between a health care insurer and a health care provider or group of providers who agree to provide specified covered services to insureds. The health care insurer in a PPA can be either an insurance company or an HMO. The providers who enter into such a contract with a health care insurer are known as *preferred providers*. Providers who have not contracted with a health care insurer are known as *nonpreferred providers*. As described earlier in Insight 6-1, one specific type of health benefit plan that includes a preferred provider arrangement is known as a *preferred provider organization (PPO)*.

When a PPA is included as part of an indemnity insurance plan, the plan is regulated by state insurance laws that govern all medical expense insurance coverages. When a PPA is included as part of an HMO, the HMO is regulated by state laws governing HMOs. In addition, many states have adopted laws or regulations that impose specific requirements on preferred provider arrangements, whether those arrangements are part of an indemnity insurance plan or an HMO. In these states, a health benefit plan that includes a PPA must comply with both the general insurance laws applicable to the type of health plan and the specific laws that govern PPAs.

The NAIC has adopted a *Preferred Provider Arrangements Model Act* that establishes minimum standards for preferred provider arrangements and the health benefit plans that include such arrangements. Requirements in only a few states are based on the Model Act, but its provisions are representative of the types of requirements often imposed.

The Model Act requires a preferred provider arrangement to establish the amount and manner of payment to the preferred providers. The arrangement also must include mechanisms designed to minimize the cost of the health benefit plan. These mechanisms may include procedures for reviewing or controlling utilization of health care services and for determining whether health care services rendered are medically necessary. Preferred provider arrangements must provide insureds with reasonable access to covered services, and health benefit plans that include a PPA must include an adequate number of preferred providers to render those services. The Model Act also prohibits preferred provider arrangements from unfairly denying health benefits for medically necessary covered services.

The Preferred Provider Arrangements Model Act permits health care insurers to issue health benefit policies that provide incentives for insureds to use the services of preferred providers. These policies must provide coverage for emergency care for covered services rendered by a nonpreferred provider when an insured cannot reasonably reach a preferred provider. In such cases, the cost of emergency care must be reimbursed as though the insured had been treated by a preferred provider. Policies also must clearly identify the differences in benefit levels for services of preferred providers and for services of nonpreferred providers. Covered persons typically receive greater benefits for using the services of preferred providers as opposed to using nonpreferred providers. The amount of such differences in benefit levels must be no greater than necessary to provide a reasonable incentive for covered persons to use preferred providers.

LEGISLATIVE CONCERNS

Although managed care has been successful in helping to slow the increase in health care costs, state and federal regulators continue to consider imposing additional requirements on the operation of managed care plans. Studies indicate that most people covered by managed care health benefit plans are satisfied with their plans. Nevertheless, some consumers believe their managed care plans have denied them access to necessary medical care, and they have pushed state and federal regulators to adopt more laws designed to protect the interests of patients covered by managed care health benefit plans.

A number of states have responded to consumer complaints by enacting comprehensive consumer rights laws designed to ensure that health care consumers have appropriate and timely access to medical care. Other states have enacted more limited requirements, such as creating specific appeals procedures that managed care plans must provide to patients who disagree with a plan's decision about whether a health care service is covered by the plan.

Federal legislators also are considering patients' rights legislation that would allow consumers to file lawsuits against HMOs. Figure 6-1 discusses the obstacles involved in drafting such legislation.

FIGURE 6-1 Patients' Rights Legislation.

In August 2001, the U.S. House of Representatives drafted legislation that would allow consumers to sue health plans and employers that directly participate in health care coverage decisions. Legislation regarding patients' rights has caused concern for almost everyone involved in the health care industry and has created dissension among Democrats and Republicans in Congress that is not likely to be resolved in the near future.

Members of organizations such as the Health Insurance Association of America (HIAA), as well as other industry experts, are concerned about patients' rights legislation because they believe that expanding liability to employers will cause many employers to stop offering health care coverage to their employees. Experts also predict that allowing consumers to sue health plans and employers will lead to higher insurance premiums and cause employees to decline health insurance coverage through their employers.[1]

While both Democrats and Republicans agree on the need for a patients' rights bill, debate between the two parties centers around two key issues in proposed legislation. First, under the bill proposed by the House, patients can sue a health plan only after completing an external review process. However, health plans argue that the language of the legislation allows consumers to sue health plans even if an external review panel upholds a health plan's decision regarding whether care is "medically necessary." Second, under currently proposed legislation, punitive damage awards would be capped at $1.5 million for cases heard in federal court. Democrats, in particular, are opposed to such a cap on punitive damages, arguing that the legislation could preempt state law that would allow higher punitive damage awards.[2]

External review panel procedures and the potential for higher premiums have prompted most health plans to oppose the recently drafted legislation. In addition, many experts believe that Democrats and Republicans will continue to disagree over punitive damage awards and other issues. All of these factors will make it difficult for lawmakers to draft legislation that is acceptable to all sides.

KEY TERMS AND CONCEPTS

indemnity plan
managed care plan
enrollee
Health Maintenance Organization Act of 1973
Health Maintenance Organization Model Act
health maintenance organization (HMO)
basic health care services
certificate of authority
quality assurance program
net worth
uncovered expenditures
uncovered expenditures insolvency deposit
letters of credit
evidence of coverage
Managed Care Plan Network Adequacy Model Act
Health Care Professional Credentialing Verification Model Act
Quality Assessment and Improvement Model Act
quality assessment program
Health Carrier Grievance Procedure Model Act
preferred provider arrangement (PPA)
preferred provider
nonpreferred provider
preferred provider organization (PPO)
Preferred Provider Arrangements Model Act

ENDNOTES

1. Steven Brostoff, "Health Plans Contend Patient Protection Bill Will Cause Millions to Lose Coverage," *National Underwriter* Life & Health/Financial Services ed. (23 July 2001): 33.

2. Jill Wechsler, "Showdown or Slowdown on Patients' Rights Bill?" *Managed Healthcare Executive* (September 2001): 11.

CHAPTER 7

Regulation of Reinsurance Agreements

LEARNING OBJECTIVES

After studying this chapter, you should be able to

- Distinguish between assumption reinsurance and indemnity reinsurance

- Recognize the requirements imposed on insurers by state laws based on the NAIC Assumption Reinsurance Model Act

- Explain the effect of a reserve credit and the situations in which an insurer is entitled to reinsurance reserve credits

- Identify the types of requirements the states impose on reinsurance intermediaries

When most people think of insurance products, they typically envision those products that insurance companies sell to individuals and businesses in the consumer marketplace. Insurers, however, also purchase insurance. *Reinsurance* is insurance that an insurer buys to transfer some or all of its own risk on insurance policies; as such it is an important tool that insurers use for risk management and financial management.[1]

In each reinsurance transaction, one insurer—known as the ***ceding company***—transfers or *cedes* a portion of risk to a second insurer—known as a ***reinsurer***. An insurer may be the ceding company in some of its reinsurance transactions, and it may be the reinsurer in other transactions. Relatively few companies operate solely as professional reinsurers.

Because reinsurance transactions are entered into by insurers that are knowledgeable about reinsurance, the parties do not especially need governmental protection. As a result, relatively few state laws and regulations govern reinsurance as compared to the number of laws and regulations that govern life and health insurance products. In addition, the laws and regulations that have been enacted to regulate reinsurance are relatively uniform across the United States.

The states' primary goal in regulating reinsurance is to keep reinsurers solvent. State regulation consists of several components, including:

- **Licensing of reinsurers.** State licensing requirements focus on solvency issues. Some states allow foreign and alien insurers to engage in reinsurance transactions within the state without being licensed by the state if the insurers meet specified requirements.

- **Solvency standards.** When operating within a state, reinsurers become subject to the jurisdiction of the state insurance department, and they must submit financial statements and other relevant information to the insurance department as required.

We begin our discussion of reinsurance regulation by describing two types of reinsurance agreements and how the states regulate those agreements. Then we describe some of the business purposes that reinsurance serves and how the states regulate insurers' use of reinsurance. Finally, we describe how the states regulate reinsurance intermediaries.

Types of Reinsurance Agreements

The parties to a reinsurance agreement have a great deal of flexibility in negotiating the terms of their agreement. As a result, reinsurance contracts can contain a variety of terms, and reinsurance is offered under a variety of arrangements. Every reinsurance agreement, however, can be classified as either an assumption reinsurance agreement or an indemnity reinsurance agreement.

- *Assumption reinsurance* is the type of reinsurance used to effect a complete, permanent, and total transfer of in-force insurance business, and it can be viewed as the reinsurer's purchase of the business that is transferred.

- *Indemnity reinsurance* is the type of reinsurance used to effect, in most cases, a partial transfer of business and to form a basis for sharing the risks of the insurance business. By partial transfer of business we mean that the ceding company transfers only a portion of the risk represented by specified insurance policies.

Assumption Reinsurance

Once business is transferred under an assumption reinsurance agreement, the ceding company's obligations under the transferred insurance policies generally are fully extinguished; the reinsurer becomes totally and directly liable to all policyowners. The reinsurer becomes a party to the insurance policies that were transferred and is said to "stand in the place" of the original insurer. The reinsurer must issue new insurance certificates, known as *assumption certificates*, to all affected policyowners, indicating the reinsurer has assumed all of the risk under the policies. Figure 7-1 illustrates an assumption reinsurance transaction.

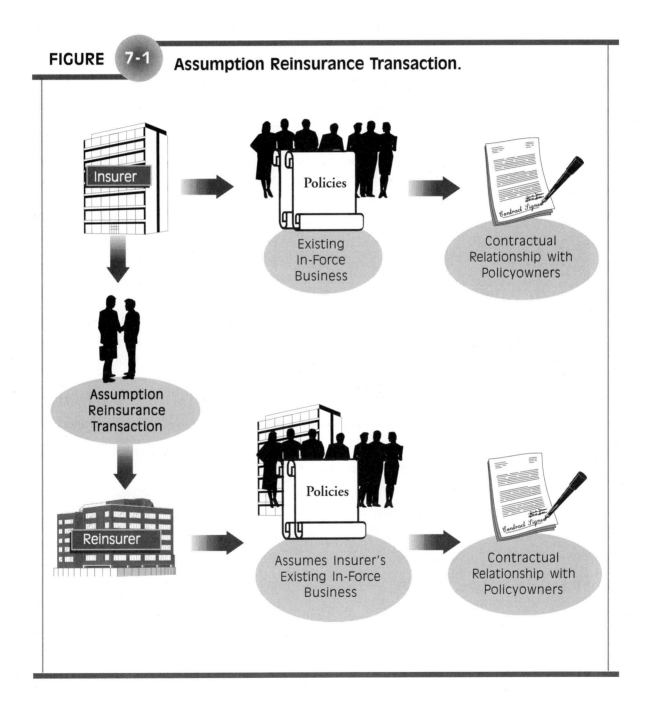

FIGURE 7-1 **Assumption Reinsurance Transaction.**

Assumption reinsurance is the most common method of buying and selling blocks of insurance business. An assumption reinsurance transaction can be used to

- Effect the sale of an entire insurance company
- Permit a licensed insurer to exit a line of business by ceding the business to a reinsurer
- Permit a licensed insurer to enter a new line of business by assuming or reinsuring a line of business from another insurer

Assumption reinsurance also is used by state guaranty associations to transfer the business of a failed insurer to other insurers.

A number of states have enacted laws based on the NAIC *Assumption Reinsurance Model Act*, which applies to any insurer that is authorized to conduct business in a state that has enacted such a law and that either assumes or transfers insurance risks under an assumption reinsurance agreement. In these states, assumption reinsurance agreements are subject to a variety of regulatory requirements designed to protect and define the rights and obligations of policyowners and the parties to the agreements.

Notice to Policyowners and Producers

The Assumption Reinsurance Model Act requires that, before completing an assumption reinsurance transaction, the transferring insurer must notify all affected policyowners and the transferring insurer's producers of record for the affected policies. The insurer must mail to each affected policyowner and producer a *notice of transfer* that includes the following information:

- The date the transfer of the policyowner's policy is proposed to occur
- The name, address, and telephone number of the assuming insurer and of the transferring insurer
- The policyowner's right to consent to or reject the transfer and the time limit the policyowner is given for consenting to or rejecting the transfer
- The procedures the policyowner should follow to consent to or reject the transfer
- Specified financial information for both insurers
- The address and phone number of the state insurance department where the policyowner resides so that the policyowner can contact the department for more information about the assuming insurer's financial condition
- An explanation of the reasons for the transfer

Along with the notice of transfer, the insurer must include a pre-addressed, postage-paid response card that the policyowner may return to indicate written acceptance or rejection of the policy transfer. Figure 7-2 contains a sample notice of transfer form taken from the Assumption Reinsurance Model Act.

FIGURE 7-2 Sample Notice of Transfer to Policyowners Affected by an Assumption Reinsurance Agreement.

NOTICE OF TRANSFER
IMPORTANT: THIS NOTICE AFFECTS YOUR CONTRACT RIGHTS. PLEASE READ IT CAREFULLY.

Transfer of Policy

The [ABC Insurance Company] has agreed to replace us as your insurer under [insert policy/certificate name and number] effective [insert date]. The [ABC Insurance Company's] principal place of business is [insert address] and certain financial information concerning both companies is attached, including (1) ratings for the last five years, if available, or for such less period as is available from two nationally recognized insurance rating services; (2) balance sheets for the previous three years, if available, or for such lesser period as is available and as of the date of the most recent quarterly statement; (3) a copy of the Management's Discussion and Analysis that was filed as a supplement to the previous year's annual statement; and (4) an explanation of the reason for the transfer. You may obtain additional information concerning [ABC Insurance Company] from reference materials in your local library or by contacting your Insurance Commissioner at [insert address and phone number].

The [ABC Insurance Company] is licensed to write this coverage in your state. The Commissioner of Insurance in your state has reviewed the potential effect of the proposed transaction, and has approved the transaction.

Your Rights

You may choose to consent to or reject the transfer of your policy to [ABC Insurance Company]. If you want your policy transferred, you may notify us in writing by signing and returning the enclosed pre-addressed, postage-paid card or by writing to us at:

[Insert name, address and facsimile number of contact person.]

Payment of your premium to the assuming company will also constitute acceptance of the transaction. However, a method will be provided to allow you to pay the premium while reserving the right to reject the transfer.

> **Figure 7-2. Sample Notice of Transfer to Policyowners Affected by an Assumption Reinsurance Agreement,** *continued.*
>
> **Your Rights** *(continued)*
>
> If you reject the transfer, you may keep your policy with us or exercise any option under your policy. If we do not receive a written rejection you will, as a matter of law, have consented to the transfer. However, before this consent is final you will be provided a second notice of the transfer twenty-four months from now. After the second notice is provided, you will have one month to reply. If you have paid your premium to the [ABC Insurance Company], without reserving your right to reject the transfer, you will not receive a second notice.
>
> **Effect of Transfer**
>
> If you accept this transfer, [ABC Insurance Company] will be your insurer. It will have direct responsibility to you for the payment of all claims, benefits and for all other policy obligations. We will no longer have any obligations to you.
>
> If you accept this transfer, you should make all premium payments and claims submissions to [ABC Insurance Company] and direct all questions to [ABC Insurance Company].
>
> If you have any further questions about this agreement, you may contact [XYZ Insurance] or [ABC Insurance].
>
> Sincerely,
>
> _____
>
> [XYZ Insurance Company] [ABC Insurance Company]
> 111 No Street 222 No Street
> Smithville, USA Jonesville, USA
> 555/555-5555] 333/333-3333]
>
> For your convenience, we have enclosed a pre-addressed postage-paid response card. Please take time now to read the enclosed notice and complete and return the response card to us.
>
> [Notice Date]
>
> **Source:** Excerpted from NAIC, *Assumption Reinsurance Model Act,* Appendix A, 1999. Reprinted with permission from the National Association of Insurance Commissioners.

Prior Approval Requirements

States that have enacted laws based on the Assumption Reinsurance Model Act impose a prior approval requirement on all assumption reinsurance transactions, which must be approved by state insurance regulators before insurers issue notices of transfers to policyowners. Under the Model Act, each state has primary responsibility for approving the assumption reinsurance transactions of its domiciliary insurers. Before transferring or assuming risks under an assumption reinsurance agreement, a domiciliary insurer must obtain the state insurance department's approval of both the notice of transfer and the assumption reinsurance transaction. Thus, the transferring insurer must obtain the approval of the insurance department of its domiciliary state, and the assuming insurer must obtain the approval of the insurance department of its domiciliary state.

Other states also have an interest in reviewing assumption reinsurance transactions that affect their residents. When a licensed foreign insurer proposes to transfer or assume risks on insurance policies issued to or owned by residents of a state that has enacted the Model Act, the insurer must file the following information with the insurance department of that state:

- The assumption certificate

- A copy of the notice of transfer

- An affidavit that the transaction is subject to substantially similar regulatory requirements in the state of domicile of both the transferring and assuming insurers

If an insurer's domiciliary state does not have substantially similar requirements for assumption reinsurance transactions, then the foreign insurer proposing to transfer or assume risk must obtain approval of the insurance department of the state whose residents are affected by the transaction.

The Model Act lists the factors the state insurance department must consider when evaluating a request for approval of an assumption reinsurance transaction. These factors include

- The financial condition of both insurers and the effect the transaction will have on the financial condition of each insurer

- The competence, experience, and integrity of the people who control the operation of the assuming insurer

- The assuming party's plans for administering the policies that will be transferred

- Whether the transfer is fair and reasonable to the policyowners of both insurers

- Whether the notice of transfer is fair, adequate, and not misleading

We noted earlier that when an insurer assumes business under an assumption reinsurance agreement, it then "stands in the place" of the transferring insurer. Each state has an interest in ensuring that when an insurer assumes business within the state the insurer is licensed to conduct business there. As a result, insurers licensed in a state that has adopted the Assumption Reinsurance Model Act are prohibited from transferring risks on insurance contracts issued to or owned by residents of that state to an insurer that is *not* licensed in that state. Insurers domiciled in the state may not assume risks on insurance contracts issued to or owned by policyowners residing in another state unless (1) the assuming insurer is licensed in that other state or (2) the insurance department of that other state has approved the transaction.

It is important for insurers to comply with all regulatory requirements concerning assumption reinsurance agreements, because failure to comply can negate the effects of the transaction. For example, if a policyowner does not receive notice of the transfer and is not given the opportunity to reject the transfer, then the transfer of that policy is likely to be ineffective. In other words, a transferring insurer that fails to provide a policyowner with notice of the transfer will remain contractually liable on that insurance policy.

Indemnity Reinsurance

Unlike assumption reinsurance agreements, indemnity reinsurance agreements create an ongoing contractual relationship between the parties to the agreement. Also, the existence of an indemnity reinsurance agreement is not disclosed to affected policyowners as is an assumption reinsurance agreement. While an indemnity reinsurance agreement is in effect and business is reinsured, the ceding company pays periodic reinsurance premiums to the reinsurer. In exchange, the reinsurer agrees to reimburse the ceding company for some stated portion of claims that are incurred under the reinsured business.

Traditional indemnity reinsurance is used to effect a partial transfer of newly written business. Although the transfer is intended to be permanent, traditional indemnity reinsurance agreements typically include a *recapture provision* that specifies a procedure by which the ceding company may end the reinsurance arrangement on a given block of reinsured business. Insight 7-1 provides an example of a typical indemnity reinsurance transaction and introduces some basic terminology of the reinsurance business.

INSIGHT 7-1 — Example of an Indemnity Reinsurance Transaction.

Simon Alcott applied for a $3 million whole life policy from the Neptune Insurance Company. Very few insurance companies are large enough to issue a $3 million life policy without reinsurance, and Neptune was no exception. In the event of Mr. Alcott's early death, the $3 million benefit payment would have seriously weakened Neptune's financial condition.

Long before Mr. Alcott's purchase, however, Neptune had entered into a contractual agreement with Atlas Reinsurance Company under which Atlas Re agreed to reinsure part of the mortality risk of very large policies. Such a contract for reinsurance is known as a **reinsurance treaty**. The treaty between Neptune and Atlas Re contained two typical provisions setting lower and upper limits on the amounts of the risks to be reinsured:

- Under the **scheduled retention limit** provision, Neptune agreed that whenever it issued life insurance in an amount of at least $50,000, Neptune would reinsure with Atlas Re the amount greater than $50,000. According to the terms of the reinsurance treaty, Neptune's scheduled retention limit was $50,000.

- Under the **automatic binding limit** provision, the treaty limited the maximum amount that Neptune could automatically transfer to Atlas Re on any one policy. The treaty set this maximum at four times the amount that Neptune retained on the policy—in other words, four times $50,000, or $200,000. For a policy amount of $250,000 or less, the reinsurance treaty permitted Neptune to *automatically* transfer the entire amount above its retention limit ($200,000). Any such automatic cession is a type of **automatic reinsurance**, because Atlas Re agreed to automatically accept the risk upon Neptune's issuance of a policy.

Because Mr. Alcott's policy amount exceeded the automatic binding limit, the reinsurance treaty required Neptune to submit the application and all pertinent underwriting documentation to the reinsurer. Atlas Re then made its own underwriting decisions about (1) whether to approve the case as a standard risk and (2) whether to assume the major part of the risk. A reinsurance treaty that gives the reinsurer the option of accepting or declining a risk based on its own underwriting evaluation is classified as **facultative reinsurance**.

When the underwriting documentation reached Neptune's underwriter, she classified Mr. Alcott as a standard mortality risk. She also provided the underwriting documentation to Atlas Re and notified Atlas Re that Neptune was prepared to assume $50,000 of the risk, leaving $2,950,000 to be reinsured. Atlas Re's underwriters, however, decided not to retain the entire $2,950,000, and so they passed along, or **retroceded**, a portion of the risk to other reinsurers, which in this situation acted as **retrocessionaires**. Only after Atlas Re notified Neptune that reinsurance coverage for the remaining $2,950,000 had been arranged at a standard rating did Neptune's underwriter give approval for issuing the policy. Atlas Re provided Neptune with administrative data on the policy.

As with many reinsurance situations, the treaty entered by Neptune and Atlas Re specified the **yearly renewable term (YRT) reinsurance method** of premium payment for the shared risk. According to this method, on the anniversary date of each policy reinsured, Neptune

> **Insight 7-1. Example of an Indemnity Reinsurance Transaction,** *continued*.
>
> became liable to pay Atlas Re a one-year term premium based on the amount reinsured. For Mr. Alcott's policy, the amount of the reinsurance premium was calculated as if for one-year term life insurance, even though Mr. Alcott had a whole life policy. Whereas reinsurance premiums are typically remitted monthly, the amount of the premiums is calculated for a period of one year in advance.
>
> Upon Mr. Alcott's death, Atlas Re collected from its retrocessionaires the amounts that they had reinsured for his policy. Atlas in turn paid Neptune the total amount of the death benefit that was reinsured—$2,950,000. Then, Neptune paid the beneficiary the full amount due. The insured and the beneficiary were never aware that a reinsurance situation existed, nor did they need to know. By using reinsurance, the Neptune Insurance Company was able to issue a single policy large enough to cover Mr. Alcott's insurance needs.
>
> **Source:** Excerpted and adapted from Eli A. Grossman, *Life Reinsurance* (Atlanta: LOMA, © 1980), 3–5. Used with permission; all rights reserved.

BUSINESS PURPOSES FOR REINSURANCE

A decision to transfer or assume reinsurance is accompanied by a predictable set of marketing, tax, accounting, and administrative effects that can enable insurers to achieve a number of business purposes. Although a full discussion of such effects is beyond the scope of this text, we will briefly describe two broad business purposes for reinsurance—relief of surplus strain and achievement of marketing objectives—so that we can illustrate some additional regulatory concerns that relate to reinsurance. Some other business purposes for reinsurance are identified in Insight 7-2.

Relief of Surplus Strain

When an insurer issues insurance policies, it incurs acquisition expenses and must establish new reserves for those policies. As a result of issuing new business, an insurer increases the amount of its liabilities, which decreases the amount of its capital and surplus. This effect is commonly called *new business strain* or *surplus strain*. The strain arises partly because of U.S. statutory accounting principles, which require an insurer to allocate all acquisition expenses to the year in which an insurance policy is issued. The insurer, however, records premium revenue for the policy for only one year at a time. The insurer also must establish a reserve for every new policy—

> **INSIGHT 7-2 Business Uses for Reinsurance.**
>
> **Redistributing risks:** The primary purpose of reinsurance is to avoid having any one insurer placed in financial jeopardy at the time of a benefit payment. Reinsurance minimizes the risk to an insurer from large claims or unexpectedly large numbers of claims during a given period of time. For example, reinsurers are heavily involved in the payment of claims for the losses of life and property that occurred as a result of the September 11, 2001, terrorists' attacks in New York City, Washington, D.C., and Pennsylvania. At the time of this writing, it is estimated that the total of all covered claims will be between $30 billion and $40 billion.[2]
>
> **Gaining underwriting experience:** Reinsurance companies tend to develop a high level of underwriting skill and knowledge, and are expert at evaluating risks for complex and unusual cases. Because reinsurers work with many ceding companies, reinsurers collect and maintain large amounts of underwriting information from many sources. Reinsurers then are able to share valuable information with ceding companies.
>
> **Sharing expenses and profits:** Reinsurance enables an insurer and a reinsurer to share the expenses and profits associated with a block of business. In exchange for accepting a stated portion of a ceding company's accepted risk, a reinsurer receives periodic payments known as **reinsurance premiums**. Under some agreements, the reinsurer pays the ceding insurer a **reinsurance allowance**—a share of the ceding insurer's acquisition expenses and maintenance expenses for items such as commissions, underwriting costs, policy issue costs, and premium taxes. Reinsurance allowances are sometimes known as **expense allowances**, and they also are known as a **reinsurance commission** or a **ceding commission**.
>
> **Source:** Adapted from Susan Conant, *Capital Management for Insurance Companies* (Atlanta: LOMA, © 2001), 145–163. Used with permission; all rights reserved.

even though the first-year premium revenue the insurer receives usually is not enough to cover even the acquisition expenses.

Insurers have historically used traditional indemnity reinsurance to transfer a portion of their new insurance business in order to relieve the effects of surplus strain. An insurer can transfer to a reinsurer the responsibility for holding reserves on reinsured business. The accounting treatment for recording such a transfer of reserves on the books of the ceding company is known as a *reserve credit*. Thus, when it issues a policy, the insurer establishes the required reserve on its books and then reduces the amount of that reserve by recording a reserve credit to reflect the reinsurance transaction.

Almost all of the states have enacted legislation based on the NAIC *Credit for Reinsurance Model Law* and have adopted regulations based on the *Credit for Reinsurance Model Regulation*. Together, the provisions of these models restrict the situations in which an insurer is entitled to such reinsurance reserve credits. The requirements are designed to ensure that reinsurance companies remain solvent and are able to pay claims as they come due. In order for an insurer to receive reinsurance reserve credits in most states, the insurer must purchase reinsurance from a reinsurer that meets at least one of the following requirements:

- The reinsurer is licensed by the ceding company's domiciliary state as an insurer or reinsurer. Licensing ensures that the state insurance department can oversee the reinsurer's solvency.

- The reinsurer is an *accredited reinsurer*, which is a reinsurer that is not licensed in the ceding company's domiciliary state but that meets specified financial and reporting requirements of that state and is licensed to transact insurance or reinsurance in at least one other state. Because solvency regulation is relatively uniform across the United States, states often rely on the insurance departments of other states to oversee the solvency of their own domestic insurers.

- The reinsurer is licensed as a reinsurer by another state that has laws and regulations governing reinsurers that are similar to those of the ceding company's domiciliary state. The reinsurer also must maintain a stated minimum surplus and must submit its books and records for examination by the ceding company's domiciliary state.

- The reinsurer maintains a trust fund in a qualified U.S. financial institution and in a prescribed amount for the payment of valid claims. The form of the trust must meet specific requirements, and the reinsurer must meet reporting and examination requirements of the ceding company's domiciliary state.

A reinsurer that does not meet at least one of the foregoing requirements is referred to as an *unauthorized reinsurer*. When an insurer deals with an unauthorized reinsurer, the insurer is entitled to receive reinsurance reserve credits only on risks that are located in jurisdictions where the reinsurance is required by law.

Most states also have adopted regulations based on the NAIC *Life and Health Reinsurance Agreements Model Regulation*, which seeks to prevent licensed insurers from ceding reinsurance for the purpose of relieving surplus strain, typically on a temporary basis, while not transferring the significant risks inherent in the business being reinsured. In other words, the Model Regulation prohibits a licensed insurer from taking a reserve credit under a reinsurance agreement that does not significantly change the ceding company's potential liability for ceded business. The Model Regulation lists a variety of conditions which, if they result from a reinsurance agreement, whether in substance or effect, mean the ceding insurer may not reduce any liability or establish any asset in any financial statement filed with the applicable state insurance department.

Meeting Marketing Objectives

In addition to relieving surplus strain, insurers often use indemnity reinsurance arrangements to meet marketing objectives. An insurer, for example, can accomplish a strategic goal of entering a new market by assuming new risk on policies issued by another company. Another option for entering a new geographic territory is through a joint venture with another insurer. A *joint venture* is a type of partnership arrangement between two otherwise independent businesses that agree to undertake a specific project together for a specified time period. An insurer can enter a territory where it has no product distribution outlet by first manufacturing and then reinsuring insurance sold by another insurer that does have a distribution system operating in the chosen territory. To effect such a marketing partnership, a direct writer and a reinsurer typically use indemnity reinsurance to partially transfer the risks under newly written business on a permanent, but recapturable basis.

For example, consider the case of Saturn Insurance and Armor Assurance. Saturn has an agency distribution system in State X and is licensed to sell life insurance there. Although Armor is also licensed in State X, it has no distribution outlet there and would like to market universal life there. For its part, Saturn does not write universal life coverage, although its agents would like to be able to offer universal life coverage to their clients. To address their common needs, Saturn and Armor enter into a marketing joint venture agreement under which Armor will manufacture, underwrite, service, and administer a type of universal life coverage for issuance in State X. Saturn will issue the coverage in its own name and its sales force will market the coverage in State X. Upon issuing a policy, Saturn will transfer the entire risk to Armor. Note that both insurers are licensed to conduct business in State X and are subject to the jurisdiction of the state insurance department.

Another type of joint venture between a reinsurer and an insurer is sometimes referred to as fronting. *Fronting* is an arrangement in which one insurer, known as the *fronting company*, acts as a primary insurer and issues policies that another company, the *reinsurer*, has underwritten; then, the primary insurer immediately transfers most of the risk to the reinsurer. Fronting arrangements permit a reinsurer to in effect sell business in a state where the reinsurer is not licensed to write insurance and may or may not be authorized as a reinsurer.

Fronting arrangements have been the focus of regulatory attention because regulators have a duty to protect the public against the activities of reinsurers indirectly doing business in states where the state insurance department lacks jurisdiction over them. Not surprisingly, some states prohibit fronting, and most states have adopted regulations designed to discourage the practice. These limitations include (1) limiting the volume of fronting business permitted, (2) limiting the percentage that an originating insurer may cede in a fronting arrangement, and (3) requiring audits and other monitoring designed to detect any illegal applications of fronting. In addition, under some circumstances, insurers are required to establish an extra reserve related to transactions with unauthorized reinsurers.

REGULATION OF REINSURANCE INTERMEDIARIES

A reinsurance transaction is sometimes effected through the efforts of a third party, known as a *reinsurance intermediary*, that acts as a go-between for the insurer and reinsurer. Almost all of the states have adopted laws based on the NAIC *Reinsurance Intermediary Model Act*, which regulates the activities of reinsurance intermediaries, as well as insurers and reinsurers that use the services of reinsurance intermediaries. The Model Act identifies the following types of reinsurance intermediaries:

- A *reinsurance intermediary—broker (RB)* is any person, firm, or corporation that solicits, negotiates, or places reinsurance cessions or retrocessions on behalf of a ceding insurer but that is not authorized to enter into a binding reinsurance contract on behalf of the ceding insurer.

- A *reinsurance intermediary—manager (RM)* is any third party that acts as an agent of a reinsurer and either has authority to bind the reinsurer to a reinsurance contract or manages all or part of the reinsurer's assumed business.

Note the distinction between an RB, who represents the ceding company, and an RM, who represents the reinsurer. Although an RM is authorized to bind a reinsurer to a reinsurance contract, an RB is not authorized to bind a ceding company to such a contract.

In order to act as a reinsurance intermediary in a state that has enacted the Model Act, an intermediary who maintains an office in the state must be a licensed producer in the state. If the intermediary does not maintain an office in the state, then the intermediary must (1) be a licensed producer in the state, (2) be a licensed producer in another state that has a law substantially similar to the Model Act, or (3) be licensed in the state as a nonresident reinsurance intermediary.

The Model Act governs how reinsurance intermediaries conduct their businesses and imposes a number of duties on insurers and reinsurers that deal with intermediaries. Here, we will focus on the requirements insurers and reinsurers must meet.

Transactions between an insurer and an RB may be entered into only by means of a written agreement that contains specified provisions. The insurer, for example, must have the ability to terminate the RB's authority at any time. Other requirements impose duties on the RB. An insurer is prohibited from engaging the services of any person, firm, or corporation to act as an RB on the insurer's behalf unless the intermediary is licensed in accordance with the licensing requirements we described earlier. The insurer also is required to obtain annual financial statements of each RB with which it conducts business.

Transactions between a reinsurer and an RM also are governed by provisions of the Reinsurance Intermediaries Model Act. Such transactions must be entered into by means of a written contract that contains specified provisions governing the conduct of the RM. The following are examples of the required provisions:

- The reinsurer may terminate the contract for cause upon written notice to the RM.

- The RM will provide the reinsurer with monthly accounts of all material transactions.

- The RM cannot assign the contract.

- The RM will provide the reinsurer with annual financial statements, and the reinsurer shall periodically conduct on-site reviews of the RM's operations.

The Model Act requires the reinsurer's board of directors to approve contracts between the reinsurer and an RM. At least 30 days before a reinsurer assumes or cedes business through an RM, a copy of the written contract between the reinsurer and the RM must be filed with the state insurance department for its approval. Reinsurers are prohibited from engaging the services of an RM who is not properly licensed. Within 30 days of termination of a contract with an RM, the reinsurer must notify the state insurance department in writing.

KEY TERMS AND CONCEPTS

reinsurance
ceding company
reinsurer
assumption reinsurance
indemnity reinsurance
assumption certificate
Assumption Reinsurance Model Act
notice of transfer
recapture provision
new business strain
surplus strain
reserve credit
Credit for Reinsurance Model Law
Credit for Reinsurance Model Regulation
accredited reinsurer
unauthorized reinsurer
Life and Health Reinsurance Agreements Model Regulation
joint venture
fronting
fronting company
reinsurance intermediary
Reinsurance Intermediary Model Act
reinsurance intermediary—broker (RB)
reinsurance intermediary—manager (RM)

ENDNOTES

1. Portions of this chapter are adapted from Susan Conant et al., *Managing for Solvency and Profitability in Life and Health Insurance Companies* (Atlanta: LOMA, © 1996), 457–484. Used with permission; all rights reserved.

2. Mark A. Hofmann, "U.S. Insurers Seek Reinsurance Pool for Terrorism Risks," *Business Insurance* (1 October 2001): 3.

CHAPTER 8

State Regulation of Group Life and Health Insurance

LEARNING OBJECTIVES

After studying this chapter, you should be able to

- Identify the types of groups that are eligible for group life and health insurance coverage and, for each type of group, identify the individuals who are eligible for life or health insurance coverage

- Recognize the policy provisions that all group life and group health insurance policies must contain

- Identify the features of the conversion provision that group life insurance policies must include and the conversion provision that must be included in group health insurance policies

- Identify the types of regulatory requirements that the states impose on health insurers that market insurance to small groups

- In a given situation, determine which state(s) has jurisdiction to regulate a group insurance policy

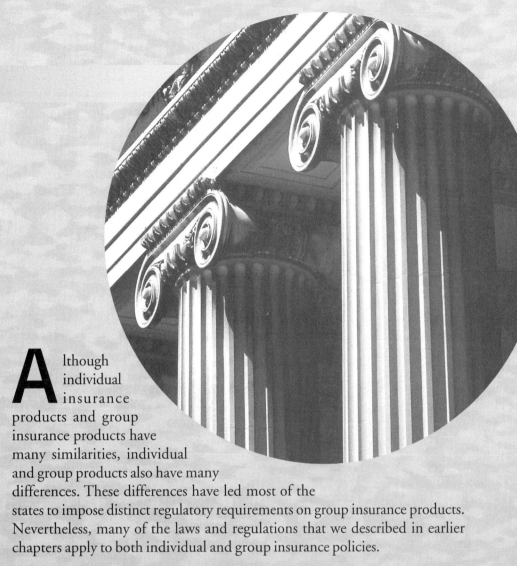

Although individual insurance products and group insurance products have many similarities, individual and group products also have many differences. These differences have led most of the states to impose distinct regulatory requirements on group insurance products. Nevertheless, many of the laws and regulations that we described in earlier chapters apply to both individual and group insurance policies.

In this chapter, we describe the regulatory requirements that the states specifically impose on group life and health insurance products. We begin our discussion by describing the state regulatory requirements that insurers must consider as they develop group life and health insurance products. First, we describe the types of groups that are eligible for group life and health insurance. Next, we describe state regulatory requirements governing the provisions that group policies must include. We also describe the requirements that some states impose on insurers that market health insurance to small groups. We end the chapter by describing the issues that affect which state or states have jurisdiction to regulate a given group insurance policy. Chapter 9 is devoted to the topic of federal regulation of group life and health insurance products. Figure 8-1 is a glossary of group insurance terminology.

FIGURE 8-1 Glossary of Group Insurance Terminology.

Certificate of insurance: A document that describes the coverage provided by a group insurance policy and that is provided by the insurer for the group policyholder to distribute to each group insured.

Contributory plan: A group insurance plan for which insured group members must contribute some or all of the premium for their coverage.

Eligibility period: A specified time, usually 31 days, during which a new group member who is eligible for group insurance coverage may first enroll for that coverage.

Enrollment: The procedures by which an eligible group member signs up for group insurance coverage. In employer-employee groups, for example, new employees generally enroll for group insurance when they are hired.

Group insured: An individual who is covered by a group insurance policy.

Group policyholder: The employer or other party that enters into a group insurance contract with an insurer.

Late entrant: An eligible group member who enrolls for group insurance coverage after the expiration of her eligibility period. Unless they enroll during an open-enrollment period, late entrants generally must provide satisfactory evidence of insurability in order to enroll for group insurance coverage.

Master group insurance contract: An insurance contract that insures a specific group of people.

Noncontributory plan: A group insurance plan for which premiums are paid entirely by the employer or group policyholder.

Open-enrollment period: A specified period during which group members who did not enroll during their eligibility periods may enroll for group insurance coverage without providing evidence of insurability.

Probationary period: A specified period that a new group member must wait before becoming eligible to enroll in a group insurance plan. A probationary period is sometimes referred to as a *waiting period*.

GROUP INSURANCE PRODUCT DEVELOPMENT

Insurers follow the same general stages in the process of developing group life and health insurance products as they follow in developing individual insurance products. The procedures used to develop group policy forms, however, differ from the procedures used to develop individual policy forms. As we described in earlier chapters, insurers develop standardized policy forms for individual life and health insurance policies. By contrast, group life and health insurance agreements quite often are subject to some negotiation between the parties to the agreements. For example, the larger the group proposed for insurance, the more likely that the parties will negotiate the terms of a group insurance policy. Because the benefits provided by large group policies tend to be unique, insurers do not develop standard group insurance packages by standardizing their policy forms. Insurers do, however, tend to develop standardized policy provisions that they include in most of the group life and health insurance policies they issue.

Insurers also develop standard group life and health insurance certificates that will be provided to all group insureds to describe the terms of their group life and health insurance plans. Insurance laws in most states require group life and health insurance policy forms and certificates to be filed with and approved by the state insurance department before they are delivered or issued for delivery in the state.

In this section, we describe the regulatory requirements insurers must meet as they develop group life and health insurance products. Most states have enacted a law based on the NAIC *Group Life Insurance Definition and Group Life Insurance Standard Provisions Model Act (Group Life Insurance Model Act)*. This Model Act defines the types of groups that are eligible for group life insurance and specifies standard provisions that group life insurance policies must include. The NAIC also has adopted a *Group Health Insurance Definition and Group Health Insurance Standard Provisions Model Act (Group Health Insurance Model Act)*. This Model Act specifies the types of groups eligible for group health insurance and the standard provisions that group health policies must contain. Although most states impose specific regulatory requirements on group health policies, only a dozen states have modeled their requirements on the Group Health Insurance Model Act.

Eligible Groups

Both the Group Life Insurance Model Act and the Group Health Insurance Model Act prohibit a policy of group insurance from being delivered in a state that has adopted the applicable Model Act unless the policy insures one of seven specified types of eligible groups. For each type of eligible group, the model acts (1) identify the party or parties that are permitted to be the group policyholder and (2) impose requirements concerning the individuals who are eligible for coverage under the policy. For each type of eligible group, the model acts give the insurer the right to exclude or limit coverage on any group member who does not present evidence of individual insurability satisfactory to the insurer. As we describe in Chapter 9, the federal Health Insurance Portability and Accountability Act (HIPAA) imposes limitations on an insurer's right to require such evidence of insurability. Insurers often do not require evidence of individual insurability because group insurance underwriting focuses on evaluating the insurability of a group as a whole rather than evaluating the insurability of individual group members. Insight 8-1 describes some of the fundamental principles of group insurance underwriting. In the past, many of these fundamental principles of group underwriting were required by state insurance laws. Over time, most states have relaxed such requirements so that more people can have access to group insurance. Regardless of whether insurers are legally required to consider these principles, good business practices dictate that companies include them in the underwriting guidelines they use to evaluate a group that applies for group life or health insurance.

According to the model acts, a policy may be issued to cover any of the following types of groups: (1) a single employer group, (2) a debtor-creditor group, (3) a labor union group, (4) a multiple employer group, (5) an association group, (6) a credit union group, or (7) a discretionary group. Throughout this discussion, we describe the provisions of the Group Life Model Act and the Group Health Model Act. Keep in mind that specific requirements vary a great deal from state to state.

Single Employer Group

A policy insuring a single employer group insures the employees of one employer for the benefit of persons other than the employer. According to the model acts, a single employer group policy may be issued to an employer or to the trustees of a trust fund established by an employer. A *trust* is a fiduciary relationship in which a person, known as a ***trustee***, holds legal title to property—known as the ***trust property*** or *trust fund*—for the benefit of another person, the ***trust beneficiary***. When insurance is issued to the trustees of such a fund, the trustees own the policy for the benefit of the group insureds.

Each group policy must identify the individuals who are eligible for coverage. According to the model acts, the individuals eligible for coverage under a single employer group policy are all of the employees of the employer or all employees of any designated class or classes of employees. Under most group

INSIGHT 8-1: Some Fundamentals of Group Insurance Underwriting.

The goal of group insurance underwriting is to produce a group of insureds who present similar underwriting risks and whose mortality or morbidity experience is reasonably predictable. The underwriter's focus is on the risk characteristics of the group proposed for insurance rather than on characteristics of individual group members. Here, we describe some of the most important risk factors considered in group underwriting. Keep in mind that the scope of the group selection process is much broader than simply deciding whether to approve a group and, if so, whether to charge an extra premium. When group underwriters decline an application, they often are asked to suggest ways in which features of the group plan can be modified so that the application can be approved.

- **Purpose for the group's existence.** To guard against antiselection, a group proposed for insurance should have been formed for purposes other than to obtain group insurance for its members. With the acceptance of discretionary groups by some states, this requirement may sometimes be waived by state insurance departments.

- **Source of premium payment.** For contributory employer-employee plans, insurers generally require the employer to pay at least a portion of the premium. This requirement helps reduce the employees' premium costs and, thus, tends to increase employee participation in the plan.

- **Participation requirements.** Because group members who elect to participate in a contributory group insurance plan tend to be poorer risks than those who do not participate, insurers generally impose minimum participation requirements on contributory plans. For most groups, insurers require that at least 75 percent of eligible group members participate. If the group is very small, the insurer may impose a higher participation requirement; if the group is very large, the participation requirement may be reduced.

- **Stability of group membership.** The cost of group insurance largely depends on the group's age distribution. In order to keep the costs of group insurance down, a group should expect some turnover in group membership. Otherwise, as the group members all grow older, the cost of insurance would constantly spiral upwards. In addition, a group that experiences an unusually high rate of turnover in membership will result in increased administrative costs. Thus, group underwriters seek to approve groups that have a steady, and not unreasonably high, rate of turnover in group membership.

- **Automatic determination of benefits.** A group insurance plan must be designed so that the benefits provided to each individual insured are determined automatically. Allowing the group insured or the group policyholder to determine the benefit levels provided any individual would subject the insurer to a great deal of antiselection. Group life insurance plans typically contain a benefit formula that establishes the amount of life insurance provided to each insured based on some objective factor, such as position in the company, seniority, or salary level.

- **Policy administration.** The ability of insurers to provide cost-effective group insurance rests to a large extent on the administrative economies presented by group policy administration compared to individual policy administration. Group underwriters evaluate the willingness and ability of the group policyholder to perform certain administrative functions for the group insurance plan.

Other characteristics of each group that are considered in underwriting include the size of the group, the geographic location of group members, and the nature of the industry in which they work. If a group proposed for insurance has been previously insured, the group underwriter will evaluate the group's claim experience and the reasons the group policyholder is considering changing insurance carriers.

life and health insurance policies, for example, all of the employer's full-time employees are eligible for group insurance coverage once they have completed any required probationary period. The model acts permit a group policy to define the term *employees* to include

- Employees of subsidiary corporations
- Employees of affiliated corporations, proprietorships, and partnerships that are under common control
- Retired employees, former employees, and directors of a corporate employer

According to the model acts, the premiums payable for an employer-employee group life or health insurance policy may be paid either by the employer, the insured employees, or both the employer and the employees. Insurers' group underwriting guidelines, however, generally require that the employer pay at least a portion of the policy premiums.

The model acts require noncontributory group insurance plans to cover all eligible employees except those who reject the coverage in writing. Contributory group insurance plans are generally subject to minimum participation requirements, but such requirements are imposed by insurers as part of their underwriting guidelines rather than by regulatory requirements. Thus, for example, insurers usually require that at least 75 percent of eligible employees participate in a contributory group insurance plan.

The model acts do not impose minimum requirements on the size of eligible employer-employee groups. Nevertheless, most states require that an employer-employee group life insurance policy insure at least a specified minimum number of group members. Depending on the state, employer-employee group life policies must insure from at least 2 to at least 10 group members. Note that employer-employee group health policies usually are not subject to such minimum size requirements.

Debtor-Creditor Group

A debtor-creditor group policy insures individuals who have borrowed money from a specific lender or lenders. According to the model acts, such a policy may be issued to the creditor or to a parent holding company of the creditor. In cases in which a policy insures debtors of more than one creditor, the policy may be issued to one or more trustees or to an agent designated by the creditors. The model acts state that the individuals eligible for group insurance are all of the debtors of the creditor or all of any class or classes of debtors. The policy may define the term *debtors* to include

- Individuals who borrow money or who purchase or lease goods, services, or property for which payment is arranged through a credit transaction
- The debtors of one or more subsidiary corporations
- The debtors of one or more affiliated corporations, proprietorships, or partnerships that are under common control

The premium payable for a debtor-creditor group life or health insurance policy may be paid entirely by the creditor, entirely from charges collected from insured debtors, or from both the creditor and the insured debtors. If the creditor pays the entire premium, however, then the policy must insure all of the creditor's eligible debtors.

For both group life and group health insurance, the amount of insurance payable with respect to an indebtedness may not exceed the greater of the scheduled amount or the actual amount of unpaid indebtedness. In open-ended credit arrangements that extend the debtor an open-ended credit limit of more than $10,000, the amount of insurance available on the life of the debtor may not exceed the amount of the credit limit.

If an insured debtor dies or becomes disabled, the policy benefit is payable to the creditor, and the amount of the benefit paid to the creditor is used to reduce or extinguish the unpaid indebtedness of the debtor. If any funds remain after paying the unpaid debt, those funds are payable to the insured, the insured's designated beneficiary, or the estate of the insured. Note that the only type of group policy under which policy benefits are payable to the group policyholder is a debtor-creditor group policy. Policies issued to all other types of groups typically prohibit benefits from being payable to the policyholder.

Regulatory requirements imposed on debtor-creditor group policies differ quite a bit from the requirements imposed on other group life and health insurance policies. The remainder of this chapter will address regulatory requirements imposed on group life and health insurance policies *other than* credit insurance policies. We describe state regulation of credit life and health insurance in detail in Chapter 10.

Labor Union Group

State insurance laws permit a group policy to be issued to a labor union or similar organization to insure members of the union for the benefit of persons other than the union or any of its officials, agents, or representatives. The individuals eligible for group insurance under a labor union group policy are all of the members of the union or all of any class or classes of union members. The policy premium may be paid from funds of the union, of the insured union members, or of both. If the entire premium is paid by the union, then all eligible union members, except those who reject coverage in writing, must be insured.

Although state insurance laws permit a group insurance policy to be issued to a labor union, the federal Labor Management Relations Act of 1947, known as the *Taft-Hartley Act*, prohibits an employer from paying anything of value to a labor union.[1] As a result, if a labor union is the policyholder of a group policy insuring union members, then the employers of those members are prohibited from contributing premiums on behalf of their employees because that would require making payments to the labor union. The Taft-Hartley Act, however, permits employers to make premium contributions on behalf of their employees if the following requirements are met:

- Payments must be placed in trust to purchase insurance.

- The employers and the union must be equally represented in administering the funds placed in trust. In other words, the number of trustees who represent the employers must equal the number of trustees who represent the union members.

In order to comply with federal requirements, when employers contribute to premium payments, the group policy insuring the members of a labor union must be issued to a trust established for the purpose of purchasing insurance for union members. Because of the effect of the Taft-Hartley Act, these groups are often referred to as *Taft-Hartley trusts*. Such groups also are sometimes referred to as *negotiated trusteeships* because they are created by the negotiation of an agreement between a labor union and the employers of union members.

Multiple Employer Group

A multiple employer group may be insured under a life or health insurance policy issued to a trust or to the trustees of a fund established or adopted by (1) two or more employers, (2) two or more labor unions, or (3) one or more employers *and* one or more labor unions. The policy must insure the employees of the employers or the members of the unions for the benefit of persons other than the employers or the unions. The policy may define the term *employees* to include all the individuals we described earlier as employees of a single employer. In addition, the term *employees* may include the trustees and/or their employees if their duties are principally connected with the trusteeship. Other requirements imposed on such group life and health insurance policies are the same as those imposed on employer-employee group policies.

Association Group

An association group policy may be issued to an association or to a trust or the trustees of a fund established, created, or maintained for the benefit of members of one or more associations. For regulatory purposes, an *association* is defined as an association of employers or individuals formed for a purpose other than to obtain insurance. Figure 8-2 describes some of the types of association groups that are eligible for group life and health insurance coverage.

FIGURE 8-2 Types of Association Groups.

Trade Association	Association of Individuals
An association of firms that operate in a specific industry.	An association of individuals who share a common bond other than the common purpose of obtaining insurance. The following types of associations of individuals typically are eligible for group life and health insurance: ▸ **Professional association.** An association of individuals who share a common occupation, such as an association of medical doctors, attorneys, or engineers. ▸ **Public employee association.** An association of individuals employed by a state, county, or city government or by a state or local school board. ▸ **Common interest association.** An association of individuals who share a common status or a common interest. Examples include associations of retired persons, gun owners, participants in a specific sport, or alumni of a specific college.

The model acts provide that, in order to qualify for such a policy, an association must meet the following requirements:

- The association initially must have at least 100 members.

- The association must have been formed for a purpose other than to obtain group insurance coverage.

- The association must have been in existence for at least two years to be eligible for group *life* insurance. By contrast, the association must have been in existence only one year to be eligible for group *health* insurance.

- The association must have a constitution and bylaws that (1) provide for regular meetings and (2) give the members voting privileges and representation on the governing board and committees.

Other requirements that the model acts impose on association group insurance policies are the same as those the model acts impose on employer-employee group policies.

Credit Union Group

A credit union group policy insures members of a credit union for the benefit of persons other than the credit union. Such a policy may be issued to either (1) a credit union or (2) a trustee, trustees, or agent designated by two or more credit unions. The premium for the policy must be paid by the policyholder from the credit union's funds and must insure all eligible members.

Discretionary Group

The Group Life Insurance Model Act and the Group Health Insurance Model Act provide that a life or health policy may be issued to any other type of group, known as a *discretionary group*, only if the applicable state insurance department specifically approves the policy for issuance to such a group. In states that have enacted laws based on the model acts, the laws provide that the insurance department will approve a discretionary group policy if the following three conditions are met:

- Issuing the policy is not against the best interest of the public.

- Issuing the policy would result in economies of acquisition or administration.

- The policy benefits are reasonable in relation to the premiums charged.

Coverage may be offered in a state that has enacted the Group Life Insurance Model Act or the Group Health Insurance Model Act under a discretionary group policy issued in another state only if the insurance department of one of the states determines that the policy meets the foregoing requirements. Premiums payable for a discretionary group policy may be payable by the policyholder, the insured individuals, or both.

Most states have adopted laws based on the model acts' requirements concerning the issuance of insurance to discretionary groups, and, thus, most states allow insurers to issue discretionary group policies. Regulatory interpretations of the requirements for the issuance of discretionary group policies, however, vary a great deal from state to state. Some states are quite lenient in approving groups as discretionary groups eligible for group insurance. Other states are quite strict and tend to impose more stringent requirements. Types of discretionary groups that are eligible for group insurance range from customers of a bank to customers of a mail order company. Small employers with only one or two employees sometimes are able to purchase group coverage under a discretionary group insurance policy.

Dependent Coverage

A group life insurance policy subject to the Group Life Insurance Model Act may insure the covered individuals against loss due to the death of their spouses and dependent children. Likewise, the Group Health Insurance Model Act allows group health policies to extend group health coverage to the family members and dependents of covered individuals. The premium for dependent coverage may be payable by the policyholder, the covered individuals, or both. If the policyholder pays the entire premium, then the policy must insure all eligible individuals against covered losses. The model acts, however, permit the insurer to exclude or limit coverage on any spouse or dependent child—other than a newborn child—who does not present evidence of individual insurability satisfactory to the insurer. The amount of group life insurance provided for any spouse or child may not exceed 50 percent of the amount of insurance provided on the life of the covered group member.

Standard Policy Provisions

Most state insurance laws require that specified provisions be included in group life and health insurance policies that are delivered or issued for delivery within the state. These required policy provisions may be modified if the state insurance department determines that the terms of any such modified provisions are either (1) more favorable to the insured individuals or (2) at least as favorable to the insured individuals and more favorable to the policyholder. The following provisions must be included in all group life and health insurance policies:

- A *grace period provision* giving the policyholder a grace period of 31 days for the payment of renewal premiums. Coverage remains in force during the grace period, unless the insurer is notified by the policyholder that it has elected to discontinue coverage in accordance with the terms of the policy. The policy may provide that the policyholder will be liable to pay any premium for the time the policy was in force during the grace period.

- An *incontestability provision* stating that, after the policy has been in force for two years, the insurer may not contest the validity of the group insurance contract except for nonpayment of premium. This provision also limits the insurer's ability to contest the validity of an insured's coverage under a group policy after that coverage has been in force for two years during the insured's lifetime. Such a contest may not be based on statements made by an insured person relating to his insurability unless those statements are contained in a written statement signed by the insured. When an insured is required to provide evidence of insurability, that evidence is contained in a questionnaire included in or attached to the insured's enrollment form. Group members usually are required to complete an *enrollment form* as a prerequisite to group insurance coverage. The enrollment form serves a number of purposes, including providing the insurer with identifying information about the group member and allowing the group member to make beneficiary designations. In employer-employee contributory plans, enrollment forms contain the group members' written authorizations for the employer to make payroll deductions to pay the employees' share of required premiums.

- An *entire contract provision* stating that a copy of the application shall be attached to the policy when issued, that all statements made by the policyholder or the insureds shall be deemed representations and not warranties, and that no statement made by an insured shall be used in any contest unless a copy of the document containing the statement has been furnished to the insured or, if the insured is deceased or incapacitated, to the insured's beneficiary or personal representative.

- An ***evidence of insurability provision*** specifying the conditions, if any, under which the insurer reserves the right to require a person eligible for insurance to furnish evidence of individual insurability satisfactory to the insurer as a condition to part or all of her coverage.

- A *misstatement of age provision* that specifies an equitable adjustment of premiums, of benefits, or of both premiums and benefits if the age of an insured is misstated. The provision must clearly state the method to be used to make such an adjustment.

- A *certificate of coverage provision* stating that the insurer will issue a certificate to the policyholder for delivery to each insured. The certificate must describe the insured's coverage, the person to whom the benefits are payable, and any dependent coverage provided.

Group insurance policies contain a variety of provisions that are not found in individual life and health policies. For example, as individuals enter and leave a covered group, the group insurance policy defines when they become eligible for group coverage and when that coverage begins and ends.

Other provisions that must be included in group insurance policies vary depending on whether they are life or health insurance policies. Figure 8-3 identifies the provisions that must be included in both group life and group health insurance policies.

Group Life Insurance Policy Provisions

Group life insurance policies must contain a provision stating that the benefit payable following an insured's death will be paid to the beneficiary named by the insured. In addition, group life policies must include a *conversion provision* that gives the insured the right to obtain an individual life insurance policy if her group coverage terminates because of specified reasons. An eligible insured is entitled to obtain individual life insurance coverage without providing evidence of insurability by applying for the individual policy and paying the initial premium within 31 days after termination of group coverage.

The conversion provision gives an insured the right to obtain individual life insurance in two situations.

- If the group coverage terminates because the insured's employment terminates or the insured is no longer a member of a class eligible for coverage, then the insured must be given the right to purchase any type of individual policy the insurer is then issuing at the insurer's customary premium rate for that policy based on the insured's age. The exception to this rule is that the group life policy may exclude the option of purchasing term insurance. The amount of insurance provided by the

FIGURE 8-3 Provisions Required in Group Life and Group Health Insurance Policies.

Provisions found in *both* group life and group health insurance policies

- ☑ Grace period provision
- ☑ Incontestability provision
- ☑ Entire contract provision
- ☑ Evidence of insurability provision
- ☑ Misstatement of age provision
- ☑ Certificate of coverage provision
- ☑ Conversion provision

Provisions found in group health insurance policies *only*

- ☑ Claimants for disability benefits must provide the insurer with written proof of loss within 90 days after the beginning of the period for which the insurer is liable
- ☑ All benefits payable under the policy, other than disability, will be payable not more than 60 days after the insurer receives proof of loss
- ☑ Benefits payable upon the death of an insured are payable to the beneficiary designated by the insured
- ☑ Insurers have the right and opportunity to have physical examinations conducted of a claimant at the insurers' expense while a claim is pending
- ☑ No legal action may be brought to recover benefits under the policy until at least 60 days after the claimant has provided the insurer with proof of loss

Provision found in group life insurance policies *only*

- ☑ Nonforfeiture provision, if the policy is issued on a plan of insurance other than term insurance individual policy is limited to the amount of group life insurance that terminated, less any amount of group life insurance for which the insured becomes eligible within 31 days after termination. For example, assume that Ephraim Wise terminated his employment with the ABC Corporation, where he was insured for $75,000 under ABC's group life policy. Ten days later, Mr. Wise began employment with the XYZ Company, where he was eligible for $50,000 of life insurance coverage. The maximum amount of group coverage Mr. Wise would have been able to convert under the ABC group life insurance policy was $25,000 ($75,000 minus $50,000). If an individual insured under a group life policy dies, then the insured's surviving dependents who were covered under the group plan at the insured's death must have the right to obtain individual coverage on the terms we just described. In addition, if a dependent insured by a group life policy no longer qualifies for group coverage, then the dependent must have the right to obtain individual coverage on the terms just described.

- If the insured's group coverage terminates because the group policy terminates or is amended so as to terminate the coverage of any class of insureds, then each individual whose coverage terminates—including insured dependents of covered persons—and who has been insured under the group policy for at least five years is entitled to obtain an individual life insurance policy. With one exception, this conversion privilege is subject to the same terms described above. The exception is that the amount of insurance provided by the individual policy is limited to the smaller of (1) $10,000 or (2) the amount of group life insurance that terminated less the amount of group life insurance for which the insured becomes eligible within 31 days after termination.

Group life insurance policies must provide that if an insured or covered dependent dies during the 31-day conversion period and has not been issued an individual policy, then the insurer is liable to pay a death benefit equal to the amount of individual insurance that the insured was entitled to purchase under the conversion provision. This provision has the effect of extending group life insurance coverage throughout the 31-day conversion period.

The Group Life Insurance Model Act requires that individuals who become eligible to convert their group coverage under a conversion provision must be notified of their conversion privilege. According to the Model Act, an individual who is not notified of the privilege within 15 days of the end of the conversion period will have additional time in which to exercise the conversion privilege. The additional period ends 15 days after the individual is given the notice except that the period will not extend beyond 60 days after the expiration of the original 31-day conversion period. Although the individual in such a case has additional time in which to apply for individual life insurance, this requirement does not affect the time during which a death benefit is payable following the termination of group coverage.

Many group life policies condition eligibility for coverage upon an individual's active employment. When active employment is a condition of insurance, the group life policy must give insureds the right to continue their coverage during a period of total disability if they pay the policyholder any premium they would have been required to pay had they not become disabled. Coverage may be continued for a period of six months unless (1) the insurer approves the continuation of coverage under a disability provision in the group life policy or (2) the group life insurance policy terminates.

If a group life insurance policy is issued on a plan of insurance other than term insurance, then the policy must contain a *nonforfeiture provision* that the state insurance department determines is equitable to the insureds and the policyholder.

Group Health Insurance Policy Provisions

In addition to the provisions described earlier in the chapter, the Group Health Insurance Model Act requires group health insurance policies to include the following provisions:

- A provision that a claimant for disability benefits must provide the insurer with written proof of loss within 90 days after the beginning of the period for which the insurer is liable. Subsequent written proofs of continuing disability must be furnished to the insurer as often as the insurer may reasonably require. For all other covered losses, a claimant must provide the insurer with written proof of loss within 90 days after the loss.

- A provision that all benefits payable under the policy, other than disability, will be payable not more than 60 days after the insurer receives proof of loss. Disability income benefits must be paid at least as frequently as every month.

- A provision that benefits payable upon the death of an insured are payable to the beneficiary designated by the insured. If the policy contains conditions relating to family status, however, the beneficiary of any death benefits payable may be the family member specified by the policy terms. Some policies, for example, contain a beneficiary provision stating that, if the insured does not name a beneficiary, then benefits are payable in a stated order of preference. Typically, benefits are payable to the insured's spouse, if living; if not, then to the insured's children, if living; if not, then to the insured's parents, if living; if none are living, then to the insured's estate. All other benefits payable under the group health policy are payable to the person insured.

- A provision that the insurer has the right and opportunity to have a physical examination of a claimant conducted at the insurer's expense while a claim is pending.

- A provision that no legal action may be brought to recover benefits under the policy until at least 60 days after the claimant has provided the insurer with proof of loss. Claimants lose the right to bring such an action after a period of three years following the end of the period within which proof of loss was required. The specific time limit imposed varies somewhat from state to state.

In addition to the provisions required by the Group Health Insurance Model Act, most states require group health insurance policies to contain other provisions, including a *conversion provision*. Most states base their requirements on the NAIC ***Group Health Insurance Mandatory Conversion Privilege Model Act***. The Model Act applies to group policies that provide hospital, surgical, or major medical expense insurance on an expense-incurred basis but not to medical expense policies that provide accident-only coverage or that provide benefits only for specific diseases. A policy subject to this Model Act may not be delivered or issued for delivery in a state that has enacted the Model Act unless the policy contains the specified conversion privilege. This privilege gives an insured group member the right to obtain an individual health policy from the insurer without providing evidence of insurability if the following conditions are met:

- The group member must have been insured under the group health policy for at least three months.

- The group policy is discontinued and is not replaced with similar coverage within 31 days or the group member's coverage under the group policy is terminated for reasons other than the individual's failure to pay a required premium.

- The group member applies in writing for a conversion policy and pays the first premium for the conversion policy within 31 days after termination of group coverage.

Subject to some exceptions that we describe later in the section, when an insured group member meets these conditions, the insurer must issue an individual policy that provides coverage effective on the date following the termination of the insured's group health insurance coverage. The Model Act refers to such an individual policy as a *converted policy*. The Mandatory Conversion Privilege Model Act limits the premium rates an insurer may charge for converted policies. These requirements seek to ensure that converted policies will be affordable to policyowners while recognizing that individuals who elect such coverage often are substandard risks.

The Model Act identifies the following situations in which an insurer is *not* required to issue a converted policy:

- The insured is covered by Medicare.

- The insured is covered by or eligible for—regardless of whether she is covered by—another medical expense policy or program, *and* the benefits provided by that policy or program together with the benefits provided by the converted policy would result in the insured's being overinsured according to the insurer's underwriting standards. The insurer's standards must bear a reasonable relationship to the actual health care costs in the area where the insured lives. In addition, the insurer must file its underwriting standards with the state insurance department before using them to deny coverage to insureds.

The Mandatory Conversion Privilege Model Act specifies the scope of benefits that a converted policy must provide. These requirements are designed to provide insureds with benefits that are substantially similar to the benefits they had under their group health insurance policies.

Most states also have adopted regulations based on the NAIC *Group Coordination of Benefits Model Regulation*, which permits group health insurance plans to include a coordination of benefits (COB) provision and requires COB provisions to comply with requirements in the Model Regulation. A ***coordination of benefits (COB) provision*** is a group medical expense insurance policy provision that is designed to prevent a group member who is insured under more than one group insurance policy from receiving benefit amounts greater than his actual incurred medical expenses. The COB provision prevents duplicate benefit payments by defining the group health plan that is the primary provider of benefits and the plan that is the secondary provider for insured group members who have duplicate group medical expense coverage.

As a general rule, an insured's primary plan must pay benefits as if the secondary plan did not exist. Then, the secondary plan reduces the amount of benefits it pays so that total benefits provided by both plans are not more than the total amount of covered expenses. By contrast, some group medical expense policies contain another type of COB provision, referred to as a *nonduplication of benefits provision*, which more strictly limits the benefits payable when an insured is covered by more than one group insurance policy. According to a nonduplication of benefits provision, the plan designated as the secondary provider of benefits is required to provide a benefit amount equal to the difference, if any, between the amount paid by the primary plan and the amount that would have been payable by the secondary plan had it been the primary plan.

By standardizing COB provisions, state insurance regulations based on the COB Model Regulation establish a uniform order of benefit determination under which each group insurance policy pays claims. Figure 8-4 provides examples to illustrate the operation of the COB provision.

Minimum Policy Standards

In Chapter 3, we described the Accident and Sickness Insurance Minimum Standards Model Act and the Model Regulation to Implement the Accident and Sickness Insurance Minimum Standards Model Act, which a number of states have adopted. The regulatory requirements contained in the Model Act and Model Regulation apply not only to individual health insurance policies but also to group supplemental health insurance policies that provide any of the following coverages:

- Hospital confinement indemnity coverage
- Accident only coverage
- Specified disease coverage
- Specified accident coverage
- Limited benefit health coverage

In states that have enacted such requirements, group policies that provide any of the foregoing coverages must comply with the minimum benefit standards specified by applicable state regulations.

FIGURE 8-4 Examples of the Operation of the COB Provision in Group Medical Expense Policies.

EXAMPLE 1

Sean Poe is covered by two group medical expense plans. Both plans include a standard coordination of benefits (COB) provision, and each plan specifies a $100 deductible and a 20 percent coinsurance requirement. Mr. Poe incurred $5,100 in allowable medical expenses during the calendar year. **Allowable medical expenses** are those reasonable and customary expenses that the group insured incurred and that are covered under at least one of the insured's group insurance plans.

The plan designated as Mr. Poe's primary plan is responsible for paying benefits equal to $4,000. The calculations used to determine this benefit amount are as follows:

$$\$5,100 - \$100 \text{ (deductible)} = \$5,000$$
$$\$5,000 \times 0.80 \text{ (coinsurance factor)} = \$4,000$$

Because both plans contain the same deductible and coinsurance features, Mr. Poe's secondary plan also would provide him with a $4,000 benefit payment if it were deemed the primary plan. Under the COB provision, however, the secondary plan would provide only a $1,100 benefit payment; that is, the secondary plan will pay the difference between the amount of total allowable expenses ($5,100) and the amount the primary plan paid in benefits ($4,000). Mr. Poe incurs no out-of-pocket costs.

EXAMPLE 2

Using the same example, assume that the plan designated as Mr. Poe's secondary plan contains a nonduplication of benefits provision. In this case, the plan designated as the primary plan would pay a $4,000 policy benefit calculated as above. The secondary plan, however, would provide no benefit amount, because the primary plan has already paid the full $4,000 benefit amount to which Mr. Poe was entitled under the secondary plan. In this example, Mr. Poe is required to pay a portion of the cost of his covered medical expenses.

Mandated Benefits

As described in Chapter 3, most states require that specified benefits be provided by individual health insurance policies. These regulatory requirements mandating specified benefits that must be provided generally are imposed on both individual and group health insurance policies. In many states, mandated benefits are considered to be provided by health policies covering state residents regardless of the terms of those policies. Thus, a group health insurance policy that did not provide a benefit mandated by state laws would be deemed by state law to provide the benefit to covered state residents.

REGULATION OF INSURANCE ISSUED TO SMALL GROUPS

State and federal regulators continue to seek ways to promote the availability and affordability of medical expense coverages. Although most people obtain medical expense coverages through their employment, many people remain uninsured. Figure 8-5 gives information on the numbers of people without health insurance in the United States. Small businesses, in particular, often are unable to afford to provide medical expense insurance benefits to their employees.

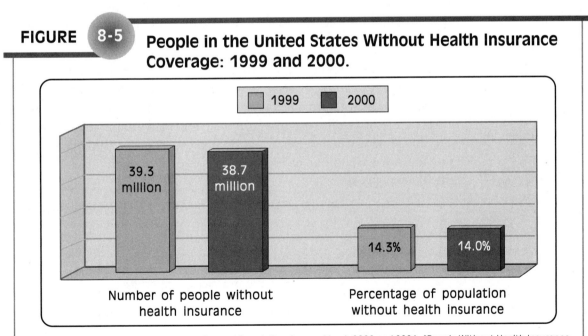

FIGURE 8-5 People in the United States Without Health Insurance Coverage: 1999 and 2000.

Source: Data from U.S. Census Bureau, Current Population Survey, March 2000 and 2001. "People Without Health Insurance Coverage: 1999 and 2000," http://www.census.gov/hhes/hlthins/hlthin00/fig01.jpg (27 November 2001).

Most states have enacted statutes to promote the availability of medical expense coverages for individuals employed by small businesses, and laws in most states are based on NAIC model laws. Nevertheless, the regulatory requirements vary a great deal from state to state, and even the definition of *small employer* varies quite a bit. The NAIC model laws we describe in this section define a small employer as a group of 25 or fewer employees who are eligible for group coverage; many states include groups with as many as 50 or even 100 employees within the definition of a small employer.

After studying the small group market, the NAIC found that some states wanted to regulate that market to improve the availability and affordability of medical expense coverages. The NAIC has adopted the following model laws designed to give the states several options for how they regulate small group medical expense plans:

- *Premium Rates and Renewability of Coverage for Health Insurance Sold to Small Groups* is the earliest model law adopted by the NAIC. It imposes restrictions relating to premium rates and renewability of small group medical expense coverages and imposes disclosure requirements on insurers that market health insurance to small groups.

- The *Small Employer Health Insurance Availability Model Act* includes many provisions similar to those in the earlier model law and imposes a number of additional requirements on carriers that provide small group health benefit coverages. To recognize the differing small group markets from state to state, the NAIC adopted two separate versions of this model.

A number of states have laws based on the NAIC model entitled *Premium Rates and Renewability of Coverage for Health Insurance Sold to Small Groups*, which is designed to provide a range of solutions to problems related to the affordability of medical expense insurance for small groups and individuals. The model law, which applies to any medical expense insurance plan that provides coverage to one or more employees of a small employer, identifies the following goals:

- To promote the availability of health insurance coverage to small employers

- To prevent abusive premium-rating practices

- To require disclosure of rating practices to purchasers

- To establish rules for continuity of coverage for employers and covered individuals

- To improve the efficiency and fairness of the small group health insurance marketplace

The model law prohibits the premium rate for any class of an insurer's business from exceeding by more than 20 percent the premium rate for any other class of the insurer's business. The model law also limits the amount by which the premium rate charged a small employer group may increase at the start of a new premium-rating period.

Laws patterned on the model law require that plans subject to the law be renewable at the option of the small employer—not at the option of the insurer. However, insurers are not required to renew such a policy in the following circumstances:

- Nonpayment of premiums by the employer

- Fraud or misrepresentation by the employer or a group insured

- The employer's failure to comply with contractual provisions

- The number of individuals insured under the plan is less than the number specified by the plan's participation requirements

- A change in the employer's business so that it is no longer actively engaged in the business in which it was engaged on the effective date of the plan

An insurer has the right to stop renewing plans if it does so for all plans in a class of business. At least 90 days before such a termination of coverage, the insurer must notify the state insurance department in each state in which an insured individual resides.

The model law requires insurers to make specified disclosures in solicitation and sales materials used to market group insurance to small employers. Insurers must disclose the following information to small employers:

- The extent to which premium rates for the employer will be established or adjusted on the basis of the claim experience, health status, or duration of coverage of the individuals insured under the employer's medical expense plan

- The contractual provisions that concern the insurer's right to change premium rates and the factors that will affect changes in premium rates

- A description of the class of business in which the small employer will be included and a description of the applicable grouping of plans into various classes of business

- The contractual provisions that relate to the small employer's right to renew coverage

An insurer that issues small group health benefit plans must maintain at its principal place of business detailed records that describe the insurer's premium rating and renewal underwriting practices. These records also must include documentation to demonstrate that the insurer's rating methods are based on commonly accepted actuarial assumptions and are in accordance with sound actuarial principles. On an annual basis, the insurer must file an actuarial certification with the applicable state insurance department. The certification must be in the form of a written statement by a qualified actuary indicating that the actuary has examined the insurer's actuarial assumptions and methods and certifies that those assumptions and methods comply with regulatory requirements.

The second NAIC model law we mentioned earlier, the *Small Employer Health Insurance Availability Model Act*, imposes the same types of requirements as those just described, including the following:

- Restrictions are placed on premium rates and on renewal rate increases
- Renewability requirements are imposed

The Small Employer Health Insurance Availability Model Act goes further than the earlier model law by including requirements designed to broaden the availability of health care benefits to small employer groups. As we mentioned, the NAIC adopted two versions of this Model Act. Both versions require carriers that sell to small employers to provide all eligible small employers in the state with at least a basic health benefit plan and a standard benefit plan; the specific components of the basic health benefit plan and the standard benefit plan are established by a representative group of carriers, small employers, and health care providers operating within the state. The two versions of the Model Act, however, take different approaches to broadening the availability of coverage to small employer groups:

- One version of the Model Act provides for the creation of a *small employer allocation program* to which all carriers that provide coverage to small employer groups in the specific state must belong. Small groups in the state that have been unable to obtain coverage for a specified time are able to purchase health benefit coverage through the carriers participating in the allocation program. The program is designed to distribute the coverage of these groups equitably among all the carriers included in the program.

- The second version of the Model Act provides for the creation of a *small employer health reinsurance program* that enables small employers and small employer carriers to reinsure small group health benefit coverages through a nonprofit reinsurance program established pursuant to the Model Act.

REGULATORY JURISDICTION

In underwriting and issuing a group life or health insurance policy, an insurer must ensure that the policy complies with appropriate state regulatory requirements. Sometimes, determining which state has jurisdiction to regulate a group insurance policy can be difficult. For example, a group policy may be issued by an insurer domiciled in one state to an employer domiciled in another state and may insure employees residing and working in a number of states. According to laws in most states, jurisdiction to regulate a group insurance contract is held by the state in which the group master contract is delivered to the group policyholder. In a few states, however, group contracts must comply with state regulatory requirements if the contracts insure residents of the state even if the group policyholder takes delivery of the policy in another state.

The parties to a group insurance contract agree on where the insurer will deliver the policy to the policyholder. For example, employers often receive delivery of employee group policies at their principal places of business. The parties, however, are not totally free to select the site of policy delivery. State regulators require that a given state's selection as the place of policy delivery have a reasonable basis. The states generally recognize the following sites as being acceptable as the place of policy delivery for purposes of establishing regulatory jurisdiction:

- The state where the policyholder is domiciled
- The state where the policyholder's principal place of business is located
- The state where the greatest number of insured individuals are employed

When a group policy is issued to a trust, the following are acceptable as being the state in which the policy is delivered:

- The state in which the trust was created
- Any state in which an employer or labor union that is a party to the trust is located
- The state where the greatest number of insured individuals are employed

KEY TERMS AND CONCEPTS

Group Life Insurance Definition and Group Life Insurance Standard Provisions Model Act
Group Health Insurance Definition and Group Health Insurance Standard Provisions Model Act
trust
trustee
trust property
trust beneficiary
Taft-Hartley Act
discretionary group
evidence of insurability provision
certificate of coverage provision
conversion provision
Group Health Insurance Mandatory Conversion Privilege Model Act
Group Coordination of Benefits Model Regulation
coordination of benefits (COB) provision
nonduplication of benefits provision
small employer
Premium Rates and Renewability of Coverage for Health Insurance Sold to Small Groups
Small Employer Health Insurance Availability Model Act

ENDNOTE

1. 29 U.S.C.A. §§ 141 *et seq.* (2000).

CHAPTER 9

Federal Regulation of Group Life and Health Insurance Plans

LEARNING OBJECTIVES

After studying this chapter, you should be able to

- Identify the types of group insurance plans that are subject to the federal Consolidated Omnibus Budget Reconciliation Act (COBRA) and identify the qualifying events following which COBRA gives certain group insureds the right to continue their group coverage

- Identify the features of the COBRA continuation coverage an insurer must provide a qualified beneficiary

- Recognize the duties and responsibilities of the employer, employee, and plan administrator following the occurrence of a qualifying event under COBRA

- Identify the types of requirements imposed by the federal Health Insurance Portability and Accountability Act (HIPAA) on the pre-existing condition exclusion provision included in group medical expense plans

- Calculate the amount of a given individual's creditable coverage using the standard method and the alternative method specified by HIPAA

- Describe HIPAA's special enrollment period requirement, non-discrimination requirement, guaranteed availability requirement, and guaranteed renewability requirement

Although the states have primary authority to regulate group insurance plans, a number of federal regulatory requirements affect the design of group life and health insurance plans. Many federal requirements are designed to regulate employee benefit plans, and insurers must ensure that the group insurance plans they develop for employee groups comply with applicable federal requirements. The following are some federal requirements imposed on employee group life and health insurance plans:

- A number of federal laws prohibit employers from discriminating against employees on specified grounds, and employee benefit plans—including group insurance plans—must not include features that result in any such prohibited discrimination. Figure 9-1 identifies and describes the federal laws that prohibit employers from discriminating against employees on specified grounds.

- The federal *Employee Retirement Income Security Act (ERISA)*, which regulates employee welfare benefit plans, imposes disclosure and reporting requirements on such plans.[1] For purposes of ERISA, a *welfare benefit plan* is a plan that an employer establishes to provide the specified benefits listed in Figure 9-2 to plan participants and their beneficiaries. Any employer-sponsored plan that provides one of the listed benefits becomes subject to ERISA's disclosure and reporting requirements. ERISA

FIGURE 9-1 Federal Laws That Prohibit Employment Discrimination.

- ✓ The *Civil Rights Act of 1964* is a broad antidiscrimination law that applies to employers that are engaged in interstate commerce and that have 15 or more employees. Title VII of the Act prohibits employment discrimination on the basis of race, color, sex, religion, or national origin.[2]

- ✓ The *Pregnancy Discrimination Act*, which was enacted as an amendment to the Civil Rights Act of 1964, requires employers to treat pregnancy, childbirth, and related medical conditions the same as any other medical condition.[3]

- ✓ The *Americans with Disabilities Act (ADA)* protects disabled individuals against all types of discrimination, including employment discrimination. The ADA applies to all employers with 15 or more employees and requires that disabled employees have equal access to the life and health insurance coverages that are available to other employees.[4]

- ✓ The *Age Discrimination in Employment Act (ADEA)* applies to employers that have 20 or more employees and prohibits those employers from discriminating against employees who are age 40 and older because of their age.[5]

- ✓ The *Family and Medical Leave Act (FMLA)* requires employers with 50 or more employees within a 75-mile radius to allow eligible employees in specific circumstances to take up to 12 weeks of unpaid leave within any 12-month period. The Act defines *eligible employee* as an employee who has been employed by a covered employer for at least 12 months and who worked at least 1,250 hours during the 12 months preceding the start of a leave. Employers must continue to provide group health insurance coverage to employees who are on family and medical leave.[6]

also regulates many aspects of pension plans, and we describe these ERISA requirements in Chapter 11.

Our goal in this chapter is to describe federal laws that specifically regulate the provisions included in group insurance plans. We begin by describing the Consolidated Omnibus Budget Reconciliation Act (COBRA) and then we describe the Health Insurance Portability and Accountability Act (HIPAA). We also briefly describe several other federal laws that regulate group insurance plans.

FIGURE 9-2 Employee Benefits that Subject a Welfare Benefit Plan to ERISA.

- ✓ Medical, surgical, or hospital care benefits
- ✓ Sickness, accident, disability, death, or unemployment benefits
- ✓ Vacation benefits
- ✓ Day-care benefits
- ✓ Scholarship funds
- ✓ Prepaid legal services
- ✓ Apprenticeship or training programs
- ✓ Certain benefits, including severance benefits and housing benefits, described in the Labor Management Relations Act of 1947*

* The *Labor Management Relations Act of 1947*, also known as the Taft-Hartley Act, is a federal law that regulates certain union activities. 29 U.S.C. §§ 141 *et seq.* (2000).

CONSOLIDATED OMNIBUS BUDGET RECONCILIATION ACT

The *Consolidated Omnibus Budget Reconciliation Act (COBRA)* imposes requirements on group insurance plans that provide medical expense benefits and that are sponsored by employers with 20 or more employees.[7] All such employer-sponsored plans that provide medical expense benefits—whether they are indemnity insurance plans or managed care plans—are subject to COBRA's requirements; the only exceptions are employer-employee plans sponsored by a local, state, or federal government or by a church.

COBRA requires group medical expense plans to give certain covered employees and their covered spouses and dependent children the right to continue their group insurance coverage for a limited time in specified situations in which their group coverage would otherwise terminate. When an individual elects to continue group coverage under COBRA, the group coverage is often referred to as *COBRA continuation coverage*. Individuals who elect continuation coverage must pay for their coverage, and they may be required to pay a larger premium for the coverage than they paid before the qualifying event.

Qualifying Events

COBRA spells out the situations, known as *qualifying events*, in which a covered individual who otherwise would lose group health coverage has the right to continue that coverage for a specified period of time. For each qualifying event, COBRA specifies the individuals, known as *qualified beneficiaries*, who have the right to continue their group coverage without providing evidence of insurability.

- Upon the death of a covered employee, the employee's surviving spouse and dependents who were covered under the group health plan are qualified beneficiaries who are entitled to continue their group coverage if they choose to do so.

- Upon the voluntary or involuntary termination of a covered employee's employment for reasons other than the covered employee's gross misconduct, the employee and covered spouse and covered dependents are entitled to continue their group coverage. Such a termination of employment is a qualifying event whether the employee retires, quits, or is fired for reasons other than gross misconduct.

- If a covered employee's hours are reduced so that the employee is no longer eligible for group insurance coverage, the employee and covered spouse and covered dependents are entitled to continue their group coverage.

- Upon the divorce or legal separation of a covered employee, the employee's covered spouse and those covered dependent children who would otherwise lose their group coverage are entitled to continue their group coverage.

- When a covered dependent child ceases to be a dependent child for purposes of the group health plan, the child has the right to continue group coverage.

- When a covered employee becomes entitled to receive Medicare benefits, the employee's covered spouse and covered dependent children are entitled to continue group coverage.

- When an employer is the subject of a bankruptcy proceeding, a retired employee who is covered under the employer's group plan may continue that group insurance coverage. The retiree's covered spouse and covered dependent children, if any, also may elect COBRA continuation coverage.

Figure 9-3 identifies the qualifying events specified by COBRA, along with the qualified beneficiaries who are eligible for continuation coverage following a qualifying event.

COBRA Continuation Coverage

COBRA spells out the types of coverage that individuals must be offered when they elect COBRA continuation coverage. It also specifies the minimum length of time that such coverage must be available and the maximum premium a qualified individual may be charged for continuation coverage.

Required Benefits

An individual who elects to receive COBRA continuation coverage must be offered the same coverages that the employer's group plan offers to similarly situated individuals. Thus, for example, assume that a covered employee dies and his surviving spouse elects COBRA continuation coverage. The surviving spouse must be offered the same coverages that the group plan provides to spouses of covered employees. Any changes to a group plan must apply equally to qualified beneficiaries with COBRA continuation coverage as to similarly situated covered individuals. For example, if a group plan adds benefits for covered spouses, then the plan must provide those same benefits for spouses who are continuing their group coverage under COBRA.

Period of Continuation Coverage

As noted, COBRA specifies the maximum length of time following a qualifying event for which qualified beneficiaries must be permitted to continue their group health coverage. The required period of continuation coverage for a qualified beneficiary begins on the date of a qualifying event and lasts until one of the following events occurs:

- The employer stops providing any group health insurance plan to its employees
- The qualified beneficiary fails to pay a required premium
- The qualified beneficiary becomes covered as either an employee or a dependent under another group health insurance plan

FIGURE 9-3 COBRA Continuation Coverage Requirements.

Qualifying events	Qualified beneficiaries	Maximum required period of continuation coverage*
Death of a covered employee	Covered spouse	36 months after the qualifying event
	Covered dependents	36 months after the qualifying event
Termination of a covered employee's employment	Employee	18 months after the qualifying event
	Covered spouse	18 months after the qualifying event
	Covered dependents	18 months after the qualifying event
Reduction in an employee's hours resulting in the employee's loss of eligibility for group coverage	Employee	18 months after the qualifying event
	Covered spouse	18 months after the qualifying event
	Covered dependents	18 months after the qualifying event
The divorce or legal separation of an employee	Covered spouse	36 months after the qualifying event
	Covered dependents	36 months after the qualifying event
A covered dependent child ceases to be a dependent under the terms of the plan	Covered dependent	36 months after the qualifying event
A covered employee becomes entitled to receive Medicare benefits	Covered spouse	36 months after the qualifying event
	Covered dependents	36 months after the qualifying event
The employer is the subject of a bankruptcy proceeding	Retired employees covered under the plan	Own lifetimes
	Covered spouses	36 months following the retiree's death
	Covered dependents	36 months following the retiree's death

* Maximum periods specified reflect the general rules imposed by COBRA. These general rules are subject to a number of exceptions.

- The qualified beneficiary becomes eligible for Medicare benefits
- The maximum required period of COBRA continuation coverage ends

The maximum required period of COBRA continuation coverage varies depending on the qualifying event. (See Figure 9-3.) In general, when the qualifying event is the termination of employment or a reduction in hours, COBRA limits the maximum period of continuation coverage to 18 months. COBRA, however, contains the following two exceptions to this general rule:

- If the Social Security Administration determines that an employee was totally disabled when her employment was terminated or her hours were reduced, then the maximum period of continuation coverage is extended to 29 months.
- If a second qualifying event occurs during the 18-month period of COBRA continuation coverage, then the maximum period for all qualified beneficiaries usually is extended to a total of 36 months following the first qualifying event.

If the qualifying event is a bankruptcy proceeding, a covered employee may continue his group health coverage throughout his lifetime; the employee's covered spouse and covered dependents may continue their group health insurance coverage for a maximum of 36 months following the retiree's death. In most other cases, COBRA gives qualified beneficiaries the right to continue their group coverage for a maximum period of 36 months following the qualifying event.

COBRA also requires group medical expense plans to provide a conversion privilege to certain qualified beneficiaries. As we described in Chapter 8, employer-employee group health plans typically include a conversion provision that gives covered individuals the right to convert their group health coverage to a plan of individual insurance upon termination of their group insurance. For example, assume that Irene Mott has terminated her employment and has the option of converting her group coverage to individual coverage or continuing her group coverage under COBRA. If Irene elects COBRA continuation coverage, then COBRA requires that she be allowed to exercise the conversion option during the 180-day period following the expiration of her COBRA continuation coverage.

Premium Charges

Individuals who elect to continue group health coverage under COBRA must pay the premiums for their continuation coverage. COBRA, however, limits the amount of premium that may be charged to 102 percent of the cost to the group health plan for similarly situated covered individuals. The cost for similarly situated individuals must be calculated without regard to whether their premiums are paid by the employer or the employee.

Notice Requirements

COBRA requires group health plan administrators to provide written notification to an employee and the employee's spouse, if any, of the rights they have under COBRA. A ***plan administrator*** is the party responsible for handling the administrative aspects of a group insurance plan and ensuring the plan complies with applicable regulatory requirements. Depending on how the group insurance arrangement is structured, the plan administrator generally is the plan sponsor, a plan trustee, an insurance company, or a third party administrator.

The plan administrator must make this notification of COBRA rights when group insurance coverage begins. Qualified beneficiaries also must be notified of their rights under COBRA upon the occurrence of a qualifying event. Depending on the type of qualifying event, either the employer or the employee is responsible for notifying the group insurance plan administrator of the qualifying event.

The employer is responsible for notifying the plan administrator of the following qualifying events:

- A covered employee's death
- Termination of a covered employee's employment or a reduction in the employee's hours
- An employee becomes entitled to Medicare benefits
- An employer is the subject of a bankruptcy proceeding

In these cases, the employer has a period of 30 days following the qualifying event in which to notify the plan administrator of the qualifying event. Upon receiving such a notification, the plan administrator has 14 days in which to notify all qualified beneficiaries of their right to elect COBRA continuation coverage.

The employee is responsible for notifying the plan administrator of a qualifying event in the following cases:

- The employee divorces or is legally separated
- A dependent child ceases to be a dependent

In these cases, the employee has a period of 60 days following the qualifying event in which to notify the plan administrator. The plan administrator then has 14 days in which to notify all qualified beneficiaries of their right to elect COBRA continuation coverage.

Election Period

In order to continue group health insurance coverage following a qualifying event, a qualified beneficiary must elect COBRA continuation coverage within a specified time, known as the *election period*. An individual's election period begins on the date his group insurance coverage terminates because of a qualifying event. The election period ends 60 days after the later of

- The date coverage terminates or
- The date the individual was notified of his right to continue coverage under COBRA

When a qualified beneficiary elects COBRA continuation coverage during the election period, that coverage is provided retroactively from the date the individual lost group health coverage because of a qualifying event. An individual who fails to elect coverage during the election period loses the right to receive COBRA continuation coverage.

Enforcement Provisions

COBRA imposes a tax to penalize group health plans that fail to provide continuation coverage as required. In the case of a multiple employer group insurance plan, such a tax is imposed on the plan. Recall that a multiple employer policy must be issued to a trust. When a tax is imposed on such a group insurance plan, the tax is paid from funds placed into the trust. In the case of a single employer plan, such a tax is imposed directly on the employer. Note that the insurer is not subject to the imposition of such a tax when a group plan has not complied with COBRA.

In two specified situations, no tax is imposed when a plan fails to provide required continuation coverage. No tax is imposed if regulators determine that plan administrators did not know of the failure to provide coverage and would not have known of the failure by exercising reasonable diligence in administering the plan. In addition, no tax is imposed if a plan corrects its failure to provide required continuation coverage within 30 days after administrators know or reasonably should know of the failure.

Health Insurance Portability and Accountability Act

In Chapter 3, we described the requirements imposed by the federal *Health Insurance Portability and Accountability Act (HIPAA)* on individual medical expense insurance policies.[8] HIPAA also imposes requirements on employer-sponsored medical expense benefit plans that insure two or more employees. HIPAA's requirements are imposed on all such plans, including indemnity insurance plans and managed care plans, and the requirements are imposed on all carriers—insurance companies and health maintenance organizations (HMOs)—that market such plans. Group plans that provide accident-only coverage, including accidental death and dismemberment coverage, or only disability income coverage are exempt from HIPAA's requirements. Regulatory requirements in many states are more favorable to insureds than are HIPAA's requirements, and in those states, insurance plans and insurers must comply with the more stringent state requirements.

We begin this section by describing HIPAA's requirements concerning the preexisting condition exclusion provision included in group medical expense plans. We also describe HIPAA's special enrollment period requirements, nondiscrimination requirements, guaranteed availability requirement, and guaranteed renewability requirement. These requirements are summarized in Figure 9-4. Although HIPAA's requirements provide protections to group insureds, HIPAA does not protect insureds in every situation. Figure 9-5 lists some things that HIPAA does not do.

Preexisting Conditions

In order to increase the portability of medical expense coverages, HIPAA places limits on the preexisting condition exclusion that a group medical expense plan may include. These limits are designed to allow group insureds who have a preexisting condition to change jobs without losing coverage for their preexisting conditions. The following limitations are imposed on the preexisting condition provision included in group medical expense policies:

- HIPAA defines a *preexisting condition* as a physical or mental condition for which medical advice, diagnosis, care, or treatment was recommended or received within the six-month period preceding an individual's enrollment date. Note that the maximum *look-back period* for purposes of defining a preexisting condition is six months. The *enrollment date* is either the date the individual becomes covered under the group health plan or, if earlier, the first day of the waiting period for enrollment.

FIGURE 9-4 Overview of HIPAA's Requirements.

- ✓ Limits the use of preexisting condition exclusions by medical expense plans
- ✓ Prohibits group medical expense plans from discriminating by denying coverage or charging extra for coverage based on an insured's past or present poor health
- ✓ Guarantees certain small employers, and certain individuals who lose job-related coverage, the right to purchase medical expense coverage
- ✓ Guarantees, in most cases, that employers or individuals who purchase medical expense coverage can renew the coverage regardless of any health conditions of individuals covered under the insurance policy

- The *exclusionary period* during which a preexisting condition is excluded from coverage ordinarily may not exceed 12 months after the enrollment date. The exclusionary period, however, may extend for 18 months in the case of late enrollees. A *late enrollee* is an individual who enrolls in the group health plan other than during (1) the first period in which she is eligible to enroll or (2) a special enrollment period defined in the Act. We describe this special enrollment period later in the chapter.

- The length of the preexisting condition exclusion period applied to a covered individual must be reduced by the total amount of the individual's creditable coverage, which we describe below.

- Pregnancy may not be treated as a preexisting condition, and a preexisting condition exclusion may not be imposed on a newborn or adopted child under age 18 if the child is covered within 30 days of birth or adoption.

FIGURE 9-5 Some Things That HIPAA Does Not Do.

- ☒ HIPAA does NOT require employers to offer or to pay for medical expense coverage for employees or for employees' spouses and dependents.
- ☒ HIPAA does NOT guarantee medical expense coverage for all workers.
- ☒ HIPAA does NOT control the amount an insurer may charge for medical expense coverages.
- ☒ HIPAA does NOT require group medical expense plans to offer any specific benefits.
- ☒ HIPAA does NOT require that people who change jobs must be able to keep the same medical expense coverages they had in their old jobs.
- ☒ HIPAA does NOT eliminate all use of preexisting condition exclusions.
- ☒ HIPAA does NOT replace the state insurance departments as the primary regulator of medical expense insurance.

For a covered individual, the term *creditable coverage* means coverage under any of the following:

- A group health plan
- Medical expense coverage
- Medicare
- Medicaid
- Health care sponsored by the military

- A medical care program of the Indian Health Service
- A state health benefits risk pool
- Federal employee health care coverage
- A public health plan
- A health benefit plan under the Peace Corps Act

As you can see, virtually any type of individual or group health care coverage qualifies as creditable coverage. However, an individual is credited with a period of creditable coverage only if that period was *not* followed by a break in coverage of 63 days or more. A break in coverage of 63 or more days is often referred to as a *significant break in coverage*. For example, assume that Jodie Lorenzo was insured for 24 months under a group medical expense plan sponsored by her employer. Ms. Lorenzo quit her job and, thus, no longer qualified for coverage under her employer's plan. After being uninsured for 75 days, Ms. Lorenzo began another job and became eligible for coverage under her new employer's group health plan. Because Ms. Lorenzo had a significant break in coverage of more than 63 days, her 24 months of coverage under the first employer's plan does *not* qualify as creditable coverage. As a result, if Ms. Lorenzo has a preexisting condition, HIPAA permits that condition to be excluded from coverage under her new employer's group health plan for a maximum of 12 months.

A waiting period under an employer-sponsored group health benefits plan does not count as a break in coverage. For example, assume that Simpson Starr was insured for 12 months under a group health plan sponsored by his employer. Mr. Starr's employment terminated, and 60 days after his group coverage terminated, he began a new job. Under his new employer's plan, Mr. Starr was subject to a 30-day waiting period requirement before being eligible to enroll for group health coverage. On the first day he was eligible, Mr. Starr enrolled for coverage. The 30-day waiting period will not count as a break in Mr. Starr's coverage, and, thus, his total break in coverage is considered to be only 60 days and he will be credited with 12 months of creditable coverage under his prior employer's plan. Because Mr. Starr had 12 months of creditable coverage, HIPAA prohibits his new group plan from excluding any of Mr. Starr's preexisting conditions from coverage.

HIPAA specifies two methods—the standard method and an alternative method—that plans may use to calculate the amount of an individual's creditable coverage. When using the *standard method*, a group health plan counts a period of creditable coverage without regard to the specific benefits provided during the period. Our earlier examples about Jodie Lorenzo and Simpson Starr did not consider what benefits their employers' plans provided and, thus, used the standard method of calculating creditable coverage. Figure 9-6 illustrates how an individual's creditable coverage is calculated using the standard method.

A group medical expense plan may elect to use the *alternative method* of crediting coverage if it does so for all plan participants. Under the alternative method, the plan may count a separate period of creditable coverage for each of certain specified classes of benefits. Federal regulations specify the following five classes of benefits for which group plans may use the alternative method to calculate creditable coverage:

- Mental health benefits
- Treatment for substance abuse
- Prescription drug benefits
- Vision care benefits
- Dental care benefits

A group medical expense plan may use the alternative method for any or all of these categories of benefits. Plans must use the standard method to calculate the amount of creditable coverage for all other types of benefits.

The amount of creditable coverage for a given category of benefits is used to reduce the length of the preexisting condition exclusion period imposed on that category of benefits. Recall that generally the preexisting condition exclusion period may not exceed 12 months, which is 365 days. Assume, for example, that Alma Monroe had 65 days of creditable coverage for prescription drug benefits when she became eligible for coverage under her employer's group health plan. The preexisting condition exclusion period for Ms. Monroe's prescription drug benefits may not exceed 300 days—the 365-day maximum period reduced by Ms. Monroe's 65 days of creditable coverage.

The first step in calculating an individual's creditable coverage under the alternative method is to establish the period of time, known as the *determination period*, over which to calculate the amount of the individual's creditable coverage for the various categories of benefits. The determination period ordinarily is the individual's most recent period of creditable coverage up to a maximum of 365 days—or 546 days (18 months) for late enrollees. Then, the amount of creditable coverage within the determination period is calculated for each category of benefits. Figure 9-7 gives an example of calculating an individual's creditable coverage using the alternative method.

FIGURE 9-6 Calculating an Individual's Creditable Coverage Using the Standard Method.

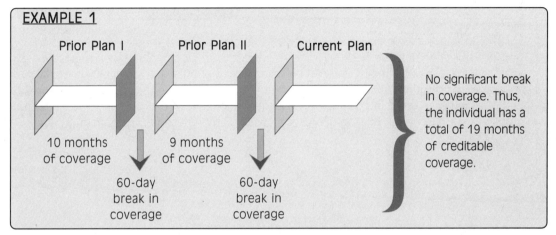

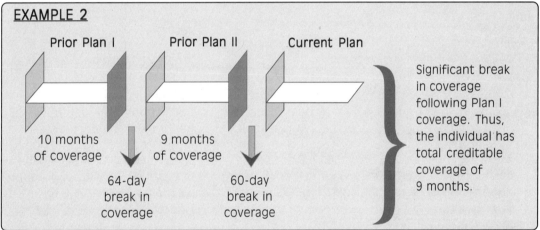

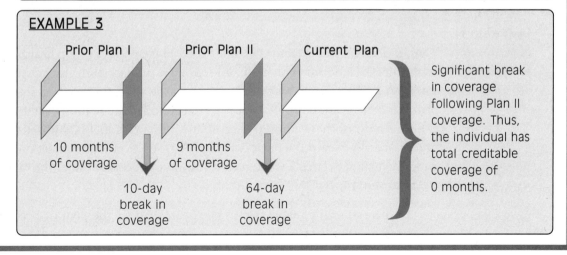

FIGURE 9-7 Calculating an Individual's Creditable Coverage Using the Alternative Method.

Willette Ingram's coverage under her prior employer's group medical expense plan became effective January 1, 2001, and terminated on December 31 of that same year. Ms. Ingram was initially covered by vision care benefits, but after 90 days that coverage was terminated from her plan. When Ms. Ingram changed jobs in 2002, she had no significant break in coverage and became eligible for coverage under her new employer's group health plan, which uses the alternative method of calculating creditable coverage.

Ms. Ingram's determination period was her most recent coverage period—that is, the 365-day period from January 1 through December 31, 2001. During the determination period, Ms. Ingram had 90 days of creditable coverage for vision care benefits. As a result, her new employer's group health plan may impose a preexisting condition exclusion period of 275 days (365 minus 90) for vision care benefits. Ms. Ingram had 365 days of creditable coverage for all other categories of benefits and, thus, will not be subject to a preexisting condition exclusion for those benefits.

An individual who becomes eligible for coverage under a group health plan establishes the amount of his creditable coverage under HIPAA by presenting a written certification of his prior coverage to the administrator of the group plan. The certification must identify (1) the period of creditable coverage and (2) the length of the waiting period, if any, the individual had to satisfy in order to be eligible for the prior coverage. A group health plan must provide an individual with such a written certification of coverage under the plan at the following times:

- When an individual ceases to be covered under the plan or becomes covered under a COBRA continuation provision

- When an individual ceases to be covered under a COBRA continuation provision

- Upon an individual's request if that request is made within 24 months following cessation of coverage

Figure 9-8 contains a sample written certification of creditable coverage.

HIPAA requires that, in order to impose a preexisting condition exclusion on an individual, a group plan must notify the individual in writing of the exclusion and of the individual's right to present evidence of creditable coverage that would reduce the length of the exclusion period.

Special Enrollment Period

HIPAA requires group medical expense plans to provide a special enrollment period for specified individuals who declined coverage when they first became eligible for it. Eligible employees and their eligible dependents must be permitted to enroll for coverage under the group plan without providing evidence of insurability if all of the following conditions are met:

- The individual already had medical expense coverage when coverage under the group plan became available.

- When group health coverage became available, the employee stated in writing that group health coverage was declined because the individual was already insured. This requirement, however, is imposed only when the plan sponsor required such a statement when an employee declined coverage and notified the employee of the requirement.

- The individual is no longer insured under another health plan because (1) her COBRA continuation coverage has ended, (2) she is no longer eligible for the coverage because of legal separation, divorce, death, termination of employment, or reduction in the number of hours of employment, or (3) her employer's contributions for the coverage ended.

- The employee requests enrollment in the group health plan within 30 days after the termination of other coverage.

Under HIPAA, group medical expense plans that provide dependent coverage must provide a special enrollment period for that coverage. A person who becomes a dependent of a covered individual through marriage, birth, adoption, or placement for adoption must be permitted to enroll for group coverage during the special enrollment period without providing evidence of insurability. The special enrollment period must extend for at least 30 days

FIGURE 9-8 **Sample Certificate of Group Health Plan Coverage.**

*IMPORTANT—This certificate provides evidence of your prior health coverage. You may need to furnish this certificate if you become eligible under a group health plan that excludes coverage for certain medical conditions that you have before you enroll. This certificate may need to be provided if medical advice, diagnosis, care, or treatment was recommended or received for the condition within the 6-month period prior to your enrollment in the new plan. If you become covered under another group health plan, check with the plan administrator to see if you need to provide this certificate. You may also need this certificate to buy, for yourself or your family, an insurance policy that does not exclude coverage for medical conditions that are present before you enroll.

1. Date of this certificate: _____
2. Name of group health plan: _____
3. Name of participant: _____
4. Identification number of participant: _____
5. Name of any dependents to whom this certificate applies: _____
   _____
6. Name, address, and telephone number of plan administrator or issuer responsible for providing this certificate: _____
7. For further information, call: _____
8. If the individual(s) identified in line 3 and line 5 has at least 18 months of creditable coverage (disregarding periods of coverage before a 63-day break), check here ____ and skip lines 9 and 10.
9. Date waiting period or affiliation period (if any) began: _____
10. Date coverage began: _____
11. Date coverage ended: _____ (or check if coverage is continuing as of the date of this certificate: ____).

Note: Separate certificates will be furnished if information is not identical for the participant and each beneficiary.

Source: *Federal Register,* Vol. 62, No. 67, 8 April 1997, Rules and Regulations, 16901.

and begins on the earlier of (1) the date dependent coverage is made available or (2) the date of the marriage, birth, adoption, or placement for adoption.

HIPAA prohibits group plans from imposing a waiting period requirement on dependents who enroll during the special enrollment period. When a covered individual's spouse enrolls for dependent coverage, the spouse's coverage must become effective no later than the first day of the first month following the date the plan sponsor received the completed request for enrollment. In the case of a dependent child, coverage must become effective on the date of the child's birth, adoption, or placement for adoption.

Nondiscrimination Requirements

HIPAA prohibits group medical expense plans from establishing eligibility rules for group coverage based on any of the following factors:

- Health status
- Medical condition, including physical and mental illnesses
- Claims experience
- Receipt of health care
- Medical history
- Genetic information
- Evidence of insurability, including conditions arising out of acts of domestic violence
- Disability

This provision of HIPAA does not require group plans to provide any particular benefits. It also does not prevent a group plan from limiting or restricting the types or levels of benefits provided as long as those limits or restrictions apply to all similarly situated individuals enrolled in the plan.

HIPAA also prohibits a group plan from requiring a higher premium contribution from any individual than is required of similarly situated individuals based on the factors listed above. In response to these HIPAA requirements, the NAIC is in the process of drafting a model regulation that the states will be encouraged to adopt. This model regulation is described in Insight 9-1.

Guaranteed Availability Requirement

As a general rule, in every state in which an insurer offers medical expense coverage to small groups, HIPAA requires the insurer to accept every small employer that applies for such coverage. HIPAA defines a *small employer* as an employer that had an average of at least 2 but not more than 50 employees

> **INSIGHT 9-1** **Proposed Model Regulation to Prohibit Discrimination in Group Health Insurance Coverage.**
>
> At the time of this writing, the NAIC is drafting the **Nondiscrimination in Health Insurance Coverage in the Group Market Model Regulation**, which is designed to incorporate requirements set forth in HIPAA.[9] The proposed Model Regulation prohibits an employee benefit plan from establishing eligibility rules that discriminate based on any health factor, including
>
> - Health status
> - Medical condition, including both mental and physical illnesses
> - Claims experience
> - Receipt of health care
> - Medical history
> - Genetic information
> - Evidence of insurability, including conditions arising out of acts of domestic violence and participation in activities, such as motorcycling, snowmobiling, all-terrain vehicle riding, horseback riding, skiing, or similar activities
> - Disability
>
> With some exceptions, the proposed Model Regulation also prohibits a group health plan or carrier from requiring an individual to pay a premium that is greater than the premium for a similarly situated individual enrolled in the plan based on any health factor. The following exceptions are included in the proposed Model:
>
> - A plan may establish a premium differential based on whether an individual has complied with the requirements of a bona fide wellness program. In other words, a plan may require insureds to participate in a wellness program and may charge a higher premium rate for insureds who do not participate in the wellness program. Likewise, a plan may impose higher deductibles or copayments on insureds who do not participate in such a wellness program.
> - A plan may charge an individual a lower rate than it charges similarly situated individuals if the lower rate is based on an adverse health factor, such as a disability.
>
> The proposed Model Regulation does not restrict the total amount that a plan or carrier may charge an employer for coverage under a group health plan.

during the preceding calendar year and had at least 2 employees on the first day of the group plan year. HIPAA contains a number of exceptions to the general requirement that small employers must be accepted for group health coverage.

- Insurers that offer coverage in the small group market only through one or more associations are not subject to this requirement.

- HIPAA contains special rules for group health coverage that is provided through a network plan, which is a health care plan that includes a network of preferred health care providers. Insurers issuing coverage through a network plan are permitted to limit the employers that may apply for guaranteed coverage to those employers with eligible employees who work or reside in the network's service area. An insurer also may deny coverage to a small employer if the insurer demonstrates to the applicable state insurance department that the insurer (1) will not have the network capacity to deliver adequate services to new enrollees and (2) is treating all employers alike when denying such coverage.

- A health insurer that can demonstrate that it does not have the financial reserves to underwrite additional coverage is permitted to deny coverage to a small employer.

- Health insurers may require employers to pay a specified percentage of policy premiums and may establish minimum participation requirements. Insurers are permitted to deny coverage to small employer groups that cannot meet such insurer requirements.

Guaranteed Renewability Requirement

HIPAA requires insurers that offer group medical expense coverages to renew such coverage at the option of the group policyholder. Although HIPAA permits insurers to increase the premium rates charged for renewal coverage, insurers must provide group policyholders with continued access to group coverage except when the following circumstances occur:

- Nonpayment of premium by a group policyholder

- Fraud or other intentional misrepresentation of material fact by a group policyholder

- Violation of participation requirements or employer contribution requirements

- The group plan provides benefits through a network plan *and* no individual enrolled through the group policyholder lives or works in the network's service area

- The insurer no longer offers group coverage in the state

Enforcement Provisions

Responsibility for enforcing HIPAA's requirements is shared between state insurance regulators and regulators in several federal departments. As noted in Chapter 3, HIPAA amended the following three federal laws:

- The Employee Retirement Income Security Act (ERISA), which is enforced by the federal Department of Labor (DOL).

- The Internal Revenue Code, which is enforced by the federal Department of Treasury. Some of the changes to federal income tax laws are described in Figure 9-9.
- The Public Health Service Act, which is enforced by the federal Department of Health and Human Services (HHS).

In general, most of the requirements that HIPAA imposes on group medical expense plans are within the jurisdiction of each of these three federal depart-

FIGURE 9-9 Changes HIPAA Made to Federal Income Tax Laws.

✓ Beginning in 1997 and extending at least through the year 2002, eligible individuals are allowed to establish a medical savings account (MSA) and to deduct a stated portion of their contributions to the account from their taxable income. A *medical savings account (MSA)* is an interest-bearing account created for the purpose of paying the account owner's qualified medical expenses that are not covered by insurance. Monies in the account belong to the individual who owns the account and may be used at any time to pay the individual's and his family's medical expenses. After age 65, the individual may withdraw funds from the MSA for any purpose. In order to be eligible to establish an MSA, an individual must be self-employed or employed by a small employer and must have health coverage that requires the individual to pay a high deductible amount. At the time of this writing, legislation is pending in Congress to extend the income-tax benefits for MSAs beyond the year 2002 and to make the requirements for eligibility to establish an MSA more lenient so that more people are able to take advantage of such products.

✓ Within stated maximum amounts, benefits received under a long-term care policy are not treated as taxable income to the recipient. In addition, premiums paid for long-term care coverage are now deductible as a medical expense.

✓ Amounts received as accelerated death benefits are not treated as taxable income to the recipient.

✓ HIPAA gradually increases over a period of years the amount of medical insurance costs that self-employed taxpayers may deduct from their taxable incomes.

ments. HIPAA seeks to avoid duplication of effort by requiring the three departments to coordinate their enforcement efforts to ensure consistency of enforcement. Each department has issued interim regulations that specify how HIPAA will be enforced and that provide more detailed information about the requirements HIPAA imposes. Although federal laws generally are enforced by the federal government, HIPAA authorizes each state government to enforce the Act's requirements on health insurers subject to its jurisdiction. If a state fails to enforce the federal requirements, then the federal departments are authorized to enforce them.

OTHER FEDERAL REQUIREMENTS

In addition to the laws we have described, three other federal laws impose requirements on group medical expense plans. Two of these laws, which apply to both individual and group medical expense plans, were described in Chapter 3.

- The federal *Newborns' and Mothers' Health Protection Act of 1996* imposes requirements on health insurers that provide benefits for maternity and newborn care. Group and individual health insurance plans that provide benefits for maternity and newborn care must comply with the requirements described earlier.

- The federal *Women's Health and Cancer Rights Act* protects patients who choose to have breast reconstruction in connection with a mastectomy. Although this federal law does not require health plans or insurers to pay for mastectomies, if a group or individual health plan or health insurance issuer chooses to cover mastectomies, then the plan or issuer is generally subject to WHCRA requirements.

The third federal law, known as the **Mental Health Parity Act (MHPA)**, imposes requirements on group health plans, health insurance companies, and health maintenance organizations that offer group mental health benefits.[10] An employer-sponsored group health plan must comply with the Act only if the employer has more than 50 employees. Like the other federal laws we described above, the MHPA does not require group policies to provide mental health benefits. Policies that provide mental health benefits may not set an annual or lifetime maximum mental health benefits limit that is lower than any such limits for medical and surgical benefits. For example, if a group policy has a $1 million lifetime limit on medical and surgical benefits, it must also have a $1 million lifetime limit on mental health benefits. A policy that does not impose an annual or lifetime limit on medical and surgical benefits may not impose such a limit on mental health benefits. The Act permits group health plans to impose the following types of restrictions on mental health benefits:

- Cost-sharing agreements may be different for mental health benefits as compared to medical and surgical benefits. For example, copayments may be larger for mental health visits than for medical and surgical benefits.

- Plans may limit the number of covered mental health visits per year.

KEY TERMS AND CONCEPTS

Civil Rights Act of 1964
Pregnancy Discrimination Act
Americans with Disabilities Act (ADA)
Age Discrimination in Employment Act (ADEA)
Family and Medical Leave Act (FMLA)
Consolidated Omnibus Budget Reconciliation Act (COBRA)
COBRA continuation coverage
qualifying events
qualified beneficiaries

plan administrator
election period
look-back period
enrollment date
exclusionary period
late enrollee
determination period
small employer
medical savings account (MSA)
Mental Health Parity Act (MHPA)

ENDNOTES

1. 29 U.S.C. §§ 1001 *et seq.* (2000).

2. 42 U.S.C. §§ 2000e *et seq.* (2000).

3. 42 U.S.C. § 2002e(k) (2000).

4. 42 U.S.C. §§ 12101 *et seq.* (2000).

5. 29 U.S.C. §§ 621 *et seq.* (2000).

6. 29 U.S.C. §§ 2601 *et seq.* (2000).

7. 26 U.S.C. § 4980D (2000).

8. Public Law 104-191 (1996).

9. The proposed model is available online at http://www.naic.org/1papers/models/models.html (24 April 2002).

10. 42 U.S.C. § 300gg-5 (2000).

CHAPTER 10

Regulation of Credit Life and Health Insurance

LEARNING OBJECTIVES

After studying this chapter, you should be able to

- Recognize consumer credit transactions that are subject to requirements imposed by state laws based on the NAIC Consumer Credit Insurance Model Act

- Identify the provisions that state insurance laws require group and individual credit life and health insurance policies to contain

- Identify the types of regulatory requirements the states impose on credit life and health insurance premium rates

- Recognize the types of regulatory requirements, including the disclosure requirements, the states impose on the marketing of credit life and health insurance

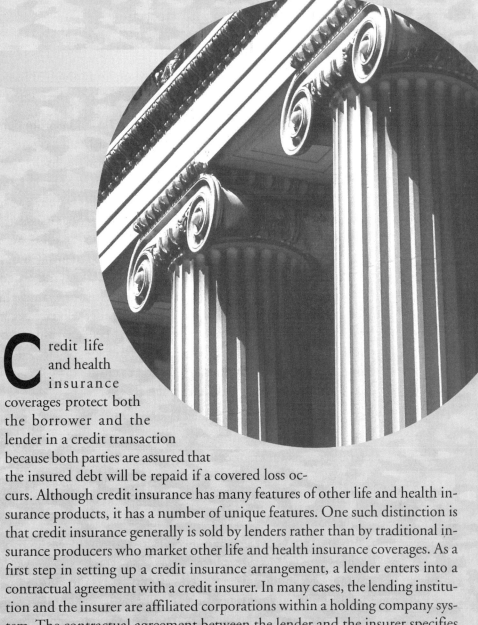

Credit life and health insurance coverages protect both the borrower and the lender in a credit transaction because both parties are assured that the insured debt will be repaid if a covered loss occurs. Although credit insurance has many features of other life and health insurance products, it has a number of unique features. One such distinction is that credit insurance generally is sold by lenders rather than by traditional insurance producers who market other life and health insurance coverages. As a first step in setting up a credit insurance arrangement, a lender enters into a contractual agreement with a credit insurer. In many cases, the lending institution and the insurer are affiliated corporations within a holding company system. The contractual agreement between the lender and the insurer specifies the types of credit insurance coverage that will be available to the lender's borrowers. Then, when an individual applies for a loan, the lender offers the borrower the opportunity to purchase credit insurance that will provide money to repay all or part of the debt if the borrower dies or becomes disabled before repaying the loan.

In most states, credit life and health coverages are offered to all qualified borrowers who are no more than 65 years old. In some states, credit insurance coverages are available up to age 70 or 71. As noted in Chapter 8, a debtor-creditor group is a type of group that is eligible for group life and health insurance, and most credit life and health insurance is issued on a group basis. The lender is both the group policyholder and the policy beneficiary. In some cases, credit life or health insurance is issued on an individual basis; the individual debtor is the owner of the policy and the lender is the named beneficiary.

Although state and federal laws prohibit a lender from denying credit to a consumer because he does not buy credit insurance offered by the lender, a borrower may feel pressured to accept the insurance in the belief that by doing so he is more likely to be approved for the requested loan. In addition, lenders have several financial incentives for selling credit insurance. As the named beneficiary of credit insurance policy benefits, the lender is assured that an insured debt will be repaid if the debtor dies or becomes disabled. As the credit insurance producer, the lender is paid by the insurer when a debtor purchases credit insurance. The amount of such payment generally is calculated as a percentage of the premium charged for the coverage. Thus, the larger the premium, the larger the amount the lender receives. The lender selects the credit insurer it will deal with and the coverages that will be made available to borrowers. State insurance laws regulating credit insurance are designed to protect the consumer's interests in such credit transactions and to ensure the solvency of the insurance companies that issue credit insurance.

In addition to state insurance laws, lenders must comply with various state and federal consumer protection laws, such as truth in lending laws, that impose requirements on creditors that engage in consumer credit transactions. Some of these consumer protection laws are described in Figure 10-1. Insight 10-1 describes how one state is poised to adopt new regulations in an effort to protect consumers from credit insurers that charge excessive premiums.

Most states have enacted specific credit insurance laws based on the NAIC *Consumer Credit Insurance Model Act*, which is designed to regulate consumer credit insurance issued or sold in connection with loans or other credit transactions for personal, family, or household purposes. State laws authorize the state insurance department to adopt regulations to carry out the laws' provisions, and most states have adopted regulations governing credit insurance. A number of states based their regulations on the NAIC *Consumer Credit Insurance Model Regulation*, which provides standards for the sale of consumer credit insurance.

In order to understand the operation of credit insurance laws and regulations, you need to understand how credit transactions are structured and how the purchase of credit insurance fits into the transaction. Credit transactions for which consumer credit insurance is available can be categorized as either closed-end credit transactions or open-end credit transactions. A ***closed-end credit transaction*** is a transaction in which a lender extends to a debtor a specified

FIGURE 10-1 Federal Consumer Protection Laws that Govern Consumer Credit Transactions.

Truth in Lending Act

Requires creditors that deal with consumers to make certain written disclosures concerning finance charges and related aspects of consumer credit transactions. Also establishes requirements for the advertising of credit terms.[1]

Fair Credit Reporting Act

Regulates the reporting and use of consumer credit information and seeks to ensure that consumer credit reports contain accurate, relevant, and recent information.[3]

Equal Credit Opportunity Act

Prohibits discrimination in the granting of credit on the basis of race, color, religion, national origin, sex, marital status, age, or receipt of public assistance. Creditors must provide applicants for credit, upon request, with the reasons for the denial of credit.[2]

Federal Trade Commission Act

Created the Federal Trade Commission (FTC) and empowered the FTC, among other things, to (a) prevent unfair methods of competition, and unfair or deceptive acts or practices in or affecting commerce; (b) seek monetary redress and other relief for conduct that injures consumers; (c) adopt trade regulation rules to define specific acts or practices that are unfair or deceptive and establish requirements designed to prevent such acts or practices; (d) conduct investigations relating to the organization, business practices, and management of entities engaged in commerce; and (e) make reports and legislative recommendations to Congress.[4]

amount of credit that will be repaid at a specified interest rate in a series of equal payments over a specified time. An *open-end credit transaction* is a transaction in which credit is extended under an agreement in which (1) the

INSIGHT 10-1: Proposed Credit Insurance Rules Will Save California Consumers Nearly $200 Million Each Year.

A proposed set of new regulations now being considered by the California Department of Insurance would save credit insurance consumers in California nearly $200 million each year according to Consumers Union.[5] The regulations have been drafted by the Department to comply with a law enacted by California lawmakers in 1999 to rein in excessive premiums and questionable sales practices by businesses that offer credit insurance.

"Credit insurance can be a useful product if it is priced right and sold fairly," said Birny Birnbaum, a consulting economist for Consumers Union and Technical Advisor for the Austin-based Center for Economic Justice. "Unfortunately, ineffective insurance regulation has allowed credit insurers to overcharge consumers by hundreds of millions of dollars each year."

"Low-income consumers are often coerced into purchasing expensive credit insurance that offers them little benefit," said Norma Garcia, Senior Attorney for Consumers Union's West Coast Regional Office in San Francisco. "Commissioner Harry Low has the authority and opportunity to curb these abuses and provide real protection for California consumers who deserve value for the insurance premiums they pay."

Credit insurance is sold in conjunction with a loan or credit agreement and may be sold by credit card companies, finance companies, auto dealers, department stores, or wherever loans are made and credit extended for the purchase of personal property. There are a number of different kinds of credit insurance. These policies make payments for the consumer to the lender for a specific loan or credit agreement in the event the borrower dies (credit life insurance), becomes disabled (credit disability insurance), loses their job (credit involuntarily unemployment insurance) or their property is lost or becomes damaged (credit property insurance).

California lawmakers took action to address credit insurance overcharges following the publication of a Consumers Union report in 1999 that documented that U.S. consumers were overcharged by more than 35 percent based on the loss ratio of the policies issued by insurers. The loss ratio is the ratio of benefits paid by insurers to the premiums paid by consumers for the insurance. From 1995 to 1997 the credit insurance industry nationwide had a loss ratio equal to 40 percent for credit life and credit disability insurance. In other words, for every dollar consumers spent in premiums, they received 40 cents in benefits. This is far lower than the 60 percent loss ratio that the National Association of Insurance Commissioners (NAIC) recommends as the minimum benefit that consumers should expect in relation to premiums paid for such policies.

Consumers Union estimates that California consumers were overcharged by 110% in 1999, the last year for which complete figures are available. During that year, the loss ratio for credit insurance was 28 percent, meaning consumers got 28 cents in benefits for every dollar they paid in premiums. As a result, consumers were overcharged by $232.2 million. The new law passed by the California legislature requires the Department of Insurance to adopt regulations that set a minimum loss ratio of 60 percent for companies issuing credit insurance.

Insurers and retail companies typically target low-income consumers for credit insurance and sometimes engage in questionable practices to coerce them into purchasing coverage. Some of these tactics include high pressure sales tactics, failure to disclose that the consumer's signature resulted in signing up for credit insurance, and misleading consumers into believing that credit insurance is required for loan approval.

> **Insight 10-1. Proposed Credit Insurance Rules Will Save California Consumers Nearly $200 Million Each Year,** *continued.*
>
> Consumers Union has recommended that the Department of Insurance strengthen the proposed rules by prohibiting many of these practices and by setting an even higher loss ratio for credit property and credit unemployment insurance.
>
> "These draft regulations go a long way towards protecting consumers from credit insurance ripoffs," said Garcia. "We hope the Department of Insurance will consider strengthening these rules to provide consumers with even more protection and savings."
>
> **Source:** © 2001 by Consumers Union of U.S., Inc. Yonkers, NY 10703-1057, a nonprofit organization. Reprinted with permission from Consumers Union for educational purposes only. No commercial use or photocopying permitted. Log onto www.Consumer.org for more information.

creditor reasonably expects repeated transactions; (2) the creditor imposes a periodic finance charge on an outstanding unpaid balance; and (3) the amount of credit that may be extended to the debtor during the term of the agreement—up to any limit set by the creditor—generally is made available to the extent that any outstanding balance is repaid. Figure 10-2 identifies the types of consumer credit transactions that often include the sale of credit life or health insurance.

Premiums for credit insurance coverage on closed-end credit transactions often are payable as a single premium, and the amount of that premium is included in the amount financed. Thus, for example, assume a consumer borrows $5,000 and purchases credit insurance at a single premium of $200. The total amount of the debt financed is $5,200. Note that by financing the amount of the credit insurance premium, the consumer must pay interest on that amount in addition to paying interest on the principal amount borrowed.

Premiums for credit insurance coverage on an open-end credit transaction generally are payable monthly at a specified rate per $1,000 of the monthly outstanding balance (MOB). For example, assume the monthly premium rate is $0.72 per $1,000 of indebtedness and the outstanding balance on the account billing date is $1,500. The monthly premium payable for credit insurance coverage is $1.08 [$1.5 \times \$0.72$]. The MOB method of premium payment also may be used for closed-end credit transactions.

Note that insurance issued or sold in connection with loans or credit transactions for business purposes is not subject to the Consumer Credit Insurance Model Act or to federal consumer protection laws. The following types of insurance written in connection with a consumer credit transaction also are exempt from requirements of the Model Act:

- Insurance issued in connection with a credit transaction that is secured by a first mortgage or deed of trust[6] and that is made to finance the purchase of real estate or the construction of a home

- Insurance sold as an isolated transaction of the insurer and not related to an agreement or plan for insuring debtors of the creditor

- Insurance for which no identifiable charge is made to the debtor

- Insurance issued to cover accounts receivable

FIGURE 10-2 Types of Consumer Credit Transactions That May Include the Purchase of Credit Life or Health Insurance.

Closed-end credit generally is made available by means of an **installment sale** in which the debtor receives goods or services in exchange for an agreement to pay for the purchase in a series of periodic installments of equal amounts over a specified period of time. For example, a consumer might purchase a household appliance from a retail store that agrees to finance the purchase by means of an installment sale.

Open-end credit is made available by either a line of credit or a credit card arrangement. A **line of credit** enables a consumer to receive cash under an agreement by a lender to make a specified maximum amount of money available to the consumer upon the consumer's request. A line of credit generally is made available to individual consumers as (1) a **personal line of credit** that is granted based on the individual consumer's overall creditworthiness or (2) a **home equity line of credit** that is granted based on the amount of the individual's ownership interest in his home.

Consumers may purchase goods and services by charging the cost to a **credit card** issued by either (1) the merchant selling the goods or services or (2) a bank or other financial institution. The consumer is billed monthly and is charged a specified rate of interest on the amount of the monthly outstanding balance.

The Model Act defines *consumer credit insurance* to include the following three types of credit insurance:

- *Credit life insurance* insures a debtor to provide funds for the payment of all or part of a specific debt owed under a credit transaction upon the debtor's death.

- *Credit accident and health insurance* insures a debtor to provide funds for the payment of amounts due under a specific credit transaction while the debtor is disabled as defined in the insurance policy. We refer to credit accident and health insurance as credit health insurance or credit disability insurance.

- *Credit unemployment insurance* insures a debtor to provide funds for the payment of amounts due under a specific credit transaction while the debtor is involuntarily unemployed as defined in the insurance policy. Credit unemployment insurance typically is classified as a type of property and casualty coverage.

PRODUCT DEVELOPMENT

Although credit insurance coverage usually is written under a group policy that is issued to the lender, policies may be issued on an individual basis. In either case, credit life and health policy forms and group certificates must be filed with and approved by the appropriate state insurance department before being delivered or issued for delivery within the state. The insurer must create a policy form or group certificate that meets the requirements of the states in which the policy or certificate will be delivered or issued for delivery. Credit life and health insurance policy forms and group certificates are developed in the same general manner as other life and health products.

Policy Form Development

In earlier chapters, we identified a variety of regulatory requirements the states impose on individual and group life and health insurance policies and group certificates. Many of these requirements apply to credit life and health insurance.

- Both group and individual credit life and health insurance policies and certificates must comply with readability requirements.

- Credit life and health policies must comply with state laws that require life and health policies to include specified provisions. These required life and health policy provisions described in earlier chapters are summarized in Figure 10-3.

FIGURE 10-3 Regulatory Requirements for Credit Life and Health Insurance Policy Provisions.

Individual credit life policies must comply with state insurance laws that define the provisions individual life insurance policies must contain. (See Chapter 1.) The provisions most states require individual credit life policies to include are:

- Entire contract provision
- Grace period provision
- Incontestability provision
- Misstatement of age provision
- Reinstatement provision

Individual credit health policies are subject to laws based in most states on the NAIC *Uniform Individual Accident and Sickness Policy Provision Law* (see Chapter 3), which requires individual credit health policies to include the following provisions, if applicable:

- Entire contract provision
- Time limit on certain defenses provision
- Grace period provision
- Reinstatement provision
- Renewal provision
- Notice of claim provision
- Claim forms provision
- Change of beneficiary provision
- Proof of loss provision
- Time of payment of claims provision
- Payment of claims provision
- Physical examinations and autopsy provision
- Legal actions provision

Group credit life policies must comply with requirements based on the NAIC *Group Life Insurance Definition and Group Life Insurance Standard Provisions Model Act* (see Chapter 8), which requires group credit life policies to include the following provisions:

- Entire contract provision
- Incontestability provision
- Grace period provision
- Misstatement of age provision
- A provision identifying the conditions on which the insurer may require evidence of insurability
- A provision stating that the insurer will issue a certificate to the policyholder for delivery to each insured
- Conversion provision

Figure 10-3. Regulatory Requirements for Credit Life and Health Insurance Policy Provisions, *continued.*

Group credit health policies must comply with requirements based on the NAIC *Group Health Insurance Definition and Group Health Insurance Standard Provisions Model Act* (see Chapter 8), which requires group credit health policies to include the following provisions:

- Entire contract provision
- Incontestability provision
- Grace period provision
- Misstatement of age provision
- A provision identifying the conditions on which the insurer may require evidence of insurability
- A provision stating that the insurer will issue a certificate to the policyholder for delivery to each insured
- Proof of loss provision

In addition to those requirements, the Consumer Credit Insurance Model Act requires individual credit life and health policies and certificates for group credit life and health coverage to include the following information:

- The name and home office address of the insurer.

- The name of the insured debtor or debtors.

- The premium payable by the debtor. If the credit transaction is an open-end loan, then the policy or certificate must specify the premium rate and the basis on which the premium will be calculated. For example, the calculation may be based on the amount of the debtor's average daily loan balance or on the amount of the prior monthly balance.

- A full description of the coverage, including the amount and term of that coverage, as well as any exceptions, limitations, and exclusions.

- A statement that (1) the policy benefit will be paid to the creditor to reduce or extinguish the unpaid debt and (2) if the amount of the benefit payable exceeds the amount of the unpaid debt, then the excess will be payable to either a beneficiary named by the debtor or the debtor's estate.

- If the scheduled term of credit insurance coverage is less than the scheduled term of the credit transaction, a statement to that effect must appear on the face page of the policy or certificate in at least 10-point boldface type.

Recall that the lender is the named beneficiary of credit insurance benefits, and, therefore, the lender is identified in the policy within the policy's beneficiary designation. State laws based on the Consumer Credit Insurance Model Act also require policies and group certificates to provide insureds with at least a 30-day free-look period.

An individual insured by a credit insurance policy must have the right to cancel the coverage at any time by notifying the insurer of cancellation. State laws based on the Model Act require individual credit insurance policies and group credit insurance certificates to provide for a refund of unearned premiums if the coverage is terminated before the scheduled maturity date of the coverage. The state insurance departments establish the minimum amount of any such premium refund that must be provided, and many insurance departments require insurers to use a specified formula to calculate the amount of such premium refunds. The Model Act requires that any formula an insurer uses to calculate premium refunds must first be filed with and approved by the state insurance department. This filing requirement is met if the refund formula is set forth in the individual policy or group certificate filed with the state insurance department as part of a policy form filing submission package.

The debtor's right to cancel credit insurance coverage may be subject to the terms of the credit transaction in addition to being subject to the terms of the credit insurance agreement. For example, a consumer credit agreement may require the debtor to secure the loan with some form of insurance coverage. Note that the debtor cannot be required to purchase credit insurance through the lender, and the creditor must inform the consumer of her right to purchase such coverage from any licensed insurer. In order for the debtor to terminate insurance coverage required by a credit agreement, the creditor may require the debtor to provide proof that she has alternative coverage.

The Consumer Credit Insurance Model Act also limits the amount of consumer credit insurance that may be issued on a specific debt, regulates the beginning and ending dates of consumer credit insurance coverage, and imposes disclosure and reporting requirements on credit insurers.

Amount of Credit Insurance Coverage

State insurance laws place maximum limits on the amount of credit life and credit disability insurance that may be issued to a debtor. In general terms, state laws based on the Consumer Credit Insurance Model Act limit the amount of credit insurance coverage provided in connection with any given credit transaction to the total amount of the insured debt. The Model Act also permits a credit insurance policy to provide coverage to pay only a specified portion of an insured debt. Although the Model Act does not place a specified maximum dollar limit on the amount of credit insurance coverage issued in connection with a consumer credit transaction, laws in a number of states do impose such limits. With some exceptions, these states generally limit the total amount of credit life or health insurance that may be issued to insure any debtor to $50,000 or $100,000.

State insurance laws specify how the amount of an insured debt is determined for purposes of establishing the amount of consumer credit insurance a policy provides. In this section, we describe the requirements of the Consumer Credit Insurance Model Act. Keep in mind that credit insurance coverage issued in connection with a closed-end credit transaction is generally decreasing term insurance—the amount of coverage provided gradually decreases over time as the debtor makes scheduled installment payments and repays the debt. (See Figure 10-4.) By contrast, the amount of credit insurance coverage issued in connection with an open-end credit transaction varies over time. The balance due on a credit card debt, for example, generally fluctuates up and down as the borrower makes purchases and periodic payments.

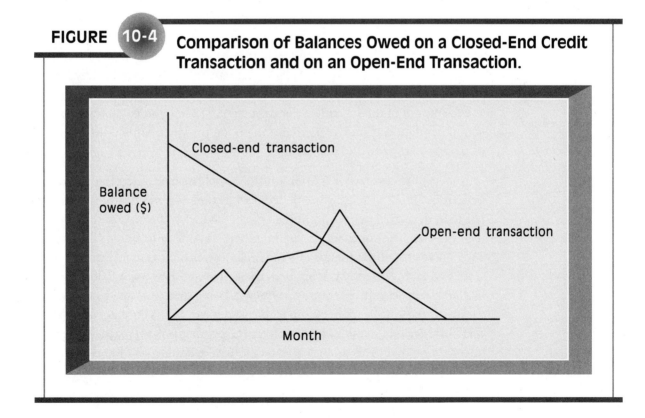

FIGURE 10-4 Comparison of Balances Owed on a Closed-End Credit Transaction and on an Open-End Transaction.

Credit life insurance. Credit life insurance is written as a promise to repay a debt, and the amount repayable may be specified as either the scheduled net debt or the actual net debt. The *scheduled net debt* is the lump-sum amount needed to pay off the debt on a given date according to the credit agreement's repayment schedule. Depending on the debtor's payment history, the amount actually needed to repay the debt on a given date may be more or less than the amount scheduled to be repaid by the credit agreement. The ***actual net debt*** is the lump-sum amount needed on any given date to pay off the debt, excluding unearned interest and any other unearned finance charges. The Consumer Credit Insurance Model Act limits the amount of credit life insurance coverage that may be provided for a given debt to the greater of the actual net debt or the scheduled net debt.

An example will help to illustrate the difference between the actual net debt and the scheduled net debt. Assume that on January 1, Ilyana Erikson borrowed $1,000 at an annual interest rate of 10 percent compounded monthly and agreed to repay the debt in 12 monthly installments. Ms. Erikson's monthly payment of $87.92 was due on the last day of each month. At the inception of the loan, the amount of both the actual net debt and the scheduled net debt was the $1,000 principal amount borrowed; Ms. Erikson had incurred no interest charges yet. Figure 10-5 contains the amortization—or repayment—schedule for Ms. Erikson's loan. Although Ms. Erikson made the first three scheduled monthly installments by the due dates of those payments, by June 1 she had failed to make the fourth, fifth, or sixth scheduled payments. On July 1, the amount of the scheduled net debt was $512.42, and the amount of the actual net debt was much larger and included the three unpaid installments plus accrued interest and penalty fees.

If credit life coverage is written on the actual net debt, then the insurance benefit payable to the creditor-beneficiary at the insured's death may not be less than the actual net debt minus any loan payments that are more than two months overdue. For example, assume that Mark Wan had credit life insurance on an installment loan. His scheduled monthly payments on the loan were $50 each. When Mr. Wan died, the actual net debt was $1,000, and he had missed the last three monthly payments. Using the actual net debt method, the amount of the death benefit payable under Mr. Wan's coverage is $950—the $1,000 actual net debt less one overdue payment of $50 each. Note that only one payment was more than two months overdue.

If credit life insurance coverage is written on the scheduled net debt, then the amount payable to the creditor-beneficiary at the time of loss depends on

FIGURE 10-5 Payment Schedule for a $1,000 Loan to Be Paid in 12 Monthly Installments at an Interest Rate of 10 Percent Compounded Monthly.

Month	Column 1 Scheduled Net Debt	Column 2 Payment	Column 3 Interest (Col. 1 × 0.0083333)	Column 4 Principal Repaid (Col. 2 − Col. 3)	Column 5 Remaining Net Debt (Col. 1 − Col. 4)
1	$1,000.00	$87.92	$8.33	$79.59	$920.41
2	$920.41	$82.92	$7.67	$80.25	$840.16
3	$840.16	$87.92	$7.00	$80.92	$759.24
4	$759.24	$87.92	$6.33	$81.59	$677.65
5	$677.65	$87.92	$5.65	$82.27	$595.38
6	$595.38	$87.92	$4.96	$82.96	$512.42
7	$512.42	$87.92	$4.27	$83.65	$428.77
8	$428.77	$87.92	$3.57	$84.35	$344.42
9	$344.42	$87.92	$2.87	$85.05	$259.37
10	$259.37	$87.92	$2.16	$85.76	$173.61
11	$173.61	$87.92	$1.45	$86.47	$87.14
12	$87.14	$87.92	$0.73	$87.19*	0

*Due to rounding, the amount of the scheduled principal to be repaid does not equal the amount of the net debt in Column 1. In reality, the amount of the final payment equals the total amount of the net debt then owed or $87.14.

whether the actual net debt is larger than the scheduled net debt. The following rules are specified by the Consumer Credit Insurance Model Act:

- If the actual net debt is less than or equal to the scheduled net debt, then the amount payable is the amount of the scheduled net debt.

- If the actual net debt is greater than the scheduled net debt but is less than or equal to the scheduled net debt plus two months of payments, then the amount payable is the amount of the actual net debt.

- If the actual net debt is greater than the scheduled net debt plus two months of payments, then the amount payable is the amount of the scheduled net debt plus two months of payments.

The Model Act also specifies the methods an insurer may use to establish the amount of credit life coverage to issue if the amount of that coverage will be less than the amount of the net debt. The following are some of the methods an insurer may use:

- The amount of insurance may be the lesser of (1) a stated level amount and (2) either the actual net debt or the scheduled net debt.

- The amount of insurance may be a constant percentage of either the actual net debt or the scheduled net debt.

Credit disability insurance. When a debtor insured under a credit disability insurance policy becomes disabled according to the terms of the policy, the insurer makes the scheduled periodic payments on behalf of the insured. In addition, credit disability policies may provide a waiver-of-premium benefit under which any premiums payable for credit health insurance are waived during a period of disability. From the insurer's perspective, the amount of the debt payable under a credit disability policy is equal to the total of the remaining scheduled payments, known as the *gross debt*. Figure 10-6 illustrates both the scheduled net debt and the gross debt over the life of the closed-end credit transaction we described in our earlier example concerning Ilyana Erikson.

According to the Consumer Credit Insurance Model Act, the total amount of periodic benefits payable under a credit disability policy is limited to the total of the periodic scheduled unpaid installments. The amount of each periodic benefit payment may not exceed the original gross debt divided by the number of periodic installments. In the case of an open-end credit transaction, the amount of each benefit payment must be at least the amount of the minimum payment required according to the creditor's minimum repayment schedule.

Term of Credit Insurance Coverage

State laws based on the Consumer Credit Insurance Model Act impose requirements as to when credit insurance coverage must begin and end. The effective date of coverage varies depending on whether the debtor elected to receive coverage at the time of the credit transaction.

- If coverage was elected at the time of the credit transaction, then that coverage must become effective when the debtor becomes legally obligated to the creditor under the terms of the credit transaction. This general requirement is subject to one exception. When the insurer requires the debtor to provide evidence of insurability as a condition of

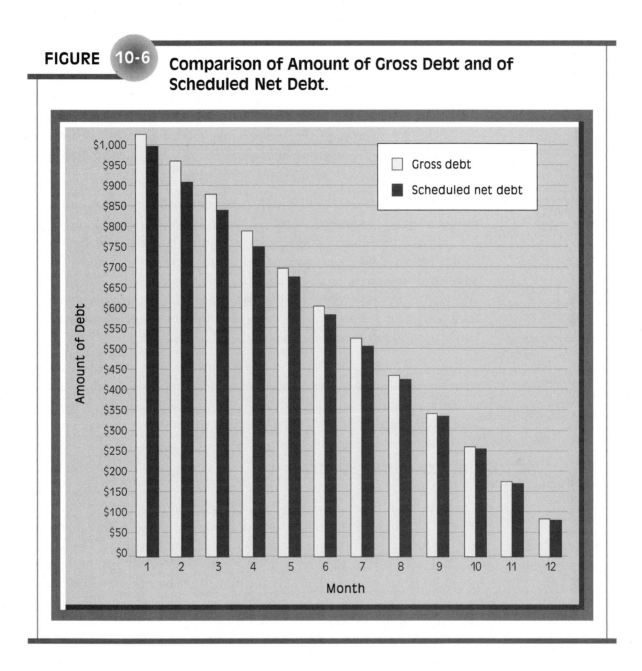

FIGURE 10-6 **Comparison of Amount of Gross Debt and of Scheduled Net Debt.**

coverage and the debtor provides such evidence more than 30 days after becoming obligated to the creditor, then coverage becomes effective when the insurer determines that the evidence of insurability is satisfactory. Recall from our discussion in Chapter 8 that state regulatory requirements imposed on group insurance permit group insurers to require individuals to provide satisfactory evidence of insurability as a condition of group insurance coverage.

- Sometimes, a debtor seeks credit insurance after the completion of a credit transaction. In these cases, credit insurance coverage must become effective no earlier than the date the debtor elected coverage *and* no later than 30 days after the insurer accepts the risk for coverage. The insurer must establish an objective method by which it establishes the effective date of such coverage. For example, the insurer may select a particular date within the creditor's billing cycle or within a calendar month on which to begin coverage for insured debtors.

Credit insurance coverage typically continues until the date on which the insured debt is scheduled to be paid. Subject to specified restrictions, credit life or disability insurance coverage may terminate before or after the scheduled payoff date. Coverage, for example, terminates when an insured debt is paid before its scheduled payoff date, and any unearned premium must be refunded to the debtor. Similarly, if an insured debt is refinanced, credit insurance coverage of the original debt must be terminated before any new insurance may be issued in connection with the refinanced debt.

Laws in a number of states also impose specific limits on the maximum term of credit insurance coverages. For example, some states prohibit the term of credit life insurance or credit disability insurance on any debtor from exceeding 10 years.

Actuarial Considerations

Credit insurance premium rates are subject to regulatory requirements in most states. The Consumer Credit Insurance Model Act requires that premium rates be filed as part of a policy form filing submission package. The Model Act also provides that the state insurance department shall disapprove such premium rates within 30 days after the filing if the benefits provided by the policy are unreasonable in relation to the premium charged. Benefits are considered reasonable in relation to premiums if the premium rate charged may reasonably be expected to develop a loss ratio of at least 60 percent. (We described loss ratio requirements in Chapter 3.) Most states specify minimum loss ratio requirements for credit life and health insurance, and the specified minimums range from around 40 percent to as much as 70 percent; a minimum loss ratio of 50 or 60 percent is most typical. Many states impose different loss ratio requirements for credit life and credit health insurance, and these states impose a higher minimum loss ratio for credit disability policies than for credit life policies. A typical requirement is 50 percent for credit life policies and 60 percent for credit disability policies. Note that the higher the loss ratio, the larger the percentage of premiums received are expected to be paid out in policy benefits.

In order to establish a benchmark for determining what premium rates satisfy this loss ratio requirement, most state insurance departments have adopted schedules that define the maximum premium rates, known as the *prima facie premium rates*, that may be charged for each type of credit insurance. A schedule of prima facie premium rates for credit disability insurance is illustrated in Figure 10-7.

A credit insurer must file its premium rates with the applicable state insurance department. If the premium rates filed exceed the state's prima facie rates, then the insurer must file actuarial calculations and memoranda that explain why the higher premium rates are necessary. An insurer may increase its premium rates by filing those rates with the state insurance department and meeting applicable loss ratio requirements. The Consumer Credit Insurance Model Regulation permits an insurer to use a premium rate that is less than its filed premium rate at any time without notifying the state insurance department. A number of states, however, require credit insurers to file all premium rates with the state insurance department.

Marketing Considerations

As with other types of life and health insurance, credit life and health insurance may be sold only by an insurer that is licensed to sell credit life or health insurance. Likewise, credit life and health insurance producers must be properly licensed by the state in which they conduct business. As noted earlier, credit insurance typically is marketed by lenders. A lender's employees who solicit the sale of credit insurance generally must be licensed by the state insurance department of each state in which those employees conduct a credit insurance business, but licensing requirements vary from state to state.

Many states provide for the licensing of *limited insurance representatives* who solicit or negotiate contracts for specified lines of insurance. A limited insurance license is not deemed to require the professional competency demanded of an insurance producer's license, and many states issue limited licenses without requiring applicants to pass a competency examination. About half of the states provide for the licensing of limited insurance representatives who sell only credit insurance. A *limited credit insurance license* permits the licensed individual to solicit the sale of credit insurance only.

FIGURE 10-7 Sample Schedule of Prima Facie Premium Rates for Credit Disability Insurance Payable in a Single Premium (Per $100 of Indebtedness).

Original number of equal monthly installments	14-day retroactive policies[a]	14-day nonretroactive policies[b]	30-day retroactive policies[c]	30-day nonretroactive policies[d]
12	$1.81	$1.15	$1.40	$0.66
24	$2.47	$1.81	$2.06	$1.31
36	$3.12	$2.47	$2.71	$1.97
48	$3.53	$2.88	$3.12	$2.38
60	$3.87	$3.21	$3.46	$2.71
72	$4.23	$3.57	$3.82	$3.07
84	$4.59	$3.93	$4.18	$3.43
96	$4.95	$4.29	$4.54	$3.79
108	$5.31	$4.65	$4.90	$4.15
120	$5.67	$5.01	$5.26	$4.51

a. Benefits are payable only after the insured has been disabled for 14 days—the elimination period—but are payable retroactively to the first day of disability.

b. Benefits are payable after the insured has been disabled for 14 days and are not payable for the elimination period.

c. Benefits are payable after a 30-day elimination period retroactively to the first day of disability.

d. Benefits are payable after a 30-day elimination period and are not payable for the elimination period.

Source: Iowa Department of Insurance, "Iowa Credit Insurance Prima Facie Rates Effective March 30, 2001," http://www.iid.state.ia.us/docs/bull0004.pdf (5 December 2001).

In many other states, individuals who sell credit life insurance must be licensed as life insurance producers and individuals who sell credit health insurance must be licensed as health insurance producers. A few states provide specified exemptions from producer licensing requirements for creditors that are group credit insurance policyholders. In these states, licenses are not required for individuals employed by a creditor that makes group credit insurance available to its debtors. A few states, however, exempt only employees who are not compensated for the solicitation of credit insurance sales.

A component of the cost of credit insurance is the compensation paid by a credit insurer to a lender that sells credit insurance coverage. Because the amount of such compensation is established by an agreement between the insurer and the lender, regulators try to keep premium costs down by limiting the amount of the compensation. The Consumer Credit Insurance Model Act defines *compensation* as any form of remuneration resulting directly from the sale of consumer credit insurance, including commissions, dividends, retrospective rate credits, service fees, expense allowances or reimbursements, gifts, or the furnishing of equipment, facilities, goods, or services. The Consumer Credit Insurance Model Regulation prohibits an insurer from paying total compensation of more than 30 percent of the net premiums written; a maximum of 25 percent of the net premium may be paid to the creditor. In many states, compensation is limited indirectly by the states' minimum loss ratio requirements. A drafting note to the Model Regulation states that the compensation limitation provision is optional and that states that have adopted prima facie premium rates based on a 60 percent loss ratio may want to do away with any specific limitation on compensation.

The Consumer Credit Insurance Model Regulation specifies a number of practices that constitute unfair methods of competition and that are subject to the applicable state's Unfair Trade Practices Act. The specified unfair practices are as follows:

- The offer or grant by an insurer to a creditor of any special advantage or any service not set out in either the group insurance contract or in the agency contract, other than the payment of agent's commissions.

- An agreement by an insurer to deposit with a bank or financial institution money or securities with the intent that the deposit take the place of a deposit that otherwise would be required of the creditor by the bank or financial institution as a compensating balance or offsetting deposit for a loan.

- The deposit by an insurer of money or securities without interest or at a lesser rate of interest than is currently being paid by the creditor, bank, or financial institution to other depositors of like amounts for similar durations. The insurer, however, may maintain demand deposits or premium deposit accounts as reasonably necessary for the ordinary course of its business.

DISCLOSURE REQUIREMENTS

The Consumer Credit Insurance Model Act requires that specified information be disclosed to debtors before they elect to purchase credit insurance in connection with a consumer credit transaction. The following information must be disclosed:

- That the purchase of the credit insurance offered by the lender is optional and not a condition of obtaining credit approval

- Whether the debtor may purchase each of several available kinds of credit insurance separately or whether multiple coverages may be purchased only as a package

- The conditions that are used to determine an individual's eligibility for credit insurance coverage

- That the consumer may already have insurance that covers the risk and, thus, may not want or need credit insurance

- That the debtor may cancel the coverage and receive a full premium refund by returning the policy or group certificate to the creditor within 30 days after receiving it; and that the debtor has the right to cancel the coverage at any time and receive a refund of any unearned premium

- A brief description of the coverage, including a description of (1) the amount of coverage, (2) the term of the coverage, (3) any exceptions, limitations, and exclusions, (4) the insured event, (5) any waiting or elimination period, (6) any deductible, (7) any applicable waiver of premium provision, (8) to whom the benefits are payable, and (9) the premium rate for each coverage or for all coverages in a package

- That if the premium is financed, the amount financed will be subject to finance charges at the interest rate applicable to the credit transaction

When credit insurance is offered at the time of the credit transaction, the foregoing disclosures must be made in writing and presented to the consumer in a clear and conspicuous manner. Likewise, the disclosures must be made in writing if credit insurance is offered by a direct mail advertisement. If credit insurance is offered after the credit transaction and by means other than direct mail, then the disclosures may be made orally. However, a written disclosure must be provided no later than the earlier of (1) 10 days after the offer of insurance or (2) the date any other written material is provided to the debtor.

CLAIMS HANDLING

The Consumer Credit Insurance Model Act contains requirements as to the payment of credit insurance claims, which must be settled as soon as possible and in accordance with the terms of the insurance contract. Only the insurer or a claim representative designated by the insurer is permitted to settle or adjust credit insurance claims. The creditor may not be designated as the insurer's claim representative. In the case of a group policy, however, the creditor as the group policyholder may draw drafts, checks, or electronic funds transfers in payment of claims due the policyholder subject to audit and review by the insurer. The Model Act also states that all claim payments must comply with requirements of the Unfair Claims Settlement Practices Act.

INSURER'S COMPLIANCE RESPONSIBILITIES

The Consumer Credit Insurance Model Regulation states that each insurer transacting credit insurance in the state is responsible for conducting a thorough periodic review of creditors with whom it conducts business. The review is designed to ensure that creditors are in compliance with applicable insurance laws and regulations. The insurer must maintain written records of all such reviews for examination by state regulators.

The Model Regulation also imposes specific reporting requirements on credit insurers. Each insurer is required to file an annual report of consumer credit insurance written during the calendar year. The report must be filed with the insurance department of each state in which the insurer conducts business and the NAIC. The NAIC has developed a standard form entitled the *Credit Insurance Supplement—Annual Statement Blank* that insurers must use to file their annual reports.

KEY TERMS AND CONCEPTS

Consumer Credit Insurance Model Act
Consumer Credit Insurance Model Regulation
closed-end credit transaction
open-end credit transaction
consumer credit insurance
credit life insurance
credit accident and health insurance
credit unemployment insurance
scheduled net debt
actual net debt
gross debt
prima facie premium rates
limited insurance representative
limited credit insurance license
compensation

ENDNOTES

1. 15 U.S.C. §§ 1601–1661e (1997).

2. 15 U.S.C. §§ 1691–1691f (1997).

3. 15 U.S.C. §§ 1681 *et seq.* (1997).

4. 15 U.S.C. §§ 41–58 (1997).

5. Consumers Union is an independent nonprofit testing, educational, and information organization serving consumers.

6. A deed of trust is a form of mortgage instrument used in some states.

CHAPTER 11

Regulation of Annuities and Retirement Products

LEARNING OBJECTIVES

After studying this chapter, you should be able to

- Identify the provisions that state insurance laws require individual annuities to contain

- Recognize the types of annuities that are subject to state nonforfeiture laws and the requirements imposed by such laws

- Describe the types of advertising and disclosure requirements the states impose on insurers that solicit the sale of annuities within those states

- Determine whether a given annuity is a variable annuity, a modified guaranteed annuity, or an equity-indexed annuity and identify the state and federal requirements imposed on each type of annuity

- Distinguish among the various types of individual and group retirement products

- Recognize the types of requirements that retirement plans must meet in order to qualify for favorable federal income tax treatment

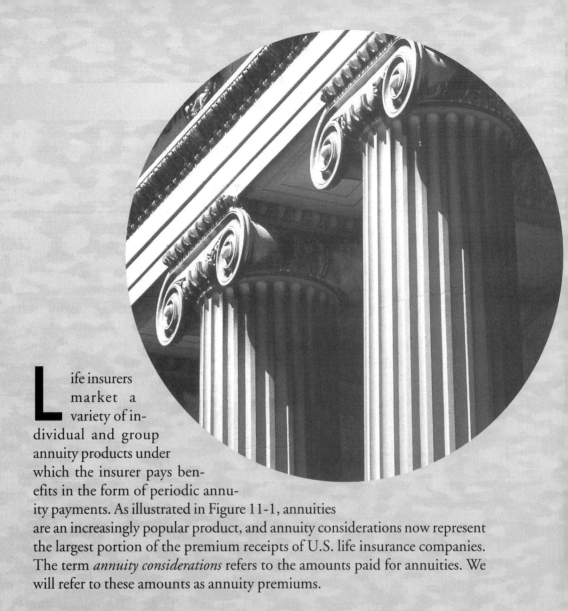

Life insurers market a variety of individual and group annuity products under which the insurer pays benefits in the form of periodic annuity payments. As illustrated in Figure 11-1, annuities are an increasingly popular product, and annuity considerations now represent the largest portion of the premium receipts of U.S. life insurance companies. The term *annuity considerations* refers to the amounts paid for annuities. We will refer to these amounts as annuity premiums.

FIGURE 11-1 **Premium Receipts of U.S. Life Insurance Companies (in Millions).**

	1990	1999	2000
Life insurance	$76,692	$120,274	$130,616
Annuity Considerations	$129,064	$270,212	$303,123
Health Insurance	$58,254	$100,049	$105,619

Source: Adapted from ACLI, *Life Insurers Fact Book: 2001* (Washington, D.C.: American Council of Life Insurers, 2001), 54. Used with permission.

In this chapter, we first describe state regulation of annuities. Then we describe the individual and group annuities that are established as retirement plans that qualify for favorable federal income tax treatment.

STATE REGULATION OF ANNUITIES

As a general rule, annuities are treated for regulatory purposes as if they were a type of life insurance. Thus, for example, in order to conduct an annuity business within a given state, an insurer generally must be licensed by that state to conduct a life insurance business and must comply with regulatory requirements imposed on life insurers. In some states, however, insurers that are licensed to sell life insurance must obtain an additional license to sell annuities. In addition, most states require an insurer to obtain specific authorization from the state insurance department before the insurer markets variable annuities. In order to solicit the sale of annuities, insurance producers generally must be licensed to sell life insurance and must comply with regulatory requirements imposed on life insurance producers.

Product Development

The same general types of regulatory compliance considerations that apply to the development of life insurance products apply to the development of annuity products. The specific regulatory requirements imposed on annuities vary somewhat depending on the specific features of a given annuity. For example, deferred annuities are subject to more regulatory requirements than are immediate annuities. (A glossary of terminology used in connection with annuities is provided in Figure 11-2.) Regardless of the features of an annuity, most states require an insurer to file an annuity contract form with and receive the approval of the state insurance department before delivering or issuing the annuity contract for delivery within the state.

FIGURE 11-2 Glossary of Terms Used in Connection with Annuities.

Accumulated value   At any given date during the accumulation period of a fixed deferred annuity, the net amount paid for the annuity, plus interest earned, less the amount of any withdrawals. The accumulated value of a variable deferred annuity on a given date is calculated based on the value of the contractholder's interest in the separate accounts used to fund the annuity.

Accumulation period   The period between the contractholder's purchase of a deferred annuity and the annuity date.

Figure 11-2. Glossary of Terms Used in Connection with Annuities, *continued*.

Annuitant — The individual whose life is used to measure the payout period of a life annuity and who usually receives the annuity benefit payments.

Annuity date — The date on which the insurer is scheduled to begin making annuity benefit payments. Often referred to as the **maturity date** or **income date**. Some insurers use the term *annuity date* to refer to a date one month before annuity benefit payments are scheduled to begin when the insurers evaluate the annuities and determine the amounts of periodic benefit payments.

Annuity period — The time span between each of the periodic annuity benefit payments due under an annuity contract. Thus, if benefits are payable monthly, then the annuity period is one month.

Contractholder — The owner of an annuity contract. The contractholder usually is also the annuitant.

Deferred annuity — An annuity under which periodic benefit payments are scheduled to begin more than 12 months after the date on which the annuity is purchased. Deferred annuities often are purchased to provide retirement incomes to contractholders.

Fixed annuity — An annuity under which the insurer guarantees that at least a defined amount of periodic annuity benefit will be provided for each dollar applied to purchasing the annuity. The insurer assumes the annuity contract's investment risk.

Flexible-premium annuity — An annuity purchased by the payment of periodic premiums; the contractholder has the right to pay any premium amount within a specified range of amounts.

Immediate annuity — An annuity under which periodic benefit payments are scheduled to begin within 12 months after the annuity is purchased.

Payout period — The period during which the insurer makes annuity benefit payments.

Single-premium annuity — An annuity purchased by the payment of a single, lump-sum premium.

Variable annuity — An annuity under which the amount of the policy's accumulated value and the amount of the periodic annuity benefit payments fluctuate in accordance with the performance of a specified pool of investments. The purchaser assumes most of the annuity contract's investment risk.

Contract Form Development

Many of the provisions included in life insurance policies also are included in annuity contracts. The state regulatory requirements that specify the provisions that are required, optional, and prohibited in life insurance policies also govern annuity contracts. (These requirements are described in Chapter 1.) State insurance laws generally require individual annuity contracts to include the following provisions:

- An *entire contract provision* stating that the entire contract consists of the annuity contract, the application if it is attached to the contract, and any attached riders and endorsements.

- A *free-look provision* that gives the contractholder a specified period, usually 10 days, within which to return the annuity and receive a full refund of all premiums paid. Most states require the free-look provision to be included on the annuity face page.

- A *misstatement of age provision* stating that if the annuitant's age was misstated, then the annuity benefits payable will be those that the premiums paid would have purchased for the correct age. As in the case of the provision included in life insurance policies, the misstatement of age provision included in annuity contracts also usually provides for the adjustment of benefits if the annuitant's sex was misstated.

- Annuities generally include an *incontestability provision*, but the terms of the provision vary depending on the types of questions contained in the application for the annuity. Typically, the application for an annuity does not contain questions relating to the insurability of the applicant, and, thus, the applicant does not make representations on which the insurer bases its decision to issue an annuity. In such cases, the incontestability provision states that, once the annuity contract becomes effective, the insurer may not contest the validity of the contract. Some insurers offer supplementary benefit riders, such as a waiver of premium for disability benefit rider. The applicant for such a rider generally must provide evidence of insurability, and the annuity's incontestability provision in such cases gives the insurer a specified period—such as one or two years—in which to contest the validity of the coverage provided by the rider based on a material misrepresentation in the application.

- Participating annuities must include a *dividend provision* that describes the contractholder's right to share in the insurer's divisible surplus, if any, and the dividend payment options available to the contractholder.

- Deferred annuities must include *nonforfeiture provisions* that we describe in the next section concerning actuarial considerations in annuity product development.

- Deferred annuities must include a *settlement options provision* that describes the contractholder's right to select the terms on which the insurer will pay periodic annuity benefits.

Although most annuities are single-premium or flexible-premium annuities, annuities may be purchased with the payment of fixed, scheduled premium payments. Because they require the payment of fixed, regular premiums, such scheduled-premium annuities must include a *grace period provision* that grants the contractholder the right to pay any premium within a specified period following the premium due date. Scheduled-premium annuities also must contain a *reinstatement provision* giving the contractholder the right to reinstate the contract to fully paid-up status by paying all unpaid and outstanding premiums.

Actuarial Considerations

As with the development of all insurance products, the development of an annuity requires the work of actuaries who must perform a variety of mathematical calculations. Actuarial features of annuities are subject to regulatory requirements that are similar to the requirements imposed on the actuarial features of life insurance products. All states have enacted laws based on the NAIC *Standard Valuation Law*, which establishes minimum requirements for the reserve liabilities that insurers must establish for both life insurance and annuity policies. In addition, almost all of the states have enacted laws based on the NAIC *Standard Nonforfeiture Law for Individual Deferred Annuities*, which requires individual deferred annuities to provide minimum nonforfeiture values. This Standard Nonforfeiture Law does *not* apply to the following types of annuities:

- Group annuities purchased under a retirement plan or deferred compensation plan established or maintained by an employer or employee organization

- Individual immediate annuities

- Variable annuities

A deferred annuity contract subject to the Standard Nonforfeiture Law must include the following provisions:

- If the contractholder stops paying required premiums, then the contract must provide a paid-up annuity benefit. The amount of the periodic annuity benefit payable must equal at least a minimum amount specified in the Standard Nonforfeiture Law.

- If the annuity provides for the lump-sum payment of annuity benefits at the maturity date, then it must provide a cash surrender benefit if the contractholder surrenders the contract or stops paying premiums before the maturity date. The amount of the cash surrender value must be calculated in accordance with the Standard Nonforfeiture Law's minimum nonforfeiture requirements.

- The annuity contract must identify the mortality table, if any, and the minimum guaranteed interest rate that will be used to calculate any paid-up annuity benefit or cash surrender benefit, along with enough information to determine the amounts of those benefits.

- The annuity contract must include an explanation of how the amounts of any paid-up annuity benefits or cash surrender benefits payable under the contract are affected by the existence of any additional amounts the insurer has credited to the contract, any indebtedness to the insurer on the contract, or any prior withdrawals from the contract.

The Standard Nonforfeiture Law imposes nonforfeiture requirements only during the accumulation period of a deferred annuity. At the annuity's maturity date, the insurer's liability to provide annuity benefit payments in accordance with the contract is fixed by the terms of the contract.

Contract Form Filing

In general, the types of materials and information included in an annuity contract filing submission package are the same as those included in a life insurance policy form submission package. The specific information included in an annuity contract form filing submission package varies depending on the features of the annuity product and how the product is purchased. For example, insurers often sell *structured settlement annuities*, which are immediate annuities issued to a person who is entitled to receive a sum of money from a third party. Typically, structured settlement annuities are issued to individuals who have agreed to settle a civil claim in exchange for a specified sum of money to be paid in the form of an annuity and to individuals who have won prizes or lotteries that are to be paid in the form of an annuity. In such cases, the insurer generally is willing to modify certain annuity contract provisions in order to tailor the annuity to fit the terms on which the third party has agreed to pay the annuitant. If the insurer knows that an annuity contract form may be modified for purposes of a structured settlement agreement, then the insurer must include that information in the filing submission package and must describe any such potential modifications to the contract form.

Advertising and Disclosure Requirements

Insurers that market annuities typically must comply with the same or similar regulatory requirements that apply to the sale of life insurance. As described in Chapter 2, many of these regulatory requirements are contained in the state Unfair Trade Practices Acts and in rules and regulations that govern the advertising of life insurance and annuities. State regulations based on the NAIC *Advertisements of Life Insurance and Annuities Model Regulation* apply equally to the advertising of annuities as they do to the advertising of life insurance.

Some states impose additional disclosure requirements on insurers that market annuities. A number of states, for example, have adopted regulations based on the NAIC **Annuity Disclosure Model Regulation**, which requires insurers to provide prospective purchasers of specified types of annuities with information to help them select an annuity appropriate to their needs. The Model Regulation applies to group annuities and individual deferred annuities. Note that individual immediate annuities are not subject to the Model Regulation. In addition, the following types of group and individual deferred annuities are exempt from the Model Regulation's requirements because they are subject to other laws and regulations that impose similar disclosure requirements:

- Variable annuities
- Charitable gift annuities and funding agreements
- Structured settlement annuities
- Contracts registered with the federal Securities and Exchange Commission (SEC)
- Individual retirement accounts and individual retirement annuities
- Contracts that are issued in connection with employee benefit plans and, thus, are subject to regulation by the federal Employee Retirement Income Security Act (ERISA)
- Contracts that are issued in connection with a governmental plan or church plan as defined by Section 414 of the Internal Revenue Code
- Contracts that are issued in connection with tax-exempt organizations as defined by Section 457 of the Internal Revenue Code
- Deferred compensation plans of a state or local government
- Nonqualified deferred compensation plans

The Annuity Disclosure Model Regulation requires an insurer to provide prospective purchasers of annuity contracts with a ***Buyer's Guide to Fixed Deferred Annuities*** that describes the differences among the various types of annuities. The Buyer's Guide discusses the following features of fixed deferred annuities:

- The method for determining interest rates for the annuity
- Any charges or fees associated with the annuity
- Benefits associated with the annuity
- Tax treatment of the annuity
- Questions or factors to consider before purchasing the annuity

In addition, the insurer must provide a prospect with a ***disclosure document*** that identifies and describes the specific annuity being considered and that includes the following types of information:

- The product name, the company name if different, the generic name of the contract, the form number, and a statement confirming that the contract is an annuity contract
- The name and address of the insurer
- The guaranteed and nonguaranteed elements of the contract
- An explanation of the initial crediting rate
- Any periodic income options
- Any value reductions caused by withdrawals or surrender of the contract
- The method by which contract values can be accessed
- Any death benefit and how it can be calculated
- The federal tax status of the contract and any penalties that may occur for withdrawing value from the contract
- The impact of any rider on the contract
- The specific dollar amount charges or percentage charges that apply to the contract
- A notice that the current guaranteed rate for new contracts is subject to change

REGULATION OF SPECIFIC ANNUITY PRODUCTS

Insurers market a variety of annuity products, and some products are subject to specific regulatory requirements. In this section, we describe state and federal regulation of variable annuities, modified guaranteed annuities, and equity-indexed annuities.

Variable Annuities

Variable annuities are subject to both federal and state regulation. Because variable annuities are securities, they are subject to federal securities laws. In addition, insurers that issue variable annuities must comply with state regulatory requirements governing annuities and specific state requirements that are imposed on only variable annuities. Requirements in almost half the states are based on the NAIC *Model Variable Annuity Regulation*, which establishes qualifications an insurer must meet in order to market variable annuities and specifies requirements that variable annuities must meet. The qualifications an insurer must meet are similar to the requirements imposed on insurers that market variable life insurance (see Chapter 1). The state insurance department must be satisfied that the insurer's financial condition will not be harmed by its sale of variable annuities. The insurer must file variable annuity contract forms with and receive approval from the state insurance department before using those forms within the state. The Model Regulation requires variable annuities to provide minimum nonforfeiture values that are generally the same as those required by the Standard Nonforfeiture Law for Individual Deferred Annuities. The Model Regulation also governs how insurers invest the assets of the separate accounts established to fund variable annuities and establishes minimum reserve requirements.

The face page of a variable annuity contract must contain a clear statement that the benefits provided by the contract are variable. The contract also must include a description of the procedures the insurer will follow to determine the amount of benefits payable.

Modified Guaranteed Annuities

Insurers market some annuity products that are hybrids containing features of various types of annuities, and the states take a variety of approaches to regulating such products. Insurers must carefully review specific requirements in each state because of the variety of regulations and the differences in how the states define specific annuity products. For example, a number of states impose specific regulatory requirements on modified guaranteed annuities, but the definitions of such annuities for regulatory purposes vary from state to state. Some states' laws are based on the NAIC *Modified Guaranteed Annuity Regulation*, which defines a *modified guaranteed annuity* as a deferred annuity for which the underlying assets are held in a separate account but the contract values are guaranteed if held for a specified time. Modified guaranteed annuities have variable premiums as opposed to fixed premiums.

In general, the Modified Guaranteed Annuity Regulation imposes requirements similar to those imposed by the Model Variable Annuity Regulation. Before an insurer markets modified guaranteed annuities within a state that has adopted the Modified Guaranteed Annuity Regulation, the state insurance commissioner must be satisfied that the insurer's financial condition will not be jeopardized by the sale of such products. In addition, the insurer's sales producers must be licensed to sell variable annuities.

Before an insurer may sell modified guaranteed annuities within a state that has adopted the Modified Guaranteed Annuity Regulation, it must submit to the state insurance commissioner a description of the types of annuities it intends to sell. The commissioner may request the following items:

- A copy of the statutes and regulations of the insurer's state of domicile under which it has received prior authorization to sell modified guaranteed annuities

- Biographical data of the officers and directors of the insurer

The Modified Guaranteed Annuity Regulation specifies that modified guaranteed annuity contracts must contain, in general, the following provisions:

- A provision outlining the specific procedures to be followed by an insurer in determining the dollar amount of nonforfeiture benefits

- A provision stating that if premium payments cease under the contract, the insurer will grant a paid-up annuity benefit in accordance with specified procedures

- A provision stating that if the contract provides for a lump sum settlement at its maturity date or at any other time, upon surrender of the contract, the insurer will pay the appropriate cash surrender benefit. The contract may specify that the insurer may defer payment of the cash surrender benefit for a period of six months

If a modified guaranteed annuity contract allows for the payment of periodic stipulated payments, then the contract must contain:

- A provision allowing a 30-day grace period during which the contract remains in force and the contractholder may make any payment due the insurer

- A provision allowing reinstatement of a policy that has lapsed within one year from the date of default. During this one year, the contractholder may pay any overdue premiums and interest to the insurer

Equity-Indexed Annuities

In the mid-1990s, a number of insurers began to offer *equity-indexed annuities*, which provide for the level of interest credits to be linked to an external standard, typically the S&P 500.[1] These products, which are also known as *interest-indexed annuities*, are similar to the interest-indexed universal life policies described in Chapter 1. Like all annuity products, equity-indexed annuities are regulated by the states. In addition, depending on the features of a given product, an equity-indexed annuity may be subject to federal regulation as a security.

At the time of this writing, most equity-indexed policies were considered to be insurance products and not securities and were, therefore, not registered with the SEC. An annuity (or life insurance) product must meet a three-part test in order to be exempt from federal registration as a security.

The first requirement for exemption from federal registration is that the contract be issued by a corporation subject to the supervision of a state insurance commissioner, bank commissioner, or similar state regulator. Annuities issued by insurers meet this requirement.

The second requirement is that the contract's investment risk must be borne by the issuer of the contract. An insurer assumes the investment risk of a contract if the following conditions are met:

- The contract's value does not vary based on the investment experience of a separate account. Equity-indexed annuities usually are general account products and, thus, meet this requirement.

- The insurer guarantees the principal amount of purchase payments and credited interest, less any deduction for sales, administrative, or other expenses or charges. Equity-indexed annuities generally guarantee the return of 90 percent of the purchase price. Note that insurers are entitled to deduct reasonable charges to cover sales, administrative, and other expenses.

- The insurer credits a specified minimum rate of interest to the principal; the required rate is the minimum required by applicable state law. Equity-indexed annuities generally guarantee a minimum annual interest rate of three percent, which is the minimum required by most state insurance laws.

- The insurer guarantees that, if it pays more than the minimum guaranteed interest rate, it will modify that interest rate no more than once a year. Any formula an insurer uses to calculate contract values using an interest index must comply with this requirement in order for the annuity to be exempt from federal registration requirements.

The final requirement for an annuity (or life insurance) product to be exempt from federal registration as a security is that the product must not be marketed primarily as an investment. The SEC has expressed concern that the nature of equity-indexed annuities makes it particularly difficult for insurers to market these products without primarily emphasizing their investment aspects.[2]

The appendix to the Buyer's Guide to Fixed Deferred Annuities contains the *Buyer's Guide to Equity-Indexed Annuities* that describes specific features of equity-indexed annuities and explains ways in which equity-indexed annuities differ from other annuities. This Buyer's Guide also discusses common contract features of equity-indexed annuities.

REGULATION OF RETIREMENT PRODUCTS

Insurers market a variety of individual and group annuity products that are designed to provide benefits in the form of a retirement income. These products enable people to pay premiums or to make contributions during their working years and then receive an income stream in their later years. Retirement annuities must comply with the various state insurance laws that govern annuities. In addition, federal laws provide income tax advantages to individuals and businesses that deposit funds into specified types of retirement savings plans.

In order to develop products that are likely to be attractive to potential purchasers, insurers seek to ensure that the retirement products they develop comply with applicable requirements and qualify for favorable federal income tax treatment. A complete discussion of the taxation of retirement products marketed by insurers is beyond the scope of this text. Rather, our focus will be on the general requirements that retirement products marketed by insurers must meet in order to qualify for favorable federal income tax treatment and insurers' compliance responsibilities for the annuity products they issue.

Individual Retirement Plans

Federal laws provide income tax benefits to individuals who establish individual retirement plans that meet specified requirements. Figure 11-3 provides a general overview of the characteristics and federal income tax treatment of individual retirement plans, which the IRS refers to as *individual retirement arrangements (IRAs)*. According to the federal income tax laws, an individual retirement arrangement may take one of two forms:

- An *individual retirement account* that is a trust account created in the United States for the exclusive benefit of an individual and his beneficiaries; the trustee must be a bank, investment company, or similar organization. Note that such organizations use the acronym IRA to refer to individual retirement accounts.

- An *individual retirement annuity* that is issued by an insurance company.[3] Insurers generally use the acronym IRA to refer to individual retirement annuity products.

In order for an individual retirement annuity to qualify for favorable federal income tax treatment, it must meet the following requirements:

- The annuity contract must be nontransferable by the owner.

- The premiums cannot be fixed. In other words, the annuity contract cannot require the contractholder to make scheduled premium payments.

- Beginning January 1, 2002, the maximum annual contribution a taxpayer may make to an IRA is $3,000. In 2005, the limit is $4,000, and in 2008, the limit increases to $5,000. The maximum annual deduction for contributions to an IRA is equal to the maximum annual contribution limit in a given year. In specified circumstances, a contractholder may be permitted to make contributions in excess of the maximum annual contribution limit. Beginning January 1, 2002, individuals age 50 and older may contribute an additional $500 to an IRA in addition to the regular maximum contribution limit. Beginning in 2006, individuals age 50 and older may contribute $1,000 to an IRA in addition to the regular contribution limit. Figure 11-4 shows the maximum annual IRA contribution amounts for years 2002 through 2008.

- Any premium refunds must be applied to the payment of future premiums or the purchase of additional benefits. Thus, dividends paid on participating annuities cannot be paid in cash.

- The owner's interest in the annuity contract must be nonforfeitable.

The insurer may include these required provisions either as part of the annuity contract itself or as an endorsement to the contract.

FIGURE 11-3 Taxation of Individual Retirement Arrangements (IRAs).

Eligible individuals can choose to contribute to a traditional or a Roth IRA. Taxpayers face different tax issues depending on the type of IRA they choose to establish. Since 1974, certain individuals have been able to establish and make contributions to an IRA, now referred to as a *traditional IRA*. A traditional IRA is subject to the following federal tax laws:

- Anyone who is less than age 70½ and who has taxable income can contribute up to $3,000 per year of earned income to a traditional IRA.
- Some or all contributions to a traditional IRA are tax-deductible. Taxation of interest earnings, however, is deferred until funds are withdrawn from a traditional IRA.
- With specified exceptions, tax penalties are imposed on withdrawals made before the taxpayer attains age 59½.
- Taxpayers must begin making annual withdrawals of at least a specified minimum amount when they reach age 70½, and after that time, they may not make additional contributions to their traditional IRAs. Traditional IRAs are subject to a 50 percent tax penalty if distributions do not begin by age 70½. If an individual has more than one IRA, he is not required to meet the specified minimum withdrawal requirement for each IRA. He may satisfy the withdrawal requirement by taking distributions from one or from more than one IRA, as long as his total withdrawals from all IRAs equal the minimum distribution requirement.

Another type of IRA available to eligible individuals since January 1, 1998, is known as a *Roth IRA*. This type of IRA operates much the same way as a regular IRA. For example, Roth IRAs have the same annual contribution limits as traditional IRAs. However, notable differences exist between a traditional IRA and a Roth IRA:

- A taxpayer may contribute to a Roth IRA only if her adjusted gross income is (1) less than $160,000 if she is married and filing a joint return, (2) less than $110,000 if she is filing a single or head-of-household return, or (3) less than $10,000 if she is married and filing a separate return.
- No tax deduction is allowed for contributions to a Roth IRA, but, unlike a traditional IRA, interest earnings from a Roth IRA are not taxable.
- Qualified withdrawals from a Roth IRA that the taxpayer has held for at least five years are not subject to income taxation. Qualified withdrawals include withdrawals taken after age 59½ and withdrawals by a qualified first-time homebuyer.
- A Roth IRA is not subject to a 50 percent tax penalty on distributions that begin after age 70½.

Taxpayers who meet specified requirements are permitted to convert a regular IRA to a Roth IRA. Generally, individuals who are eligible to make such a conversion are those who (1) have an adjusted gross income in the year of conversion of $100,000 or less *and* (2) are not married or, if married, file a joint income tax return in the year of conversion.

FIGURE 11-4 IRA Annual Contribution Limits.

Year	Regular Contribution Limit	Age 50 and Older Contribution Limit
2002	$3,000	$3,500
2003	$3,000	$3,500
2004	$3,000	$3,500
2005	$4,000	$4,500
2006	$4,000	$5,000
2007	$4,000	$5,000
2008	$5,000	$6,000

Federal tax laws require an insurer that issues individual retirement annuities to provide purchasers of such annuities with specified information. At least seven days before an individual purchases an individual retirement annuity, the insurer is required to provide the individual with the following documents:

- A *disclosure statement* that provides nontechnical explanations of the operation of an individual retirement annuity, including explanations of the statutory requirements for such an annuity, the income tax consequences of purchasing such an annuity, and the tax consequences of specific types of transactions relating to the annuity. Rather than including all of this information in the disclosure statement, the insurer may provide the purchaser with an IRS publication that contains the required information.

- A copy of the annuity contract form that will be purchased, including the individual retirement annuity endorsement.

- An IRS determination letter. Before marketing an individual retirement annuity product, the insurer usually seeks from the Internal Revenue Service (IRS) a determination as to whether the annuity contract meets the requirements of an individual retirement annuity. The IRS, which imposes a fee for each such determination, evaluates each request and sends the insurer a *determination letter* stating either that the plan appears to meet the requirements or that the plan does not meet the requirements. A favorable determination letter provides a determination only that the annuity meets the minimum regulatory requirements and does not represent a determination as to the merits of the annuity. An unfavorable determination letter identifies the plan provisions that do not comply with applicable requirements. A determination letter usually instructs insurers to inform prospects as to whether an annuity contract has received a favorable determination from the IRS. Figure 11-5 shows a sample IRS determination letter.

The insurer is permitted to provide the disclosure statement and annuity contract as late as the date of purchase if the purchaser has at least seven days in which to revoke the purchase and receive a full premium refund. Recall that states typically require individual annuities to include a free-look period of at least 10 days.

The insurer is responsible for keeping accurate records of the activity relating to each individual retirement annuity it issues. It must provide contractholders with an annual report that summarizes plan contributions, plan withdrawals, and interest earnings. When an insurer begins making taxable benefit payments under an individual retirement annuity, the insurer is responsible for reporting withdrawals to the IRS. The insurer also is responsible for withholding from annuity benefit payments a specified amount for payment of income taxes, unless the payee waives such withholding in writing.

Group Retirement Plans

Many employers provide retirement plans for their employees, and those plans are subject to federal regulation as are other employee benefit plans. As noted in an earlier chapter, the federal Employee Retirement Income Security Act (ERISA) is designed to ensure that certain minimum plan requirements are included in employee benefit plans.[4] ERISA also provides the majority of pension plan legislation in the United States. For ERISA purposes, a *pension plan* is any plan, fund, or program that is established or maintained by an employer or by an employee organization and that (1) provides retirement income to employees or (2) results in a deferral of income by employees for periods extending to the termination of employment or beyond. Figure 11-6 identifies and describes some of the various types of group retirement plans that are subject to ERISA's requirements.

FIGURE 11-5 Internal Revenue Service Determination Letter.

Internal Revenue Service

Plan Name: IRA Annuity Contract
FFN: Case: EIN:
Letter Serial No.:

Department of the Treasury
Washington, DC 20224
Person to Contact:
Telephone Number:
Date:

Dear Applicant:

In our opinion, the form of the prototype trust, custodial account, or annuity contract identified above is acceptable under Section 408 of the Internal Revenue Code, as amended by the Tax Reform Act of 1986.

Each individual who adopts this approved plan will be considered to have a retirement savings program that satisfies the requirements of Code Section 408, provided they follow the terms of the program, do not engage in certain transactions specified in Code Section 408(e), and, if the arrangement is a trust or custodial account, the trustee or custodian is a bank within the meaning of Code Section 408(n) or has been approved by the Internal Revenue Service pursuant to Code Section 408(a)(2). Please provide a copy of this letter to each person affected.

The Internal Revenue Service has not evaluated the merits of this savings program and does not guarantee contributions or investments made under the savings program. Furthermore, this letter does express any opinion as the applicability of Code Section 4975, regarding prohibited transactions.

Code Section 4089(i) and related regulations require that the trustee, custodian, or issuer of a contract provide a disclosure statement to each participant in this program as specified in the regulations. Publication 590, Tax Information on Individual Retirement Arrangements, gives information about the items to be disclosed. The trustee, custodian, or issuer of a contract is also required to provide each adopting individual with annual reports of savings program transactions.

Your program may have to be amended to include or revise provisions in order to comply with future changes in the law or regulations.

If you have any questions concerning IRS processing of this case, call us at the above telephone number. Please refer to the File Folder Number (FFN) shown in the heading of this letter. Please provide those adopting this plan with your telephone number, and advise them to contact your office if they have any questions about the operation of this plan.

You should keep this letter as a permanent record. Please notify us if you terminate the form of this plan.

Sincerely yours,

FIGURE 11-6 **Types of Group Retirement Plans.**

> **Pension plan.** A plan established by an employer to provide its employees with a pension in the form of a lifetime monthly income benefit that begins at retirement; the employer also agrees to fund at least a portion of the plan's promised benefits. Pension plans may be categorized as either defined benefit plans or defined contribution plans.
>
> **Profit sharing plan.** A type of defined contribution retirement plan that is funded primarily by employer contributions payable from the employer's profits. Contributions to a qualified plan must be substantial and recurring and cannot unduly benefit highly paid employees. Because employer contributions are based on profits, the amount of such contributions may vary from year to year. The employer, however, may make contributions in years in which its business is not profitable.
>
> **Thrift and savings plan.** A type of savings plan to which the employer is obligated to make contributions on behalf of an employee if that employee also makes a specified contribution to the plan.
>
> **Stock bonus plan.** A type of savings plan that is funded primarily by employer contributions and that provides benefits in the form of shares of stock issued by the employer.
>
> **401(k) plan.** A type of profit sharing or stock bonus plan to which participating employees may make tax-deductible contributions.

ERISA requires retirement plans to be established and maintained in accordance with a written plan document that describes the benefits provided, how the plan will be funded, and the procedure that will be followed to amend the plan. Plan participants and beneficiaries who are receiving plan benefits must be provided with a summary plan description that is understandable by the average plan participant and that reasonably apprises participants and beneficiaries of their rights and obligations under the plan. The plan description and summary plan description must contain the following types of information:

- The name and address of the *plan administrator*, which is the individual or organization designated in the plan description as being responsible for ensuring the plan complies with applicable regulatory requirements
- The names and addresses of all plan trustees, if applicable
- The plan's requirements relating to eligibility for participation and benefits
- A description of the provisions regarding nonforfeitable pension benefits
- A description of circumstances that may result in disqualification, ineligibility, or denial or loss of benefits
- The source of financing of the plan
- The identity of any organization through which plan benefits are provided
- The date of the end of the plan year and whether the plan's records are kept on a calendar-year, policy-year, or fiscal-year basis
- The procedures to be followed in presenting claims for benefits under the plan
- The remedies available for the redress of claims that are denied in whole or in part

A group retirement plan that meets requirements imposed by ERISA and the federal tax laws qualifies for favorable federal income tax treatment. Plans that meet these federal regulatory requirements are known as *qualified plans*. The tax laws provide incentives that benefit both the *plan sponsors*—the employers and unions that establish the plans—and the *plan participants*—the employees and union members who are covered by the plans.

In order to qualify for favorable income tax treatment, a group retirement plan must have been established in the United States by an employer for the exclusive benefit of its employees or the beneficiaries named by those employees. The plan also must comply with regulatory standards that impose a variety of requirements designed to protect plan participants. Although the full breadth of these regulatory requirements is beyond the scope of this text, we describe a number of the requirements imposed on qualified plans, including minimum participation requirements, minimum vesting requirements, nondiscrimination requirements, and distribution requirements. These are general requirements imposed on all qualified pension plans. In many cases, more specific regulatory requirements apply depending on the type of plan. For example, specific rules often are imposed on defined benefit pension plans and, different rules are imposed on defined contribution pension plans. These differences reflect differences in how the plans operate. A *defined benefit plan* is a retirement plan that defines the amount of the benefit each plan participant will receive at retirement; the plan sponsor is obligated to deposit enough assets into the plan to provide the promised benefits. A *defined contribution plan* is a retirement plan that describes the annual contribution the employer will deposit into the plan on behalf of each plan participant; at retirement, the amount of a participant's benefit is calculated based on the accumulated value of contributions made by or on behalf of the participant. Retirement plans generally can all be classified as either defined benefit plans or defined contribution plans. Because defined contribution plans are increasing in popularity among employers, many plan participants feel the need for professional investment advice concerning how to invest their retirement savings. Insight 11-1 discusses legislation passed by the U.S. House of Representatives that would give plan participants broader access to investment advice.

Minimum Participation Requirements

Each plan defines the requirements employees must meet in order to participate in the plan. Federal laws require plans to contain at least the following minimum participation standards:

- In order to participate in the plan, an employee cannot be required to complete a period of service beyond the later of one year or the employee's attainment of age 21. Thus, the minimum age requirement cannot be less than 21 *and* individuals who meet the age requirement must be eligible to participate after completing one year of employment. For example, an employee who is age 19 when she begins employment may be barred from participation until she attains age 21. An employee who is 21 when he begins employment may be required to complete one year of service before being eligible to participate in the retirement plan. One exception is that, if employees are fully vested after two years of service, then the plan may impose a minimum service requirement of two years. (We describe vesting in the next section.) In addition, regulatory requirements define how a year of service is measured.

- The plan generally cannot exclude employees who have attained a specified maximum age.

INSIGHT 11-1 House Passes Investment Adviser Legislation.

By a 280-to-144 vote, the House of Representatives approved H.R. 2269, "The Retirement Security Advice Act of 2001," a measure strongly supported by the American Council of Life Insurers (ACLI) that would provide pension plan participants easier access to investment advice that they want and need at the workplace.

"Perhaps more than ever, workers want and need help in managing their retirement savings. This is the right legislation, approved by the House at the right time," said Kathryn Ricard, ACLI Vice President, Retirement and Pensions.

A recent ACLI survey on investment advice found that while 51 percent of 401(k) plan participants are very comfortable making investment decisions with their retirement savings, 41 percent are only somewhat comfortable, and eight percent are not comfortable at all making the investment decisions on which their retirement security will depend.

Driving the need for the legislation is the declining popularity of traditional "defined benefit" pension plans, where employers assume all the investment risks. These were the dominant pension plans when Congress passed the Employee Retirement Income Security Act of 1974 (ERISA). They promised workers a specific, lifetime income in retirement, typically based on salary and years of service with an employer.

Today, more and more employers are setting up "defined contribution" plans, such as 401(k) plans. Some 44 million workers participate in 345,000 401(k) plans with assets totaling over $2 trillion. In 1990, by contrast, 20 million participated in less than 100,000 plans with assets of $4 billion. These plans are very popular with workers: they are portable, and they give the worker the opportunity to track the growth of their retirement nest egg. Still, they provide no guaranteed income in retirement and place all the investment risk on the worker.

"Some people may be comfortable managing their retirement savings, but many are not. Investment decisions made today can have enormous consequences in the future, which is why good advice is so critical," Ricard said.

"This legislation aims to help workers get the advice from trained financial professionals so that they can look forward to financially secure retirement," she said.

"The Retirement Security Advice Act of 2001" would allow life insurers—who already manage nearly $2 trillion in retirement savings and pension assets—and other financial services companies that provide plans and educational materials to plan sponsors and participants, to also provide them with investment advice. Presently, ERISA's conflict of interest rules bar such activity. The reform bill maintains the conflict of interest rules, but relies on a disclosure approach—modeled on federal securities laws B to replace the ERISA prohibitions against providing investment advice.

The bill also contains an important "plain English" provision, designed to ensure plan participants receive information they understand as they decide whether to seek investment advice. Examples would include explanations of fees charged to participants and conflict of interest disclosures.

The bill also ensures that advice provided by life insurers and other financial firms is in the best interest of the worker. It does this by establishing a fiduciary relationship between the investment adviser and the worker.

"'The Retirement Security Advice Act of 2001' maintains ERISA protections and addresses today's retirement savings environment. It would ensure that the landmark federal pension law that is more than a quarter century old reflects the needs of workers today," Ricard added.

The American Council of Life Insurers is a Washington, D.C.-based trade association. Its more than 400 member companies offer life insurance, annuities, pensions, long-term care insurance, disability income insurance and other retirement and financial protection products.

Source: Excerpted from Insurance News Net, "House Passes Investment Adviser Legislation," 15 November 2001, http://www.insurancenewsnet.com (26 November 2001). Used with permission.

Defined benefit plans also must meet minimum requirements as to the number of plan participants. At the time of this writing, minimum participation requirements are met if the plan covers at least a specified number of employees or a specified percentage of all employees.

Minimum Vesting Requirements

A participant is *vested* when he has the right to receive partial or full benefits under the plan even if he terminates employment prior to retirement. Qualified plans must provide that each participant is immediately vested in the accrued benefit funded by his own contributions; a participant's right to such benefits is nonforfeitable. Qualified retirement plans also must include minimum vesting standards that specify when a plan participant has the right to receive benefits funded by employer contributions. The plan must provide for each participant's vesting in benefits funded by employer contributions by one of two specified methods.

- The participant has the right to receive 100 percent of her accrued benefit after completing three years of service.

- The participant has the right to receive her accrued benefit in accordance with the following schedule:

Years of Service	Nonforfeitable %
2	20
3	40
4	60
5	80
6	100

A plan may specify that one of these methods will be used to establish the vesting schedule for one group of participants and that the other method will be used for other groups of participants.

Nondiscrimination Requirements

Three general requirements are imposed to ensure that plans do not unfairly discriminate in favor of employees who are "highly compensated" as defined by federal tax laws.

1. Contributions or benefits may not discriminate in favor of highly compensated employees. Note that this requirement contains the word "or."

Thus, either contributions or benefits can discriminate, but both contributions and benefits cannot discriminate.

2. Benefits, rights, and features provided under the plan must be made available to employees in a nondiscriminatory manner.

3. The effect of plan amendments and plan terminations must be nondiscriminatory.

The tax laws and IRS regulations contain complex rules and tests that are used to evaluate whether a plan complies with each of these requirements.

Distribution Requirements

Federal income tax laws impose several requirements on the distribution of retirement plan benefits. Some plans, primarily defined benefit pension plans, must provide that retirement benefits will be paid in the form of a qualified joint-and-survivor annuity. Thus, surviving spouses of deceased plan participants must be provided with specified survivor benefits. This requirement may be waived by a plan participant but only with the consent of the participant's spouse. The plan may provide unmarried plan participants with a life annuity.

Qualified plans must contain specified provisions regarding when plan benefits will begin to be paid. The current general rule requires that benefits begin not later than April 1 of the calendar year following the later of (1) the year in which the participant attains age 70½ or (2) the year in which the participant retires from the employer. Plans also must comply with requirements specifying the periods over which retirement benefits must be paid out. Penalties are imposed on plan participants for whom these distribution requirements are not met, and a plan's failure to meet such requirements may result in the plan's losing its tax-qualified status.

Other Requirements

A variety of additional requirements are imposed on qualified retirement plans. For example, maximum limitations are imposed on plan contributions and benefits. In addition, employer contributions are subject to minimum funding requirements and the plan must prohibit the assignment of plan benefits.

Plans must contain specified provisions that comply with ERISA rules relating to "top-heavy" plans. A ***top-heavy plan*** is a plan under which, for a given plan year, the present value of accrued benefits for key employees exceeds a specified percentage of the present value of accrued benefits for all employees. The tax laws define which individuals are considered key employees, including the employer's officers, owners, and highly paid employees. If a qualified plan becomes top heavy, then additional requirements are imposed in order for the plan to remain a qualified plan.

ERISA established a federal corporation, known as the *Pension Benefit Guaranty Corporation (PBGC)*, which is responsible for guaranteeing the payment of retirement benefits for participants in defined benefit retirement plans when those plans become financially unable to pay benefits. Covered plans are required to pay premiums to PBGC, which invests those premiums and uses the funds to pay covered benefits. Statutory limits establish the amount of plan benefits that PBGC can guarantee and the types of benefits that are guaranteed.

Other Types of Retirement Plans

Federal tax laws provide for other types of qualified retirement plans. Each type of plan must comply with specific requirements in order to qualify for favorable tax treatment. The tax laws impose the same general types of requirements on all forms of retirement plans, but the specific requirements vary depending on the type of plan. The specific tax treatment also varies depending on the type of plan.

Small employers and self-employed individuals are permitted to establish a *savings incentive match plan for employees (SIMPLE)*, which is a type of qualified savings plan under which employees may contribute a specific percentage of their compensation up to a specified maximum, and employers are required to contribute a specified amount. Only employers with 100 or fewer employees may establish a SIMPLE plan, which can be established as an individual retirement arrangement or as part of a 401(k) plan.

Two additional types of qualified retirement savings plans may be established by self-employed individuals and partnerships—simplified employee pension (SEP) plans and H.R. 10 plans. A *simplified employee pension (SEP) plan* is an individual retirement account or individual retirement annuity that is owned by an employee and that is funded by employer contributions. An *HR 10 plan*, also known as a *Keogh plan*, is an individual retirement account or individual retirement annuity that operates much like a regular IRA but with higher maximum contribution limits than a regular IRA. Specific tax code requirements vary somewhat for SEPs and HR 10 plans.

Key Terms and Concepts

settlement options provision
Standard Valuation Law
Standard Nonforfeiture Law for Individual Deferred Annuities
structured settlement annuity
Annuity Disclosure Model Regulation
Buyer's Guide to Fixed Deferred Annuities
disclosure document
Model Variable Annuity Regulation
Modified Guaranteed Annuity Regulation
modified guaranteed annuity
equity-indexed annuity
Buyer's Guide to Equity-Indexed Annuities
individual retirement arrangement (IRA)
individual retirement account
individual retirement annuity
traditional IRA
Roth IRA
disclosure statement
determination letter
pension plan
qualified plan
plan sponsor
plan participant
defined benefit plan
defined contribution plan
vested
top-heavy plan
Pension Benefit Guaranty Corporation (PBGC)
savings incentive match plan for employees (SIMPLE)
simplified employee pension (SEP) plan
HR 10 plan

Endnotes

1. The S&P 500 is described in Chapter 1.

2. SEC Concept Release, Release No. 33-7438, 20 August 1997. Available online at http://www.sec.gov/rules/concept/337438.txt (24 April 2002).

3. 26 U.S.C. § 408 (2000).

4. 29 U.S.C. §§ 1001 *et seq.* (2000).

Appendix A

ABC Insurance Company

Whole Life Insurance Plan
A Life Insurance Illustration Prepared for ALAN C. MILLER

Policy Benefits Illustration

Insurance Benefits	Definitions
Whole Life Insurance Form WL-01-01	This Whole Life Insurance policy offers level permanent life insurance coverage on the insured to age 100. This plan also provides cash values and paid up insurance. Premium payments are level.
Waiver of Premium Benefit Form WP01-05	This rider provides for the waiving of policy premiums and continuation of coverage if the insured becomes totally disabled for six months or longer, prior to his or her 60th birthday. Premiums are waived for as long as the insured is disabled.
Accidental Death Benefit Form AD01-02	This rider provides additional coverage if death results from accidental bodily injury prior to the policy anniversary following the insured's 65th birthday.

Prepared by:
John Doe
Tuesday, April 23, 2002

For:
ABC Insurance Company

ABC Insurance Company

Whole Life Insurance Plan
A Life Insurance Illustration Prepared for ALAN C. MILLER
Policy Terms Illustration

Important Terms	Definitions
Face Amount or Death Benefit	The face amount determines the life insurance death benefit amount.
Rate Class Standard Non-Smoker	The guaranteed and non-guaranteed premiums depend upon the insured's rate class. This illustration's premiums are calculated based on non-smoker rate class.
Guaranteed Premium	The guaranteed premiums illustrated in this proposal each are equal to the absolute maximum the policyowner may have to pay. It is called the maximum premium.
Non-Guaranteed Premium	This plan provides for premiums which may be less than the guaranteed premiums. These non-guaranteed premiums may change annually and are in the form of current and composite premiums. This illustration assumes that the currently illustrated non-guaranteed elements will continue unchanged for all years shown. This is not likely to occur, and actual results may be more or less favorable than those shown.
Current Premium Outlay	Current premiums are one type of this policy's non-guaranteed elements. Current premiums are calculated based on the current premium scale. These premiums may change annually and are not guaranteed.
Maximum Premium	The maximum premium illustrated in this proposal is equal to the absolute maximum that must be paid.

Prepared by:
John Doe
Tuesday, April 23, 2002

For:
ABC Insurance Company

ABC Insurance Company

Whole Life Insurance Plan
A Life Insurance Illustration Prepared for ALAN C. MILLER
Policy Terms Illustration

Important Terms	Definitions
Composite Premium Outlay	Composite premiums are one type of this policy's non-guaranteed elements. The components of the composite scale are equal to an average of the components of the maximum premium and current premium scale. These premiums may change annually and are not guaranteed.
Cash Value	This is the increasing amount of money available to you if the policy is surrendered before it becomes payable by death. This money may be borrowed for any personal need, including premium payments.
Paid Up Insurance	This benefit provides for the continuation of the original policy at a reduced amount of coverage for your whole lifetime without further premium payments. This is accomplished by using the cash value available as a single premium to purchase paid up insurance.

Prepared by:
John Doe
Tuesday, April 23, 2002

For:
ABC Insurance Company

ABC Insurance Company

Whole Life Insurance Plan
A Life Insurance Illustration Prepared for ALAN C. MILLER
Numeric Summary

Gender: Male
Age: 35
Rate Class: Standard Non-Smoker

Initial Face Amount: $100,000
Annual Contract Premium: $1,086.00

Accidental Death Benefit $100,000 to age 65
Waiver of Premium to age 60

End of Year	Age	--Guaranteed-- Maximum Premium	--Non-Guaranteed-- Composite Premium	--Non-Guaranteed-- Current Premium	--Guaranteed-- Death Benefit	--Guaranteed-- Cash Value	--Guaranteed-- Paid-Up Insurance
5	40	$1,456.00	$1,271.00	$1,086.00	$100,000	$2,464	$12,300
10	45	1,456.00	1,271.00	1,086.00	100,000	8,067	32,700
20	55	1,456.00	1,271.00	1,086.00	100,000	23,441	64,500
35	70	1,325.00	1,140.00	955.00	100,000	49,728	85,500

Assuming premiums are paid when due, the policy would provide $100,000 cash value at age 100. Both current and composite premiums are not guaranteed; the assumptions on which they are based are subject to change, and actual results may be more or less favorable. Premiums are paid at the beginning of the policy year.

I have received a copy of this illustration and understand that any non-guaranteed elements illustrated are subject to change and could be either higher or lower. The agent has told me they are not guaranteed.
Signed by:

_____
Applicant Name   Date

I certify this illustration has been presented to the applicant and that I have explained that any non-guaranteed elements illustrated are subject to change. I have made no statements that are inconsistent with the illustration. Signed by:

_____
Producer Name   Date

Prepared by: John Doe
Tuesday, April 23, 2002

For: ABC Insurance Company

ABC Insurance Company

Whole Life Insurance Plan
A Life Insurance Illustration Prepared for ALAN C. MILLER
Tabular Detail

Gender: Male
Age: 35
Rate Class: Standard Non-Smoker

Initial Face Amount: $100,000
Annual Contract Premium: $1,086.00

Accidental Death Benefit $100,000 to age 65
Waiver of Premium   to age 60

End of Year	Age	--Guaranteed-- Maximum Premium	--Non-Guaranteed-- Current Premium	Guaranteed Death Benefit	Guaranteed Cash Value	Guaranteed Paid-Up Insurance
1	36	$1,086.00	$1,086.00	$100,000	$0	$0
2	37	1,456.00	1,086.00	100,000	0	0
3	38	1,456.00	1,086.00	100,000	464	2,600
4	39	1,456.00	1,086.00	100,000	1,446	7,500
5	40	1,456.00	1,086.00	100,000	2,464	12,300
6	41	1,456.00	1,086.00	100,000	3,516	16,800
7	42	1,456.00	1,086.00	100,000	4,604	21,000
8	43	1,456.00	1,086.00	100,000	5,728	25,100
9	44	1,456.00	1,086.00	100,000	6,889	29,000
10	45	1,456.00	1,086.00	100,000	8,087	32,700
11	46	1,456.00	1,086.00	100,000	9,414	36,500
12	47	1,456.00	1,086.00	100,000	10,785	40,200
13	48	1,456.00	1,086.00	100,000	12,203	43,800
14	49	1,456.00	1,086.00	100,000	13,669	47,100
15	50	1,456.00	1,086.00	100,000	15,183	50,400
16	51	1,456.00	1,086.00	100,000	16,746	53,500
17	52	1,456.00	1,086.00	100,000	18,354	56,400
18	53	1,456.00	1,086.00	100,000	20,007	59,200
19	54	1,456.00	1,086.00	100,000	21,703	61,900
20	55	1,456.00	1,086.00	100,000	23,441	64,500
21	56	1,456.00	1,086.00	100,000	25,025	66,500
22	57	1,456.00	1,086.00	100,000	26,640	68,300
23	58	1,456.00	1,086.00	100,000	28,286	70,100
24	59	1,456.00	1,086.00	100,000	29,966	71,800
25	60	1,456.00	1,086.00	100,000	31,677	73,400
26	61	1,425.00	1,055.00	100,000	33,417	74,900
27	62	1,425.00	1,055.00	100,000	35,181	76,300
28	63	1,425.00	1,055.00	100,000	36,965	77,700
29	64	1,425.00	1,055.00	100,000	38,762	79,000
30	65	1,425.00	1,055.00	100,000	40,568	80,200

Premiums are paid at the beginning of the policy year.

Prepared by:
John Doe
Tuesday, April 23, 2002

For:
ABC Insurance Company

ABC Insurance Company
Whole Life Insurance Plan
A Life Insurance Illustration Prepared for ALAN C. MILLER
Tabular Detail

End of Year	Age	--Guaranteed-- Maximum Premium	--Non-Guaranteed-- Current Premium	Death Benefit	Guaranteed Cash Value	Guaranteed Paid-Up Insurance
31	66	1,325.00	955.00	100,000	42,382	81,400
32	67	1,325.00	955.00	100,000	44,204	82,500
33	68	1,325.00	955.00	100,000	46,036	83,500
34	69	1,325.00	955.00	100,000	47,879	84,500
35	70	1,325.00	955.00	100,000	49,728	85,500
36	71	1,325.00	955.00	100,000	51,576	86,400
37	72	1,325.00	955.00	100,000	53,413	87,200
38	73	1,325.00	955.00	100,000	55,225	88,000
39	74	1,325.00	955.00	100,000	57,000	88,800
40	75	1,325.00	955.00	100,000	58,730	89,400
41	76	1,325.00	955.00	100,000	60,414	90,100
42	77	1,325.00	955.00	100,000	62,057	90,700
43	78	1,325.00	955.00	100,000	63,667	91,300
44	79	1,325.00	955.00	100,000	65,251	91,800
45	80	1,325.00	955.00	100,000	66,811	92,300
46	81	1,325.00	955.00	100,000	68,344	92,800
47	82	1,325.00	955.00	100,000	69,839	93,300
48	83	1,325.00	955.00	100,000	71,281	93,700
49	84	1,325.00	955.00	100,000	72,658	94,100
50	85	1,325.00	955.00	100,000	73,967	94,400
51	86	1,325.00	955.00	100,000	75,211	94,800
52	87	1,325.00	955.00	100,000	76,400	95,100
53	88	1,325.00	955.00	100,000	77,549	95,400
54	89	1,325.00	955.00	100,000	78,676	95,700
55	90	1,325.00	955.00	100,000	79,804	96,000
56	91	1,325.00	955.00	100,000	80,961	96,200
57	92	1,325.00	955.00	100,000	82,181	96,500
58	93	1,325.00	955.00	100,000	83,505	96,800
59	94	1,325.00	955.00	100,000	84,976	97,200
60	95	1,325.00	955.00	100,000	86,618	97,500
61	96	1,325.00	955.00	100,000	88,427	97,900
62	97	1,325.00	955.00	100,000	90,341	98,300
63	98	1,325.00	955.00	100,000	92,213	98,600
64	99	1,325.00	955.00	100,000	93,728	98,900
65	100	1,325.00	955.00	100,000	100,000	100,000

Prepared by:
John Doe
Tuesday, April 23, 2002

For:
ABC Insurance Company

Appendix B

ABC Insurance Company
Whole Life Insurance Plan
A Life Insurance Illustration Prepared for ALAN C. MILLER
Supplemental Illustration for Whole Life

Year	Cumulative Premium	Cash Value	Annual Premium	Annual Increase in Cash Value	Annual Increase in Cash Value less Annual Premium
1	$1,086.00	$0	$1,086.00	$0	$–1,086
2	2,172.00	0	1,086.00	0	–1,086
3	3,258.00	464	1,086.00	464	–622
4	4,344.00	1,446	1,086.00	982	–104
5	5,430.00	2,464	1,086.00	1,018	–68
6	6,516.00	3,516	1,086.00	1,052	–34
7	7,602.00	4,604	1,086.00	1,088	2
8	8,688.00	5,728	1,086.00	1,124	38
9	9,744.00	6,889	1,086.00	1,161	75
10	10,860.00	8,087	1,086.00	1,198	112
11	11,946.00	9,414	1,086.00	1,327	241
12	13,032.00	10,785	1,086.00	1,371	285
13	14,118.00	12,203	1,086.00	1,418	332
14	15,204.00	13,669	1,086.00	1,466	380
15	16,290.00	15,183	1,086.00	1,514	428
16	17,376.00	16,746	1,086.00	1,563	477
17	18,462.00	18,354	1,086.00	1,608	522
18	19,548.00	20,007	1,086.00	1,653	567
19	20,634.00	21,703	1,086.00	1,696	610
20	21,720.00	23,441	1,086.00	1,738	652
21	22,806.00	25,025	1,086.00	1,584	498
22	23,892.00	26,640	1,086.00	1,615	529
23	24,978.00	28,286	1,086.00	1,646	560
24	26,064.00	29,966	1,086.00	1,680	594
25	27,150.00	31,677	1,086.00	1,711	625
26	28,205.00	33,417	1,055.00	1,740	685
27	29,260.00	35,181	1,055.00	1,764	709
28	30,315.00	36,965	1,055.00	1,784	729
29	31,370.00	38,762	1,055.00	1,797	742
30	32,425.00	40,568	1,055.00	1,806	751

THIS SUPPLEMENTAL ILLUSTRATION ASSUMES THAT THE CURRENTLY ILLUSTRATED NONGUARANTEED ELEMENTS WILL CONTINUE UNCHANGED FOR ALL YEARS SHOWN. THIS IS NOT LIKELY TO OCCUR, AND ACTUAL RESULTS MAY BE MORE OR LESS FAVORABLE THAN THOSE SHOWN.

PLEASE REFER TO THE BASIC ILLUSTRATION PRECEDING THIS SUPPLEMENTAL ILLUSTRATION FOR GUARANTEED POLICY ELEMENTS AND OTHER IMPORTANT INFORMATION.

ABC Insurance Company
Whole Life Insurance Plan
A Life Insurance Illustration Prepared for ALAN C. MILLER
Supplemental Illustration for Whole Life

Year	Cumulative Premium	Cash Value	Annual Premium	Annual Increase in Cash Value	Annual Increase in Cash Value less Annual Premium
31	33,380.00	42,382	955.00	1,814	859
32	34,335.00	44,204	955.00	1,822	867
33	35,290.00	46,036	955.00	1,832	877
34	36,245.00	47,879	955.00	1,843	888
35	37,200.00	49,728	955.00	1,849	894
36	38,155.00	51,576	955.00	1,848	893
37	39,110.00	53,413	955.00	1,837	882
38	40,065.00	55,225	955.00	1,812	857
39	41,020.00	57,000	955.00	1,775	820
40	41,975.00	58,730	955.00	1,730	775
41	42,930.00	60,414	955.00	1,684	729
42	43,885.00	62,057	955.00	1,643	688
43	44,840.00	63,667	955.00	1,610	655
44	45,795.00	65,251	955.00	1,584	629
45	46,750.00	66,811	955.00	1,560	605
46	47,705.00	68,344	955.00	1,533	578
47	48,660.00	69,839	955.00	1,495	540
48	49,615.00	71,281	955.00	1,442	487
49	50,570.00	72,658	955.00	1,377	422
50	51,525.00	73,967	955.00	1,309	354
51	52,480.00	75,211	955.00	1,244	289
52	53,435.00	76,400	955.00	1,189	234
53	54,390.00	77,549	955.00	1,149	194
54	55,345.00	78,676	955.00	1,127	172
55	56,300.00	79,804	955.00	1,128	173
56	57,255.00	80,961	955.00	1,157	202
57	58,210.00	82,181	955.00	1,220	265
58	59,165.00	83,505	955.00	1,324	369
59	60,120.00	84,976	955.00	1,471	516
60	61,075.00	86,618	955.00	1,642	687
61	62,030.00	88,427	955.00	1,809	854
62	62,985.00	90,341	955.00	1,914	959
63	63,940.00	92,213	955.00	1,872	917
64	64,895.00	93,728	955.00	1,515	560
65	65,850.00	100,000	955.00	6,272	5,317

	Year 10	Year 20	Age 65
Total Cash Value	$8,087	$23,441	$42,382
Total Premium	10,860	21,720	33,380
Net Difference	$−2,773	$1,721	$9,002

ABC Insurance Company

Whole Life Insurance Plan
A Life Insurance Illustration Prepared for ALAN C. MILLER
Supplemental Illustration for Whole Life

Annual Premium for Basic Policy	$955.00
Annual Premium for Waiver of Premium	$31.00
Annual Premium for Accidental Death Benefit	$100.00

THIS SUPPLEMENTAL ILLUSTRATION ASSUMES THAT THE CURRENTLY ILLUSTRATED NONGUARANTEED ELEMENTS WILL CONTINUE UNCHANGED FOR ALL YEARS SHOWN. THIS IS NOT LIKELY TO OCCUR, AND ACTUAL RESULTS MAY BE MORE OR LESS FAVORABLE THAN THOSE SHOWN.

PLEASE REFER TO THE BASIC ILLUSTRATION PRECEDING THIS SUPPLEMENTAL ILLUSTRATION FOR GUARANTEED POLICY ELEMENTS AND OTHER IMPORTANT INFORMATION.

Glossary

The number in brackets after a glossary entry indicates the chapter in which the term is discusssed.

Accelerated Benefits Model Regulation. An NAIC model regulation that is designed to regulate accelerated death benefit provisions and to impose disclosure standards on insurers that provide accelerated death benefits. [1]

accelerated death benefit provision. A life insurance policy provision that gives the policyowner the right to receive a portion—usually between 50 and 80 percent—of the policy benefit during the insured's lifetime when the insured is terminally ill as defined in the policy. [1]

acceptable alternative mechanism. For purposes of HIPAA, a state-approved plan that provides health insurance coverage to all eligible individuals without imposing preexisting conditions exclusions and gives eligible individuals a choice of health insurance coverage. [3]

Accident and Sickness Insurance Minimum Standards Model Act. An NAIC model law that establishes certain standards for all individual health policies other than Medicare supplement policies. [3]

accident only coverage. A type of health insurance coverage that provides coverage for death, dismemberment, disability, and/or hospital and medical care caused by accident. [3]

accredited reinsurer. In states that have enacted laws based on the Credit for Reinsurance Model Law, a reinsurer that is not licensed in the ceding company's domiciliary state but that meets specified financial and reporting requirements of that state and is licensed to transact insurance or reinsurance in at least one other state. [7]

actual net debt. For purposes of determining the benefit payable under a consumer credit insurance policy, the lump-sum amount needed on any given date to pay off the debt, excluding unearned interest and any other unearned finance charges. [10]

ADA. *See* **Americans with Disabilities Act.**

ADEA. *See* **Age Discrimination in Employment Act.**

adjusted community rate. A health insurance premium rate that reflects the medical and hospital costs to all insureds in a particular community. [3]

advertisement. According to the Advertisements of Life Insurance and Annuities Model Regulation, any material designed either (1) to create public interest in life insurance or annuities, an insurer, or an insurance producer or (2) to induce the public to purchase, increase, modify, reinstate, borrow on, surrender, replace, or retain a policy. [2]

Advertisements of Accident and Sickness Insurance Model Regulation. An NAIC model regulation designed to protect prospective purchasers by establishing minimum criteria that health insurance advertisements must meet in order to ensure they properly and accurately describe the products they advertise. [4]

Advertisements of Life Insurance and Annuities Model Regulation. An NAIC Model Regulation that establishes minimum standards that require insurers to disclose to the public all relevant information in their advertisements of life insurance and annuity policies. [2]

Age Discrimination in Employment Act (ADEA). A federal law that applies to employers that have 20 or more employees and prohibits those employers from discriminating against employees who are age 40 and older because of their age. [9]

allied medical practitioner. A licensed health care provider other than a licensed medical doctor. [3]

Americans with Disabilities Act (ADA). A federal law that protects disabled individuals against all types of discrimination, including employment discrimination. The ADA applies to all employers with 15 or more employees and requires that disabled employees have equal access to the life and health insurance coverages that are available to other employees. [9]

Annuity Disclosure Model Regulation. An NAIC model regulation that requires insurers to provide prospective purchasers of specified types of annuities with information to help them select an annuity appropriate to their needs. [11]

approval premium receipt. A type of conditional premium receipt which specifies that the temporary coverage provided by the receipt becomes effective when the insurer approves the application; should the proposed insured die before the application is approved, the receipt provides no coverage. [1]

assignment. An agreement under which one party transfers some or all of his ownership rights in a particular property to another. [1]

assignment provision. A life insurance policy provision that describes the policyowner's right to assign the policy and the responsibilities of the insurer and the policyowner when the policyowner exercises the right to assign the policy. [1]

assumption certificate. An insurance certificate issued on an existing insurance policy by a reinsurer that has assumed the risk of the policy as the result of an assumption reinsurance transaction. [7]

assumption reinsurance. A type of reinsurance used to effect a complete, permanent, and total transfer of in-force insurance business. [7]

Assumption Reinsurance Model Act. An NAIC model law that is designed to regulate insurers that assume or transfer risks under assumption reinsurance agreements. [7]

backdating. A practice by which an insurer makes the effective date of an insurance policy earlier than the date of the application. [1]

basic health benefit plan. For purposes of the Small Employer and Individual Health Insurance Availability Model Act, a low-cost health benefit plan. [3]

basic health care services. According to the Health Maintenance Organization Model Act, medically necessary services that an HMO must provide to enrollees, including preventive care, emergency care, inpatient and outpatient hospital and physician care, diagnostic laboratory services, and diagnostic and therapeutic radiological services. [6]

basic hospital expense coverage. A type of health insurance that provides coverage for a period of at least 31 days during any continuous hospital confinement for each person insured under the policy. Coverage consists of benefits for the costs of daily hospital room and board, miscellaneous hospital expenses, and hospital outpatient services. [3]

basic illustration. A spreadsheet, ledger, or proposal that is used in the sale of a life insurance policy and that shows both guaranteed and nonguaranteed policy values. [2]

basic medical expense coverage. A type of health insurance coverage that provides comprehensive hospital, medical, and surgical expense coverage, including benefits for daily hospital room and board, miscellaneous hospital services, surgical services, anesthesia services, in-hospital medical services, and out-of-hospital care. [3]

basic medical-surgical expense coverage. A type of health insurance that provides coverage for expenses each person insured under the policy incurs for necessary services rendered by a physician for treatment of an injury or sickness. Coverage consists of benefits for expenses incurred for surgical services, anesthesia services, and in-hospital medical services. [3]

benefit base. The amount to which a variable life insurance policy's net investment return will be applied periodically. [1]

binding premium receipt. A type of premium receipt that provides temporary insurance coverage from the time the applicant receives the receipt. Also known as a *temporary insurance agreement*. [1]

Buyer's Guide. A brochure designed to educate consumers about life insurance and enable them to get the most for their money when shopping for life insurance. [2]

Buyer's Guide to Equity-Indexed Annuities. An NAIC publication that describes specific features of equity-indexed annuities and explains ways in which equity-indexed annuities differ from other annuities. [11]

Buyer's Guide to Fixed Deferred Annuities. An NAIC publication that describes the various types of annuities and some of the annuity features that prospects should consider before purchasing an annuity. [11]

ceding company. In a reinsurance transaction, the insurance company that transfers risk to another insurer. [7]

certificate of authority. A document issued by a state insurance department granting an insurer the right to conduct an insurance business in the state. [6]

certificate of coverage provision. A group life and health insurance policy provision that states that the insurer will issue a certificate to the policyholder for delivery to each insured. [8]

CHAMPUS. *See* **Civilian Health and Medical Program of the Uniformed Services**.

change of beneficiary provision. An individual health insurance policy provision which states that, unless a policyowner makes an irrevocable beneficiary designation, the policyowner has the right to change a beneficiary designation and to surrender or assign the policy without the beneficiary's consent. [3]

change of occupation provision. An individual health insurance policy provision that specifies how benefits or premiums will be adjusted if the insured changes to a more or less hazardous occupation. [3]

Civil Rights Act of 1964. A federal antidiscrimination law that applies to employers that are engaged in interstate commerce and that have 15 or more employees. Title VII of the Act prohibits employment discrimination on the basis of race, color, sex, religion, or national origin. [9]

Civilian Health and Medical Program of the Uniformed Services (CHAMPUS). A federal program that provides health insurance coverage to the families of military personnel, including military retirees, military spouses, and dependents of military personnel. [3]

claim forms provision. An individual health insurance policy provision which states that the insurer will furnish the claimant with forms for filing proofs of loss when it receives notice of a claim. [3]

closed contract. A contract for which only those terms and conditions printed in or attached to the contract are considered to be part of the contractual agreement. *See also* **open contract.** [1]

closed-end credit transaction. A transaction in which a lender extends to a debtor a specified amount of credit that will be repaid at a specified interest rate in a series of equal payments over a specified time. [10]

COB provision. *See* **coordination of benefits provision.**

COBRA. *See* **Consolidated Omnibus Budget Reconciliation Act.**

COBRA continuation coverage. Group health insurance coverage provided to an individual who elected to continue group health coverage under COBRA. [9]

coinsurance. A specified amount or percentage of eligible medical expenses for which the insured—rather than the insurer—is responsible for paying. [3]

compensation. For purposes of the Consumer Credit Insurance Model Act, any form of remuneration resulting directly from the sale of consumer credit insurance, including commissions, dividends, retrospective rate credits, service fees, expense allowances or reimbursements, gifts, or the furnishing of equipment, facilities, goods, or services. [10]

complaint. For purposes of the Unfair Trade Practices Act, any written communication primarily expressing a grievance. [2]

conditional premium receipt. A type of premium receipt that specifies certain conditions that must be met before the temporary insurance coverage provided by the receipt becomes effective. [1]

conformity with state statutes provision. An individual health insurance policy provision which states that any policy provision that is in conflict with the laws of the state in which the insured resides is amended to conform to the minimum requirements of such laws. [3]

Consolidated Omnibus Budget Reconciliation Act (COBRA). A federal law that imposes requirements on group medical expense insurance plans sponsored by employers with 20 or more employees. [9]

consumer credit insurance. Credit insurance that is subject to the requirements of the Consumer Credit Insurance Model Act, including credit life insurance, credit accident and health insurance, and credit unemployment insurance. [10]

Consumer Credit Insurance Model Act. An NAIC model law designed to regulate consumer credit insurance issued or sold in connection with loans or other credit transactions for personal, family, or household purposes. [10]

Consumer Credit Insurance Model Regulation. An NAIC model regulation that provides standards for the sale of consumer credit insurance. [10]

conversion provision. A group life insurance policy provision that gives insureds the right to obtain an individual life insurance policy if their group coverage terminates because of specified reasons. [8]

coordination of benefits (COB) provision. A group medical expense policy provision that is designed to prevent a group member who is insured under more than one group insurance policy from receiving benefit amounts greater than her actual incurred medical expenses. [8]

copayment. A specified dollar amount that an insured pays for the cost of certain medical services, such as physician office visits or emergency room care. [3]

cost of benefits. For purposes of premium calculations, the total amount that an insurer is expected to pay out in contractually required benefits for a given insurance product. [1]

credit accident and health insurance. Credit insurance that insures a debtor to provide funds for the payment of amounts due under a specific credit transaction while the debtor is disabled as defined in the insurance policy. Also known as *credit health insurance* or *credit disability insurance*. [10]

credit disability insurance. *See* **credit accident and health insurance.**

Credit for Reinsurance Model Law. An NAIC model law that sp ecifies the situations in which a ceding insurer is entitled to reinsurance reserve credits. [7]

Credit for Reinsurance Model Regulation. An NAIC model regulation that supplements the Credit for Reinsurance Model Law's requirements concerning the situations in which a ceding insurer is entitled to reinsurance reserve credits. [7]

credit health insurance. *See* **credit accident and health insurance.**

credit life insurance. Credit insurance that insures a debtor to provide funds for the payment of all or part of a specific debt owed under a credit transaction upon the debtor's death. [10]

credit unemployment insurance. Credit insurance that insures a debtor to provide funds for the payment of amounts due under a specific credit transaction while the debtor is involuntarily unemployed as defined in the insurance policy. [10]

creditable coverage. For purposes of HIPAA, health insurance coverage under any of a number of specified types of health plans without a lapse of 63 days or more. [3]

debit insurance. *See* **industrial life insurance**.

deductible. A specified dollar amount of eligible expenses that an insured must pay under a medical expense insurance policy before the insurer begins to pay any benefit. [3]

defined benefit plan. A retirement plan that defines the amount of the benefit each plan participant will receive at retirement. [11]

defined contribution plan. A retirement plan that describes the annual contribution the employer will deposit into the plan on behalf of each plan participant. [11]

determination letter. A letter issued by the Internal Revenue Service (IRS) in response to a party's request that the IRS evaluate a specific product and determine whether the product meets federal tax law requirements. [11]

determination period. For purposes of HIPAA, a period of time used to calculate an individual's creditable coverage under the alternative method. The determination period ordinarily is the individual's most recent period of creditable coverage up to a maximum of 365 days; the maximum period for late enrollees is 546 days (18 months). [9]

direct response marketing. A marketing method that uses one or more media to elicit an immediate and measurable action—such as an inquiry or a purchase—from a customer. [1]

disability income protection coverage. A type of health insurance coverage that provides periodic payments, either weekly or monthly, for a specified period during the continuance of disability. [3]

disclosure document. A document that the Annuity Disclosure Model Regulation requires insurers to provide to prospective purchasers of certain types of deferred annuities; the document identifies and describes the specific annuity the customer is considering purchasing. [11]

disclosure statement. A written statement that an insurer must provide to a consumer considering the purchase of an individual retirement annuity and that provides nontechnical explanations of the operation of an individual retirement annuity. [11]

discount for advance payment of premium provision. An industrial life insurance policy provision which states the amount by which premiums due will be reduced if premiums are paid at least a specified time in advance. [1]

discretionary group. According to the Group Life Insurance Definition and Group Life Insurance Standard Provisions Model Act and the Group Health Insurance Definition and Group Health Insurance Standard Provisions Model Act, any type of group other than a single employer group, a debtor-creditor group, a labor union group, a multiple employer group, an association group, or a credit union group. A group is eligible for coverage as a discretionary group only if it is approved for group insurance by the applicable state insurance department. [8]

dividend provision. A provision that is included in participating life insurance and annuity policies and that describes the policyowner's right to share in the insurer's divisible surplus and the dividend payment options available to the policyowner. [1, 11]

dread disease coverage. *See* **specified disease coverage.**

election period. For purposes of COBRA, a specified period following a qualifying event during which a qualified beneficiary has the right to elect COBRA continuation coverage. [9]

eligible individual. For purposes of HIPAA, an individual to whom an insurer must provide individual health insurance coverage because the individual has had group health insurance coverage and meets other specified requirements. [3]

Employee Retirement Income Security Act (ERISA). A federal law designed to ensure that certain minimum plan requirements are contained in employee welfare benefit plans. [3]

enrollee. An individual who is insured by a health maintenance organization. [6]

enrollment date. For purposes of HIPAA, the date an individual becomes covered under a group health plan or, if earlier, the first day of the waiting period for enrollment in such a plan. [9]

entire contract provision. A life insurance, health insurance, and annuity policy provision that defines which documents constitute the contract between the insurer and the policyowner. [1, 3, 8, 11]

equity-indexed annuity. An annuity that provides for interest credits to be linked to an external standard, typically the S&P 500. [11]

ERISA. *See* **Employee Retirement Income Security Act.**

evidence of coverage. A written statement that outlines the essential features and services of an HMO and that is provided to individuals enrolled under a group HMO contract. [6]

evidence of insurability provision. A group life and health insurance policy provision that specifies the conditions, if any, under which the insurer reserves the right to require a person eligible for insurance to furnish evidence of individual insurability satisfactory to the insurer as a condition to part or all of his coverage. [8]

exception. A health insurance policy provision that entirely eliminates coverage for a specific hazard. [4]

exclusion. A life insurance policy provision that describes situations in which the insurer will not pay policy proceeds following the death of the insured. [1]

exclusionary period. A specified period during which a health insurance policy excludes a preexisting condition from coverage. [9]

facility of payment provision. An industrial life insurance policy provision which states that, under specified conditions, the insurer may pay policy benefits to the executor or administrator of the insured's estate, relatives of the insured, or any other person who is equitably entitled to the benefits or has incurred expenses for the care or burial of the insured. [1]

Family and Medical Leave Act (FMLA). A federal law that requires employers with 50 or more employees within a 75-mile radius to allow eligible employees in specific circumstances to take up to 12 weeks of unpaid leave within any 12-month period. [9]

flexible premium variable life policy. According to the Variable Life Insurance Model Regulation, any individual variable life insurance policy other than a scheduled premium variable life policy. [1]

FMLA. *See* **Family and Medical Leave Act.**

franchise plan. A type of individual insurance coverage that is issued to specified members of an employer-employee group or other type of group. [3]

free-look provision. An individual life insurance, health insurance, and annuity policy provision that allows the policyowner a specified period, usually 10 days, following policy delivery within which to cancel the policy and receive a refund of all premiums paid. [1, 3, 11]

fronting. An arrangement in which one insurer acts as a primary insurer and issues policies that another insurer has underwritten; then the primary insurer immediately transfers most of the risk to that other insurer. [7]

fronting company. The primary insurer in a fronting arrangement. [7]

generic name. A short title that describes the premium and benefit patterns of a policy or rider. [2]

grace period provision. A life insurance, health insurance, and annuity policy provision that gives the policyowner a specified period following a premium due date within which to pay a renewal premium. [1, 3, 8, 11]

gross debt. For purposes of determining the benefit payable under a credit disability insurance policy, the total of the remaining scheduled payments on a given date. [10]

gross premium. The amount an insurer charges a policyowner for a specific life or health insurance product. The gross premium consists of two elements: the net premium and the loading. [1, 3]

Group Coordination of Benefits Model Regulation. An NAIC model regulation that permits group health insurance plans to include a coordination of benefits (COB) provision and imposes requirements on COB provisions. [8]

Group Health Insurance Definition and Group Health Insurance Standard Provisions Model Act. An NAIC model law that defines the types of groups that are eligible for group health insurance and specifies standard provisions that group health insurance policies must include. [8]

Group Health Insurance Mandatory Conversion Privilege Model Act. An NAIC model law that requires specified types of group health insurance policies to give insureds in specified situations the right to obtain individual health insurance without providing evidence of insurability. [8]

Group Life Insurance Definition and Group Life Insurance Standard Provisions Model Act. An NAIC model law that defines the types of groups that are eligible for group life insurance and specifies standard provisions that group life insurance policies must include. [8]

guaranteed renewable policy. A health insurance policy that gives the policyowner the right to continue coverage until the insured reaches age 65 or becomes eligible for Medicare and that gives the insurer the right to change the premium rate charged for the policy if it does so for a class of policies. [3]

Guide to Health Insurance for People with Medicare. A document that was developed by the NAIC and the federal Centers for Medicare and Medicaid Services (CMS) to provide consumers who are eligible for Medicare with information to help them make informed health insurance purchase decisions. [5]

Health Care Professional Credentialing Verification Model Act. An NAIC model law that requires a managed care plan to establish a credential verification program that serves to verify the credentials of all participating health care professionals who participate in the plan. [6]

Health Carrier Grievance Procedure Model Act. An NAIC model law that is designed to ensure that covered individuals have an opportunity to resolve their grievances concerning health care decisions rendered by managed care plans. [6]

Health Insurance Portability and Accountability Act (HIPAA). A federal law that imposes a number of requirements on employer-sponsored group health insurance plans, health insurance companies, and health maintenance organizations. [3]

Health Insurance Reserves Model Regulation. An NAIC model law that establishes minimum reserve standards for all types of individual and group health insurance products except Medicare supplement and long-term care policies. [3]

health maintenance organization (HMO). A person, partnership, association, trust, or corporation that undertakes to provide or arrange for the delivery of basic health care services to enrollees on a prepaid basis, but that leaves enrollees responsible for paying copayments and deductibles. [6]

Health Maintenance Organization Act of 1973. A federal law that encouraged the growth of HMOs during the late 1970s and 1980s by providing funds to HMOs that met specified requirements and requiring employers in certain situations to provide employees with the option of participating in either a federally qualified HMO or the employers' traditional group medical expense insurance plans. [6]

Health Maintenance Organization (HMO) Model Act. An NAIC model law designed to regulate all aspects of the organization and operation of HMOs conducting business in a state that has enacted such a law. [6]

HIPAA. *See* Health Insurance Portability and Accountability Act.

HMO. *See* health maintenance organization.

HMO Model Act. *See* Health Maintenance Organization Model Act.

home service insurance. *See* industrial life insurance.

hospital confinement indemnity coverage. A type of health insurance coverage that provides a daily benefit of at least $40 per day for a period of at least 31 days during any hospital confinement. [3]

HR 10 plan. A type of qualified retirement savings plan that may be established by self-employed individuals and partnerships as an individual retirement account or individual retirement annuity that operates much like a regular IRA but with higher maximum contribution limits than a regular IRA. Also known as a *Keogh plan*. [11]

illegal occupation provision. An individual health insurance policy provision which states that the insurer will not be liable for any loss that results from the insured's committing or attempting to commit a felony or from the insured's engaging in an illegal occupation. [3]

illustration. A presentation or depiction that includes nonguaranteed values of a life insurance policy. An illustration used in the sale of a life insurance policy may be either a basic illustration or a supplemental illustration. [2]

illustration actuary. An actuary specially qualified in the actuarial standards of practice relating to life insurance sales illustrations. [2]

incontestability provision. An individual life insurance and annuity policy provision that limits the time during which the insurer may contest the validity of the insurance contract on the ground of a material misrepresentation in the application for insurance. [1, 11] In the case of group life and health insurance policies, a provision that limits the time during which the insurer may contest the validity of the insurance contract on the ground of a material misrepresentation in the application for insurance and limits the insurer's ability to contest the validity of an insured's coverage after it has been in force for two years during the insured's lifetime. [8]

indemnity plan. A medical expense insurance plan that reimburses insureds for the covered medical expenses they incur and allows insureds to select their own medical care providers. [6]

indemnity reinsurance. A type of reinsurance used to effect, in most cases, a partial transfer of business and to form a basis for sharing the risks of the insurance business. [7]

Individual Health Insurance Portability Model Act. An NAIC model law designed to increase access to individual health insurance coverage. [3]

individual retirement account. An individual retirement arrangement that consists of a trust account created in the United States for the exclusive benefit of an individual and her beneficiaries and that meets requirements specified in the federal tax laws, including a requirement that the trustee of the trust must be a bank, investment company, or similar organization. [11]

individual retirement annuity. An individual deferred annuity that qualifies for favorable federal income tax treatment as an individual retirement arrangement because it meets requirements specified in the federal tax laws. [11]

individual retirement arrangement (IRA). An individual retirement account or individual retirement annuity that meets requirements specified in the federal tax laws and thus receives favorable federal income tax treatment. [11]

industrial life insurance. Life insurance that is paid for by weekly or monthly premiums which are collected by an agent of the insurer. Also known as *home service insurance* or *debit insurance*. [1]

Industrial Life Insurance Model Bill. An NAIC model law that establishes standards for the sale of industrial life insurance. [1]

institutional advertisement. An advertisement that is designed to promote the consumer's interest in the concept of insurance or the insurer as a seller of insurance. [4]

insurability premium receipt. A type of conditional premium receipt which specifies that the temporary coverage provided by the receipt becomes effective when the receipt is issued if the insurer finds the proposed insured to be insurable. [1]

insurer's illustrated scale. According to the Life Insurance Illustrations Model Regulation, a schedule of nonguaranteed elements calculated based on the insurer's recent experience. [2]

insuring clause. An individual life insurance policy provision that contains the insurer's contractual promise to pay the policy benefits in accordance with the provisions contained in the policy. [1]

interest-indexed policy. A universal life insurance policy that provides for interest credits to be linked to an external standard, such as the Standard & Poor's 500 index. [1]

Internal Revenue Code. A comprehensive collection of laws that codifies the federal tax laws. [3]

intoxicants and narcotics provision. An individual health insurance policy provision which states that an insurer will not be liable for any loss resulting from the insured's being under the influence of alcohol or any narcotic unless taken on the advice of a physician. [3]

invitation to contract. Any insurance advertisement other than an institutional advertisement or an invitation to inquire. [4]

invitation to inquire. An advertisement that is designed to induce the audience to inquire further about a specific policy and that contains only a brief description of the coverage being advertised. [4]

IRA. *See* **individual retirement arrangement.**

joint venture. A type of partnership arrangement between two otherwise independent businesses that agree to undertake a specific project together for a specified time period. [7]

Keogh plan. *See* **HR 10 plan.**

Labor Management Relations Act. *See* **Taft-Hartley Act.**

late enrollee. For purposes of HIPAA, an individual who enrolls in a group health plan other than during (1) the first period in which he is eligible to enroll or (2) a special enrollment period defined in the Act. [9]

legal actions provision. An individual health insurance policy provision which states that a claimant may not file a legal action to recover under the policy until at least 60 days after furnishing the insurer with written proof of loss. [3]

letters of credit. Documents issued by a bank guaranteeing the payment of a customer's bank drafts up to a stated amount for a specified period. [6]

Life and Health Insurance Policy Language Simplification Model Act. An NAIC model law designed to simplify the language used in individual life and health insurance policies so that consumers are better able to understand the terms of their policies. [1]

Life and Health Reinsurance Agreements Model Regulation. An NAIC model regulation that is designed to prevent licensed insurers from ceding reinsurance for the purpose of relieving surplus strain, typically on a temporary basis, while not transferring the significant risks inherent in the business being reinsured. [7]

Life Insurance Disclosure Model Regulation. An NAIC model regulation that requires insurers to give purchasers of life insurance information that will (1) improve purchasers' ability to select the insurance plan that will best meet the purchasers' needs and (2) improve purchasers' understanding of the life insurance products they buy or consider buying. [2]

Life Insurance Illustrations Model Regulation. An NAIC model regulation designed to (1) ensure that illustrations do not mislead purchasers of life insurance and (2) make illustrations more understandable to consumers. [2]

limitation. Any health insurance policy provision that restricts coverage and that is not an exception or a reduction. [4]

limited benefit health coverage. A type of health insurance coverage that provides benefits that are less than the minimum benefit standards required for other types of medical expense coverages. [3]

limited credit insurance license. An insurance producer's license that permits the licensed individual to solicit the sale of credit insurance only. [10]

limited insurance representative. A sales representative who is licensed to solicit or negotiate contracts for specified lines of insurance. [10]

loading. An amount included in the gross premium for a life or health insurance product to cover the expenses the insurer incurs in issuing the product and the cost of the insurer's operations. [1, 3]

long-term care insurance. For regulatory purposes, a policy or rider advertised, marketed, offered, or designed to provide coverage for not less than 12 consecutive months for medically necessary care an insured receives in a setting other than a hospital, such as in the insured's home or a nursing home facility. [5]

Long-Term Care Insurance Model Act. An NAIC model law that establishes standards for both group and individual long-term care insurance and is designed to protect the public and, at the same time, promote the availability of long-term care coverage and flexibility in the design of such coverage. [5]

Long-Term Care Insurance Model Regulation. An NAIC model regulation that implements provisions of the Long-Term Care Insurance Model Act and establishes additional standards for long-term care insurance policies. [5]

look-back period. For purposes of HIPAA, a maximum period of six months preceding the date an individual enrolls in a group medical expense insurance plan during which any physical or mental condition for which medical advice, diagnosis, care, or treatment was recommended or received may be classified as a preexisting condition that is excluded from coverage for a limited period of time. [9]

loss ratio. A ratio used to evaluate the reasonableness of health insurance premiums by measuring the percentage of premiums paid out in policy benefits. [3]

major medical expense coverage. A type of health insurance coverage that provides comprehensive hospital, medical, and surgical expense coverage, including benefits for daily hospital room and board, miscellaneous hospital services, surgical services, anesthesia services, in-hospital medical services, and out-of-hospital care. [3]

managed care plan. A health benefit plan that either requires insureds to use health care providers managed, owned, under contract with, or employed by the health carrier or creates incentives for insureds to use such providers. [6]

Managed Care Plan Network Adequacy Model Act. An NAIC model law that requires managed care plans to meet specified requirements in contractual arrangements with providers. [6]

material misrepresentation. A statement made in an application for insurance that is not substantially true and that is relevant to the insurer's evaluation of the proposed insured. [1]

medical savings account (MSA). An interest-bearing account created for the purpose of paying the account owner's qualified medical expenses that are not otherwise covered by insurance. [9]

Medicare. A federal program that provides hospital and medical expense coverage for persons age 65 and older, disabled individuals, and specified others. [5]

Medicare Supplement Insurance Minimum Standards Model Act. An NAIC model law that imposes specified minimum standards on Medicare supplement policies and group certificates and requires state insurance departments to adopt regulations that impose additional standards. [5]

Medicare supplement insurance policy. A policy advertised, marketed, or designed primarily to cover the gap between the amount of hospital, medical, and surgical expenses incurred by an individual eligible for Medicare and the amount of those expenses that Medicare covers. Also known as a *Medigap policy.* [5]

Medigap policy. *See* **Medicare supplement insurance policy**.

Mental Health Parity Act (MHPA). A federal law that requires group health plans, health insurance companies, and HMOs that offer mental health benefits to impose the same annual and lifetime maximum amounts for mental health benefits as are imposed for medical and surgical benefits. [9]

MHPA. *See* **Mental Health Parity Act**.

misstatement of age provision. A life insurance, health insurance, and annuity policy provision that describes how policy benefits will be paid if the age of the insured has been misstated. [1]

Model Health Plan for Uninsurable Individuals Act. An NAIC model law that provides for the establishment of a state health insurance plan that would offer health insurance coverage to uninsurable individuals who meet certain criteria. [3]

Model Newborn Children Bill. An NAIC model law which requires that health insurance policies that provide coverage for a family member of the insured must provide coverage for a newly born child of the insured from the moment of birth.

Model Policy Loan Interest Rate Bill. An NAIC model law that places a maximum limit on the interest rate that insurers may charge on policy loans and requires insurers to state the applicable interest rate in their policies. [1]

Model Regulation to Implement the Accident and Sickness Insurance Minimum Standards Model Act. An NAIC model regulation designed to standardize and simplify the terms of individual health policies, to facilitate public understanding of health policies, and to provide full disclosure in the sale of such policies. [3]

Model Regulation to Implement the NAIC Medicare Supplement Insurance Minimum Standards Model Act. An NAIC model regulation that contains extensive requirements designed to standardize the coverages provided by individual and group Medicare supplement policies, to facilitate public understanding of such policies, and to ensure full disclosure in the sale of such policies. [5]

Model Variable Annuity Regulation. An NAIC model regulation that establishes qualifications an insurer must meet in order to market variable annuities and specifies requirements that variable annuities must meet. [11]

modified guaranteed annuity. According to the Modified Guaranteed Annuity Regulation, a deferred annuity for which the underlying assets are held in a separate account but for which the contract values are guaranteed if held for a specified time. [11]

Modified Guaranteed Annuity Regulation. An NAIC model regulation that imposes requirements on insurance producers and insurers that market modified guaranteed annuities. [11]

MSA. *See* **medical savings account.**

NAIC. National Association of Insurance Commissioners.

NAIC Model Rules Governing Advertisements of Medicare Supplement Insurance. NAIC model rules that regulate the advertising of Medicare supplement insurance by imposing requirements similar to those imposed on health insurance advertising by the Advertisements of Accident and Sickness Insurance Model Regulation. [5]

net amount at risk. The difference between the amount of the death benefit promised by a life insurance policy and the amount of the policy reserve. [1]

net premium. The amount included in the gross premium for a life or health insurance product to cover the product's expected cost of benefits. [1, 3]

net worth. According to the Health Maintenance Organization Model Act, an HMO's total admitted assets minus its total liabilities. [6]

network plan. A health care plan that provides health care through a network of preferred health care providers. [3]

new business strain. The decrease in an insurer's capital and surplus caused by high first-year costs and the reserve requirements associated with issuing new policies. Also known as *surplus strain*. [7]

Newborns' and Mothers' Health Protection Act of 1996 (NMHPA). A federal law that prohibits specified health plans and health insurance carriers from restricting benefits for a hospital stay in connection with childbirth to less than 48 hours following a vaginal delivery or 96 hours following a delivery by cesarean section. [3]

noncancellable policy. A health insurance policy that gives the policyowner the right to continue coverage until the insured reaches age 65 or becomes eligible for Medicare. [3]

nonduplication of benefits provision. A type of COB provision that more strictly limits the benefits payable when an insured is covered by more than one group insurance policy. [8]

nonforfeiture provision. A provision that is included in permanent life insurance policies that build a cash value and in deferred annuity policies and that specifies the nonforfeiture benefit options available to a policyowner who elects to stop paying required premiums. [1, 8, 11]

nonpreferred provider. A health care provider who has not contracted with a health care insurer. [6]

notice of claim provision. An individual health insurance policy provision which states that written notice of a claim must be given to the insurer within 20 days after the occurrence or commencement of a covered loss or as soon thereafter as is reasonably possible. [3]

notice of transfer. A document that an insurer must mail to its affected policyowners before the insurer transfers their policies to another insurer as part of an assumption reinsurance transaction. The document provides policyowners with information about the transfer and their right to consent to or reject the transfer of their policies. [7]

open contract. A contract that identifies the documents that constitute the contract between the parties, but the enumerated documents are not all attached to the contract. *See also* **closed contract.** [1]

open-end credit transaction. A transaction in which credit is extended under an agreement in which (1) the creditor reasonably expects repeated transactions; (2) the creditor imposes a periodic finance charge on an outstanding unpaid balance; and (3) the amount of credit that may be extended to the debtor during the term of the agreement—up to any limit set by the creditor—generally is made available to the extent that any outstanding balance is repaid. [10]

outline of coverage. According to the Model Regulation to Implement the Accident and Sickness Insurance Minimum Standards Model Act, a brief description of the coverage provided by an individual health insurance policy that an insurer must deliver to the policyowner when the policy is delivered or to the applicant when the application is completed. [4]

overinsurance provision. An individual health insurance policy provision that defines an insurer's liability to pay policy benefits for covered losses that are insured by more than one policy regardless of whether the same insurer issued all of those policies. [3]

payment of claims provision. An individual health insurance policy provision which states that claims for loss of life will be payable to the named beneficiary, and all other claims will be payable to the insured. [3]

PBGC. *See* **Pension Benefit Guaranty Corporation.**

Pension Benefit Guaranty Corporation (PBGC). A federal corporation that is responsible for guaranteeing the payment of retirement benefits for participants in defined benefit retirement plans when those plans become financially unable to pay benefits. [11]

pension plan. For purposes of ERISA, a plan, fund, or program that is established or maintained by an employer or by an employee organization and that provides retirement income to employees or results in a deferral of income by employees for periods extending to the termination of employment or beyond. [11]

permanent life insurance. Life insurance that provides coverage throughout the insured's lifetime as long as premiums are paid when due and also usually provides a savings element that builds a cash value. [1]

personal selling. A marketing method that uses commissioned or salaried sales personnel to sell products through oral presentations made to prospective purchasers. [1]

physical examinations and autopsy provision. An individual health insurance policy provision that gives an insurer the right to conduct a medical examination of the insured at the insurer's expense when reasonably necessary while a claim is pending. [3]

plan administrator. The party who is responsible for handling the administrative aspects of a group insurance plan or a group retirement plan and ensuring that the plan complies with applicable regulatory requirements. [9, 11]

plan participant. An employee or union member who is covered by a group retirement plan. [11]

plan sponsor. An employer or union that establishes a group retirement plan. [11]

policy loan provision. A provision that is included in permanent life insurance policies that build a cash value and that specifies the terms on which the policyowner may obtain a policy loan. [1]

policy reserve. A liability that identifies the amount that the insurer expects to need in order to pay future policy benefits for a given life or health insurance product. [1, 3]

policy rider. An insurance policy amendment that becomes a part of the insurance contract and either expands or limits the benefits payable under the contract. [1]

policy summary. A written statement that describes specific guaranteed elements of a life insurance policy that a prospect is considering for purchase. [2]

PPA. *See* **preferred provider arrangement**.

PPO. *See* **preferred provider organization**.

preexisting condition. For purposes of the Model Regulation to Implement the Accident and Sickness Insurance Minimum Standards Model Act, the existence of symptoms which would cause an ordinarily prudent person to seek diagnosis, care, or treatment within a five-year period preceding the effective date of the insured's coverage or a condition for which medical advice or treatment was recommended by a physician or received from a physician within a five-year period preceding the effective date of the insured's coverage. [3] For purposes of HIPAA, a physical or mental condition for which medical advice, diagnosis, care, or treatment was recommended or received within the six-month period preceding the date of an individual's enrollment in a group medical expense insurance plan. [9]

preexisting conditions policy provision. A health insurance policy provision that excludes preexisting conditions from coverage for a specified period following the effective date of coverage. [3]

preferred provider. A health care provider who enters into a preferred provider arrangement with a health care insurer. [6]

preferred provider arrangement (PPA). A contract between a health care insurer and a health care provider or group of providers who agree to provide specified covered services to insureds. [6]

Preferred Provider Arrangements Model Act. An NAIC model law that establishes minimum standards for preferred provider arrangements and the health benefit plans that include such arrangements. [6]

preferred provider organization (PPO). A specific type of health benefit plan that includes a preferred provider arrangement. [6]

Pregnancy Discrimination Act. A federal law that was enacted as an amendment to the Civil Rights Act of 1964 and that requires employers to treat pregnancy, childbirth, and related medical conditions the same as any other medical condition. [9]

Premium Rates and Renewability of Coverage for Health Insurance Sold to Small Groups. An NAIC model law that regulates small group medical expense plans by imposing restrictions relating to premiums rates and renewability of coverage. The model also imposes disclosure requirements on insurers that market health insurance to small groups. [8]

premium receipt. A receipt that is provided in exchange for the payment of an initial life insurance policy premium and that provides the proposed insured with some type of temporary insurance coverage while the application for insurance is being underwritten. [1]

premiums. The amounts that insurance companies charge for insurance products. [1]

pre-need funeral contract. An agreement by or on behalf of an individual before her death relating to the purchase of funeral or cemetery merchandise or services. [2]

prima facie premium rates. The maximum premium rates that most state insurance departments permit insurers to charge for specific types of consumer credit insurance. [10]

probationary period. A period following a health insurance policy's effective date during which no benefits are payable. Also known as a *waiting period*. [3]

proofs of loss provision. An individual health insurance policy provision that specifies the time limits within which claimants must provide the insurer with proof of a covered loss. [3]

Public Health Service Act. A federal law that established the authority to award grants for research and for the construction of hospitals and laboratories. [3]

qualified beneficiaries. For purposes of COBRA, specified individuals who have the right to continue their group health insurance coverage following a qualifying event without providing evidence of insurability. [9]

qualified long-term care insurance policy. A long-term care insurance policy that meets requirements specified in the federal tax code and, thus, qualifies for favorable federal income tax treatment. [5]

qualified plan. A group retirement savings plan that meets specified requirements imposed by ERISA and federal tax laws and, as a result, is subject to favorable federal income tax treatment. [11]

qualifying events. For purposes of COBRA, events that would otherwise result in the termination of an individual's group health coverage and that entitle the individual to continue that group coverage for a specified period of time. [9]

Quality Assessment and Improvement Model Act. An NAIC model law that requires a managed care plan to develop a quality assessment program. [6]

quality assessment program. A program established by a managed care plan to measure and evaluate the quality of health care services rendered by health care professionals who participate in the plan. [6]

quality assurance program. A program that establishes procedures to ensure that health care services provided to enrollees of a health maintenance organization are rendered under reasonable standards of quality of care consistent with prevailing professionally recognized standards of medical practice. [6]

quality rating. A letter grade or score on a numerical scale representing a rating agency's opinion of an insurer's financial condition. [2]

rating agencies. Organizations, owned independently of any insurer or government body, that evaluate the financial condition of insurers and provide information to potential customers of and investors in insurance companies. [2]

RB. *See* **reinsurance intermediary—broker**.

rebating. A prohibited sales practice in which an insurance producer or insurer offers a prospect an inducement to purchase an insurance policy from the producer or insurer and the inducement is not offered to all applicants in similar situations and is not stated in the policy itself. [2]

recapture provision. A provision that is sometimes included in indemnity reinsurance agreements and that specifies a procedure by which the ceding company may end the reinsurance arrangement on a given block of reinsured business. [7]

recurrent disability. A disability that results from the same cause as an original disability and that reappears after the original disability ends and after the insured returns to work. [3]

reduction. A health insurance policy provision that reduces the amount of the benefit payable when specified conditions are met. [4]

reinstatement provision. An individual life insurance, health insurance, and annuity policy provision that gives the owner of a policy that has lapsed for nonpayment of premium the right to reinstate the policy by meeting specified requirements. The provision also gives the owner of an individual life insurance policy that has been continued under the extended term or reduced paid-up nonforfeiture options the right to reinstate the policy by meeting specified requirements. [1, 3, 11]

reinsurance. Insurance that an insurer buys to transfer some or all of its own risk on insurance policies. [7]

reinsurance intermediary. A third party that acts as a go-between for an insurer and a reinsurer in effecting a reinsurance transaction. [7]

reinsurance intermediary—broker (RB). According to the Reinsurance Intermediary Model Act, any person, firm, or corporation that solicits, negotiates, or places reinsurance cessions or retrocessions on behalf of a ceding insurer but that is not authorized to enter into a binding reinsurance contract on behalf of the ceding insurer. [7]

reinsurance intermediary—manager (RM). According to the Reinsurance Intermediary Model Act, any third party that acts as an agent of a reinsurer and either has authority to bind the reinsurer to a reinsurance contract or manages all or part of the reinsurer's assumed business. [7]

Reinsurance Intermediary Model Act. An NAIC model law that is designed to regulate the activities of reinsurance intermediaries and of insurers and reinsurers that use the services of reinsurance intermediaries. [7]

reinsurer. In a reinsurance transaction, the insurance company that accepts risks from another insurer. [7]

renewal provision. A term life insurance policy provision that gives the policyowner the right, within specified limits, to renew the insurance coverage at the end of the specified term without submitting evidence of insurability. [1] An individual health insurance policy provision that describes the conditions under which the insurer has the right to cancel or refuse to renew the coverage and describes the insurer's right to increase the policy's premium rate at the time of a renewal. [3]

representation. A statement made by a party to a contract that will invalidate the contract if the statement is not substantially true. [1]

reserve credit. The accounting treatment by which a ceding insurance company records the transfer of reserves to a reinsurer as a result of an indemnity reinsurance transaction. [7]

reserves. Liabilities that represent amounts that an insurer expects to pay to meet its future business obligations. [1]

RM. *See* **reinsurance intermediary—manager**.

Roth IRA. A type of IRA that has been available to eligible individuals since 1998 and that has the same contribution limits as traditional IRAs. Roth IRAs have the following features: (1) a taxpayer may contribute if his adjusted gross income is (a) less than $160,000 if he is married and filing a joint return, (b) less than $110,00 if he is filing a single or head-of-household return, or (c) less than $10,000 if he is married and filing a separate return; (2) no tax deduction is allowed for contributions made to the IRA; (3) qualified withdrawals that the taxpayer has held for at least five years are not subject to income taxation; (4) no tax penalty exists if distributions begin after age 70½. [11]

savings incentive match plan for employees (SIMPLE). A type of qualified savings plan that may be established by small employers and self-employed individuals and that qualifies for favorable federal tax treatment if it meets specified requirements. [11]

scheduled net debt. For purposes of determining the benefit payable under a consumer credit insurance policy, the lump-sum amount needed to pay off the debt on a given date according to the credit agreement's repayment schedule. [10]

scheduled premium variable life policy. According to the Variable Life Insurance Model Regulation, an individual variable life policy for which the insurer fixes both the time and amount of premium payments. [1]

SEP plan. *See* **simplified employee pension plan**.

settlement options provision. A deferred annuity contract provision that describes the contractholder's right to select the terms on which the insurer will pay periodic annuity benefits. [11]

Shopper's Guide to Long-Term Care Insurance. A publication developed by the NAIC to provide consumers with information about the long-term care insurance coverages that are available and to help consumers make informed purchase decisions. [5]

significant break in coverage. A period of 63 consecutive days during which an individual does not have creditable health insurance coverage. [3]

SIMPLE. *See* **savings incentive match plan for employees**.

simplified employee pension (SEP) plan. A type of qualified retirement savings plan that may be established by self-employed individuals and partnerships as an individual retirement account or individual retirement annuity that is owned by the employee and is funded by employer contributions. [11]

small employer. For purposes of HIPAA, an employer that had an average of at least 2 but not more than 50 employees during the preceding calendar year and had at least 2 employees on the first day of the group plan year. [9]

Small Employer and Individual Health Insurance Availability Model Act. An NAIC model law designed to increase the availability of health insurance coverage to small employers and to individuals who are not covered by or eligible for group health insurance or other state-required health benefits. [3]

Small Employer Health Insurance Availability Model Act. An NAIC model law that regulates the renewability of and the premium rates charged for small group medical expense plans and that imposes requirements on carriers that provide small group health benefit coverages. [8]

specified accident coverage. A type of health insurance coverage that provides benefits for death or dismemberment resulting from a specifically identified type of accident. [3]

specified disease coverage. A type of health insurance coverage that pays benefits for the diagnosis and treatment of a specifically named disease or diseases. Also known as *dread disease coverage*. [3]

spokesperson. According to the NAIC Advertisements of Accident and Sickness Insurance Model Regulation, a spokesperson may include (1) a person who makes a testimonial or endorsement and who has a financial interest in an insurer, (2) a person who is in a policy-making position and is affiliated with an insurer, (3) a person who is in any way directly or indirectly compensated for making a testimonial or endorsement, or (4) a person who speaks on behalf of an entity formed or controlled by an insurer. [4]

standard health benefit plan. For purposes of the Small Employer and Individual Health Insurance Availability Model Act, a more expensive health benefit plan that my contain more extensive benefits than a basic health benefit plan. [3]

Standard Nonforfeiture Law for Individual Deferred Annuities. An NAIC model law that requires individual deferred annuities to provide specified minimum nonforfeiture values. [11]

Standard Nonforfeiture Law for Life Insurance. An NAIC model law that specifies how a life insurance policy's minimum cash surrender value is calculated. [1]

Standard Valuation Law. An NAIC model law that establishes minimum requirements for the reserve liabilities that insurers must establish for life insurance and annuity policies. [11]

structured settlement annuity. An immediate annuity issued to a person who is entitled to receive a specified sum of money from a third party; the terms of the annuity contract are tailored to carry out the terms of the agreement between the annuitant and the third party. [11]

suicide exclusion provision. A life insurance policy provision which states that policy proceeds will not be paid if the insured dies as the result of suicide within a specified period following the date of policy issue. [1]

suitability requirement. A regulatory requirement that imposes a duty on insurance producers and/or insurers to have reasonable grounds on which to decide that a specific product is suitable for a customer's needs. [2]

supplemental illustration. A life insurance policy illustration that is provided along with a basic illustration and that presents the information in a different format than that used in the basic illustration. [2]

surplus strain. *See* **new business strain.**

Taft-Hartley Act. A federal law that regulates labor-management relationships and that prohibits an employer from paying anything of value to a labor union. Also known as the *Labor Management Relations Act*. [8]

temporary insurance agreement. *See* **binding premium receipt.**

term life insurance. Insurance that provides a death benefit if the insured dies during a specified period. [1]

time limit on certain defenses provision. An individual health insurance policy provision that limits the time during which an insurer may contest the validity of an insurance contract on the ground of misrepresentation or may reduce or deny a claim on the ground it results from a preexisting condition. [3]

time of payment of claims provision. An individual health insurance policy provision which states that after receiving written proof of loss for which the policy provides periodic benefit payments, the insurer will pay those benefits as described in the policy. [3]

top-heavy plan. A retirement plan under which, for a given plan year, the present value of accrued benefits for key employees exceeds a specified percentage of the present value of accrued benefits for all employees. [11]

traditional IRA. An IRA available to eligible individuals since 1974 for which (1) anyone who is less than age 70½ and who has taxable income can contribute up to a specified amount of earned income each year; (2) some or all contributions are tax-deductible, but taxation of interest earnings is deferred until funds are withdrawn; (3) with specified exceptions, tax penalties are imposed on withdrawals made before the taxpayer attains age 59½; (4) taxpayers must begin making annual withdrawals of at least a specified minimum amount by age 70½. [11]

trust. A fiduciary relationship in which a person, known as the trustee, holds legal title to property for the benefit of another person, known as the trust beneficiary. [8]

trust beneficiary. A person for whose benefit another person holds legal title to trust property. [8]

trust property. Property that is held in trust. [8]

trustee. A person who holds legal title to trust property for the benefit of another person, known as the trust beneficiary. [8]

unauthorized reinsurer. A reinsurer that does not meet requirements specified in state insurance laws based on the Credit for Reinsurance Model Law. [7]

uncovered expenditures. The costs to an HMO for health care services that are the obligation of the HMO *and* for which an enrollee may also be liable if the HMO is insolvent. [6]

uncovered expenditures insolvency deposit. A deposit that an HMO may be required to make and that is held in trust to be used by the state insurance commissioner to pay claims for uncovered expenditures if the HMO becomes insolvent. [6]

underwriting guidelines. General rules that an insurer's underwriting staff use in assigning applicants to different risk classifications. [1]

underwriting philosophy. A body of standards and goals for guiding all of an insurer's risk selection and risk classification procedures. [1]

Unfair Trade Practices Act. An NAIC model law that identifies a number of general practices that are prohibited as unfair trade practices in the business of insurance. [2]

Uniform Individual Accident and Sickness Policy Provision Law (UPPL). An NAIC model law that specifies the provisions that individual health insurance policies must contain. [3]

uninsurable individual. An individual who represents a risk of loss that is too great for an insurer to cover at all or at standard risk rates. [3]

unit of coverage. A basic amount of coverage that insurers use when calculating premium rates for their products. For life insurance, a unit of coverage usually is $1,000 of coverage. [1]

Universal Life Insurance Model Regulation. An NAIC model regulation that is intended to provide states with a means to supplement their insurance laws and regulations to accommodate the issuance of universal life insurance. [1]

universal life insurance policy. A life insurance policy for which the insurer periodically makes separately identified (1) interest credits, other than credits for dividend accumulations, premium deposit funds, or other supplementary accounts; (2) mortality charges; and (3) expense charges. [1]

unpaid premiums provision. An individual health insurance policy provision which states that when a claim is paid, any premium due and unpaid may be deducted from the claim payment. [3]

UPPL. *See* **Uniform Individual Accident and Sickness Policy Provision Law**.

Variable Life Insurance Model Regulation. An NAIC model regulation that establishes qualifications an insurer must meet in order to market variable life insurance within a state and specifies requirements variable life insurance policies must meet. [1]

variable life insurance policy. For purposes of the Variable Life Insurance Model Regulation, an individual policy that provides life insurance coverage which varies in amount or duration according to the experience of one or more separate accounts established and maintained by an insurer. [1]

vested. The status of a retirement plan participant who has met requirements giving her the right to receive partial or full benefits under the plan even if she terminates her employment prior to retirement. [11]

waiting period. *See* **probationary period**.

warranty. A statement made by a party to a contract that will invalidate the contract if the statement is not literally true. [1]

Women's Health and Cancer Rights Act of 1998 (WHCRA). A federal law that requires health insurance plans that cover mastectomies to provide specified benefits for patients who choose to have breast reconstruction following a mastectomy. [3]

Index

Aa

Accelerated Benefits Model Regulation, 13–14, 20
accelerated death benefits, 7, 13, 130–31, 221
acceptable alternative mechanism, 89
access persons, 29
accidental death benefit coverage, 15
accidental death and dismemberment coverage, 80, 81
accident and health insurance. *See* health insurance
accident only coverage, 77, 79
accident and sickness insurance. *See* health insurance
Accident and Sickness Insurance Minimum Standards Model Act, 74, 107, 189
accredited reinsurer, 164
accumulated value, 250
accumulation at interest option, 12
accumulation period, 250
activities of daily living, 125–26
actual net debt, 236–38
actuarial certification, 194
actuarial considerations, 18–19
   annuities, 253–54
   credit insurance, 240–41
   individual health insurance, 92–93
actuarial memorandum, 20
actuarial values
   characteristics of, 48
   illustrations used in sales, 48–49
ADA. *See* Americans with Disabilities Act
additional term insurance dividend option, 12
ADEA. *See* Age Discrimination in Employment Act
adjusted community rate, 89
advertisements
   compliance responsibilities, 47–48
   defined, 43, 98
   regulatory requirements, 44–47
   responsibility for, 43–44, 47–48
Advertisements of Accident and Sickness Insurance Model Regulation, 97–105, 116, 127
Advertisements of Life Insurance and Annuities Model Regulation, 43–48, 60, 255
advertising requirements
   annuities, 255–56
   health insurance, 99–105
   long-term care insurance, 127
   Medicare supplement insurance, 116
   insurer's responsibility for, 22
   regulation of, 43–48
   terms prohibited, 46
Age Discrimination in Employment Act, 200
alcoholism, 85
allied medical practitioner, 85
allowable medical expenses, 190
A.M. Best Company, 45
Americans with Disabilities Act, 200
annual reports, for policies, 55
Annual Statement, 48, 105
annuitant, 251
annuities
   actuarial considerations, 253–54
   advertising and disclosure requirements, 255–56
   contract form development, 252–53
   contract form filing, 254–55
   product development, 250–55
   product regulation, 257–60
   state regulation, 250
   treated like life insurance, 250
annuity considerations, 249
annuity contract form filing submission package, 254
annuity contracts, not covered by Life Insurance Illustrations Model Regulation, 49
annuity date, 251
Annuity Disclosure Model Regulation, 255–56
annuity period, 251
antitrust laws, 42
application for insurance, 16
   industrial life insurance, 33–35
   long-term care insurance, 126–27
   variable life insurance, 30, 31
approval premium receipt, 17
assignment, 12–13
assignment provision, 7, 12–13
association, defined for group insurance purposes, 179
association group, 179–80
assumption certificate, 155
assumption reinsurance, 154–60

Assumption Reinsurance Model Act, 156–60
automatic binding limit, 161
automatic reinsurance, 161
aviation exclusion, 7, 15

Bb

backdating, 7, 16
basic health benefit plan, 89
basic health care services, 140
basic hospital expense coverage, 76, 78
basic illustration, 49, 275–80
basic medical expense coverage, 77
basic medical-surgical expense coverage, 76, 78
beneficiary provision, 69
benefit base, 28
benefits, required under COBRA continuation coverage, 203
benefit standards, Medicare supplement insurance, 113–14
benefit triggers, long-term care insurance, 125–26
binding premium receipt, 17
Birnbaum, Birny, 228
boycott, 41, 42
Buyer's Guide, 56–58
Buyer's Guide to Equity-Indexed Annuities, 260
Buyer's Guide to Fixed Deferred Annuities, 256

Cc

California Department of Insurance, 228
cancellation provision, 144
capitation, 139
cash dividend option, 12
ceding commission, 163
ceding company, 153
Centers for Medicare and Medicaid Services, 121, 135 n.2
certificate of authority, 24, 26, 141
certificate of coverage provision, group insurance, 183, 184
certificate of insurance, 172
CHAMPUS. *See* Civilian Health and Medical Program of the Uniformed Services
change of beneficiary provision, 72, 232
change of occupation provision, 72–73
charitable gift annuities, 255

Civilian Health and Medical Program of the Uniformed Services, 75
Civil Rights Act of 1964, 200
claim forms provision, 71, 113, 232
claim reserves, 93
claims handling, credit insurance, 245
closed contract, 9
closed-end credit, 230
closed-end credit transaction, 226–29
closed panel HMO, 139
CMS. *See* Centers for Medicare and Medicaid Services
COB provision. *See* coordination of benefits provision
COBRA. *See* Consolidated Omnibus Budget Reconciliation Act
COBRA continuation coverage, 202–7
code of ethics, Investment Company Act, 29
coercion, 41, 42
cognitive impairment, 125–26
Cohen, Charles, 106
coinsurance, 76–79, 137, 138
cold lead advertising, 117, 128
common interest association, 179
compensation, defined for credit insurance remuneration, 243
complaint, 42
complaint handling procedures, failure to maintain, 41–42
compliance
    advertising, 47–48
    long-term care insurance, 128
compliance responsibilities
    long-term care insurance, 133–35
    Medicare supplement insurance, 120–21
comprehensive business analysis, 5
conditional premium receipt, 17, 70
conformity with state statutes provision, 73
congenital anomalies, 83
Conning & Company, 45
Consolidated Omnibus Budget Reconciliation Act, 88, 201–7
consumer credit insurance, 231
Consumer Credit Insurance Model Act, 226, 233–45
Consumer Credit Insurance Model Regulation, 226
Consumers Union, 228–29
contestable period, universal life insurance, 32
continuation of coverage provision, 144

contract form development, annuities, 252–53
contract form filing, annuities, 254–55
contractholder, 251
contract reserves, 93
contributory plan, 172
convalescent benefits, 80
conversion privilege, 74
conversion provision, 144, 183–86, 187, 205, 232
converted policy, 188
coordination of benefits provision, 188–89, 190
copayment, 76–79, 114
cost of benefits, 19
creditable coverage, 88, 210–15, 216
credit accident and health insurance, 231
credit card, 230
credit disability insurance, 238
credit insurance, 225–31
    actuarial considerations, 240–41
    claims handling, 245
    compliance responsibilities, 245
    coverage, right to cancel, 234
    disclosure requirements, 244–45
    disclosures, 245
    marketing considerations, 241–44
    policies, 177
    policy form development, 231–40
    product development, 231
    term of coverage, 238
    unique aspects of, 225
credit life insurance, 231, 236–38
    not covered by Life Insurance Illustrations Model Regulation, 49
    not subject to Life Insurance Disclosure Model Regulation, 56
    requirement to file premium rates, 19
Credit for Reinsurance Model Law, 163–64
Credit for Reinsurance Model Regulation, 163–64
credit unemployment insurance, 231
credit union group, 180

Dd

debit insurance. *See* industrial life insurance
debtor-creditor group, 176–77, 225
debtors, defined for group insurance, 177
deductible, 76–79, 114, 137, 138
defamation, 41
deferred annuity, 251, 253
deferred compensation plans, 255
defined benefit pension plans, 271
defined benefit plan, 268
defined contribution plan, 268
dependent coverage, 181
determination letter, 264, 265
determination period, 212
direct contract HMO, 139
direct response marketing, 20–21, 121, 127
direct response solicitations, 130
direct response system, 117
disability income benefits, 65, 81
disability income policies, pregnancy, 85
disability income protection coverage, 77, 78
disclosure
    general requirements, 56–58
    pre-need funeral contracts, 60–61
    variable life insurance requirements, 58–60
    credit insurance, 245
    Truth in Lending Act, 227
disclosure document, 256
disclosure requirements
    accelerated death benefits, 14
    annuities, 255–56
    credit insurance, 244–45
    health maintenance organizations, 145
    insurer's responsibility for, 22
    Medicare supplement insurance, 117–18
Disclosure for Small Face Amount Life Insurance Policies Model Act, 62
disclosure statement, 263
discount for advance payment of premium provision, 33
discounted fee-for-service, 139
discretionary group, 180–81
discrimination, 23
    Equal Credit Opportunity Act, 227
    laws prohibiting, 199, 200
    unfair, 41, 42
distribution method, 20–22
distribution requirements, retirement plans, 271
dividend provision, 7, 9, 12, 252
dread disease coverage. *See* specified disease coverage
Duff & Phelps, 45

Ee

EDI. *See* electronic data interchange
election period, 207
electronic data interchange, 71
Electronic Signatures in Global and National Commerce Act, 21–22
eligibility period, 172
eligible groups, 173–81
eligible individual, 88
e-mail, 21
Employee Retirement Income Security Act, 59, 86, 90, 199, 201, 219, 255, 264–67, 272
employees, defined for group insurance, 176, 178–79
employer-employee contributory plans, 182
employer-employee group health plans, 205
endowment insurance, 4, 46
enforcement provisions
 COBRA coverage, 207
 under HIPAA, 219–20
enrollee, 139
enrollee contracts, health maintenance organizations, 143–44
enrollment, 172
enrollment date, 208
enrollment form, 182
enrollment periods, 90
entire contract provision
 annuities, 252
 credit insurance, 232, 233
 group insurance, 182, 184
 HMO contracts, 144,
 individual health insurance, 68, 69
 individual life insurance, 7, 9–10
 long-term care policies, 113
 Medicare supplement policies, 113
 variable life insurance, 27
Equal Credit Opportunity Act, 227
equity-indexed annuity, 259–60
ERISA. *See* Employee Retirement Income Security Act
ESIGN. *See* Electronic Signatures in Global and National Commerce Act
evidence of coverage, 144
evidence of insurability provision, group insurance, 182–83, 184
exception, 102
exclusion, 7, 14–15, 18, 82, 124–25, 143
exclusionary period, 209

expense allowances, 163
extended care benefits, 80
extranets, 21

Ff

face amount, 8
face page, variable life insurance, 27
facility of payment provision, 33
facultative reinsurance, 161
Fair Credit Reporting Act, 227
false advertising, 41
false entries, 41
false information, 41
false statements, 41
family coverage, 67, 80, 83, 85
Family and Medical Leave Act, 200
fax machines, used in health insurance advertising, 106
federal regulation
 group insurance, 199–222
 variable life insurance, 25
Federal Trade Commission Act, 227
fee schedule payment structure, 139
field intranets, 21
filing and reporting requirements, health maintenance organizations, 144–45
fixed annuity, 251
Flesch reading ease test, 7
flexible-premium annuity, 251
flexible premium variable life policy, 24
FMLA. *See* Family and Medical Leave Act
401(k) plans, 269
franchise plan, 74
fraternal insurers, open contracts, 9–10, 68
fraud, 87
fraud warning, 16
free-look period, 58, 123, 234
free-look provision, 7, 8, 9, 27, 67, 113, 252
fronting, 165–66
fronting company, 165–66
funding agreements, 255

Gg

Garcia, Norma, 228
generic name (for policies and riders), 57
grace period, 258

grace period provision
   annuities, 253
   credit insurance, 232, 233
   group insurance, 182, 184
   HMO contracts, 144
   individual health insurance, 68–70
   individual life insurance, 7, 9, 10
   industrial life insurance, 33
   long-term care policies, 113
   Medicare supplement policies, 113
   scheduled-premium variable life insurance, 28
   universal life insurance, 32
graded benefits, advertising for, 45
grievance procedures, filed in HMO licensing, 141
gross debt, 238, 239
gross premium, 19
group annuities, 253
Group Coordination of Benefits Model Regulation, 188–89
Group Health Insurance Definition and Group Health Insurance Standard Provisions Model Act, 173–81, 186–87, 233
Group Health Insurance Mandatory Conversion Privilege Model Act, 187–88
Group Health Insurance Model Act. *See* Group Health Insurance Definition and Group Health Insurance Standard Provisions Model Act
group insurance
   dependent coverage, 181
   eligible groups, 173–81
   federal requirements, 199–200
   mandated benefits, 191
   policy provisions, standard, 181–89
   product development, 173–91
   regulation of policies issued to small groups, 191–95
   regulatory jurisdiction, 195
   terminology, 172
   underwriting, 174, 175, 176
group insured, 172
group life insurance, not subject to Life Insurance Disclosure Model Regulation, 56
Group Life Insurance Definition and Group Life Insurance Standard Provisions Model Act, 173–81, 185, 232
Group Life Insurance Model Act. *See* Group Life Insurance Definition and Group Life Insurance Standard Provisions Model Act

group medical expense plans
   effect of COBRA on, 201–7
   special enrollment period under HIPAA, 215–17
group mental health benefits, 220–22
group model HMO, 139
group policyholder, 172
group retirement plans, 264–72
groups exempt from HIPAA, 208
guaranteed availability, 88–91, 217–19
guaranteed renewability, 87–88, 217–19
guaranteed renewable, 81, 113, 124
guaranteed values, 51
guaranty associations, 142
Guide to Health Insurance for People with Medicare, 120–21

Hh

hazardous avocation exclusions, 15
hazardous occupation exclusions, 15
Health Care Financing Administration, 135 n.2
Health Care Professional Credentialing Verification Model Act, 146–47
Health Carrier Grievance Procedure Model Act, 147–48
health insurance
   advertising compliance responsibilities, 105
   advertising regulation, 97–105
   advertising requirements, 99–105
   mandated benefits, 84–91
   policy provisions, 102–3
   premium rate filing requirements, 93
   reserves, 92–93
   solicitation disclosure requirements, 105–8
   testimonials in advertising for, 104–5
   words prohibited in advertisement, 99, 100, 102, 103
health insurance, individual
   actuarial considerations, 92–93
   availability and renewability of, 86–91
   coverage limitations and exclusions, 82
   discontinuing, 88
   mandated benefits, 84–91
   policy face page requirements, 66–67
   policy form development, 66–83
   policy provisions, 67–83
   policy readability requirements, 66
   product development, 66–91
   terms defined in policy, 75

health insurance continuum, 138
Health Insurance Portability and Accountability Act, 81, 83, 86–91, 122, 174, 208
    enforcement provisions, 219–20
    guaranteed availability requirement, 217–19
    guaranteed renewability requirement, 219
    nondiscrimination requirements, 217
    preexisting conditions, 208–15
    special enrollment period, 215–17
health insurance pricing, 92
Health Insurance Reserves Model Regulation, 92–93
health maintenance organization, PPA as part of, 148
Health Maintenance Organization Act of 1973, 137, 140
Health Maintenance Organization Model Act, 140–42, 145
health maintenance organizations, 138, 140
    deposits with state insurance department, 142
    disclosure requirements, 145
    enrollee contracts, 143–44
    filing and reporting requirements, 144–45
    licensing of, 141
    regulation of, 139–40
    regulatory supervision and enforcement, 145
    solvency requirements, 142–43
    types of, 139
    UPPL not applicable to, 67
high-pressure sales tactics, 128
HIPAA. *See* Health Insurance Portability and Accountability Act
HMO. *See* health maintenance organization
home equity line of credit, 230
home service insurance. *See* industrial life insurance
hospital confinement indemnity coverage, 76, 78
HR 10 plan, 272

Ii

idea generation, 5
idea screening, 5
illegal occupation provision, 73
illustration, 49
illustration actuary, 55–56
immediate annuity, 251
incontestability provision
    annuities, 252
    credit insurance, 232, 233
    group insurance, 182, 184

individual health insurance, 69
individual life insurance, 7, 9, 10
    variable life insurance, 27
indemnity insurance, 138, 208
indemnity plan, 137
indemnity reinsurance, 154, 160–62
individual health insurance, mandated benefits, 191
Individual Health Insurance Portability Model Act, 90–91
individual health policies, types exempt from Model Regulation to Implement the Accident and Sickness Insurance Minimum Standards Model Act, 74–75
individual immediate annuities, 253
individual practice association, 139
individual retirement account, 255, 261
individual retirement annuity, 255, 261–64
individual retirement arrangement, 261–63
individual retirement plans, 260–64
industrial life insurance, 33–35
    assignment provision restricted, 13
    product regulation, 33–35
Industrial Life Insurance Model Bill, 33–35
inflation protection option, 125
insider trading, 29
installment sale, 230
institutional advertisement, 99
insurability premium receipt, 17
insurance, limits on amounts, 23
insurance certificates, group life and health insurance, 173
insurer qualifications, variable life insurance, 24–26
insurer's identity, in health insurance advertising, 101
insurer's illustrated scale, 52
insuring clause, 8
interest-indexed annuities, 259
interest-indexed policy, 32, 34
interest-indexed universal life policies, 32, 34, 259
Internal Revenue Code, 86, 90, 220, 255
Internal Revenue Service, 263–64, 265
Internet, doing business on, 21–22
intimidation, 41, 42
intoxicants and narcotics provision, 74
intranet, 21
investment companies, 25
Investment Company Act of 1940, 25, 29
invitation to contract, 99, 102, 103–4
invitation to inquire, 99

IPA. *See* individual practice association
IRA. *See* individual retirement arrangement, individual retirement annuity

Jj

joint venture, 165
jurisdiction, establishing for group insurance, 195

Kk

Keogh plan, 272
Klug, Erin, 106

Ll

Labor Management Relations Act of 1947. *See* Taft-Hartley Act
labor union group, 177–87
lapse, 134–35
late enrollee, 209
late entrant, 172
legal actions provision, 72, 113, 232
letters of credit, 143
licensing
    for conducting insurance business, 24
    health maintenance organizations, 141
    reinsurers, 154
    for selling credit insurance, 243
Life and Health Insurance Policy Language Simplification Model Act, 7, 66
Life and Health Reinsurance Agreements Model Regulation, 164–65
Life Insurance Disclosure Model Regulation, 56–58, 61
Life Insurance Illustrations Model Regulation, 49–56
limitations, 102, 124–25, 143
limited benefit health coverage, 77, 79
limited credit insurance license, 241
limited insurance representative, 241
line of credit, 230
loading, 19, 92
long-term care benefits, 221
long-term care insurance, 67, 75, 121–23, 128
    additional requirements, 132–33
    advertising requirements, 127
    application forms, 126–27
    benefit triggers, 125–26
    compliance responsibilities, 133–35
    definitions required in policies, 126
    disclosure form, 132–33
    marketing standards, 127–28
    policy provisions, 123–25
    reinstatement provision, 234
    required provisions, 112, 113
    solicitation disclosure requirements, 129–31
    suitability standards, 131–32
Long-Term Care Insurance Model Act, 122–24, 129–32
Long-Term Care Insurance Model Regulation, 122–35
Long-Term Care Insurance Personal Worksheet, 132
look-back period, 208
loss ratio, 93

Mm

major medical expense coverage, 77, 78
Managed Care Plan Network Adequacy Model Act, 146
managed care plans, 137, 208
    state regulation, 145–48
    theory of, 138
    types of, 138
mandated benefits
    group insurance, 191
mandated benefits, individual health insurance, 84–91, 191
market conduct, emerging issues in, 61–62
marketing considerations, credit insurance, 241–44
marketing objectives, meeting with reinsurance, 165–66
marketing records, failure to maintain, 41
marketing standards
    long-term care insurance, 127–28
    Medicare supplement insurance, 116–17
master group insurance contract, 172
material misrepresentation, 10, 11, 16, 87
maternity benefits, 85
medical expense coverage, 65
medical savings account, 221
Medicare, 111
Medicare Part A, 114, 115, 135 n.1
Medicare Part B, 114, 115, 135 n.1
Medicare Supplement Insurance Minimum Standards Model Act, 74, 112–13, 117

Medicare supplement insurance policies, 67, 74, 112
   additional requirements, 118
   advertising requirements, 116
   benefit standards, 113–14
   compliance responsibilities, 120–21
   disclosure requirements, 117–18
   marketing standards, 116–17
   policy provisions, required, 112–13
   reporting requirements, 121
   standard benefit plans, 114–15
Medicare Supplement Model Act. *See* Medicare Supplement Insurance Minimum Standards Model Act
Medicare Supplement Model Regulation. *See* Model Regulation to Implement the NAIC Medicare Supplement Insurance Minimum Standards Model Act
Medigap policies. *See* Medicare supplement insurance policies
Mental Health Parity Act, 220–22
MHPA. *See* Mental Health Parity Act
military service exclusion, 80
minimum benefit standards, individual health insurance, 76–83
Minimum Reserve Standards, 93
Minimum Standards Act. *See* Accident and Sickness Insurance Minimum Standards Model Act
Minimum Standards Model Regulation. *See* Model Regulation to Implement the Accident and Sickness Insurance Minimum Standards Model Act
misleading, capacity to, 44
misrepresentation, 124, 128
   insured, 10, 11, 16
   insurer, 40–41, 69
misstatement of age provision
   annuities, 252
   credit insurance, 232, 233
   group insurance, 183, 184
   group insurance, 69
   individual health insurance, 73
   individual life insurance, 7, 9, 10–11
   variable life insurance, 27
misstatement of age and sex provision, 11
misstatements, 68
mixed model HMO, 139
Model Health Plan for Uninsurable Individuals Act, 91
Model Newborn Children Bill, 85–86
Model Policy Loan Interest Rate Bill, 12
Model Regulation to Implement the Accident and Sickness Insurance Minimum Standards Model Act, 74–83, 105–7, 189
Model Regulation to Implement the NAIC Medicare Supplement Insurance Minimum Standards Model Act, 112–23
Model Rules Governing Advertisements of Medicare Supplement Insurance, 116
Model Variable Annuity Regulation, 257, 258
modified benefits, advertising for, 45
modified guaranteed annuities, 257–59
Modified Guaranteed Annuity Regulation, 258–59
Moody's Investors Service, 45
morbidity rates, 92
MSA. *See* medical savings account
multiple employer group, 178–79

Nn

NAIC, 120–21
   Accelerated Benefits Model Regulation, 13–14, 20
   Accident and Sickness Insurance Minimum Standards Model Act, 74, 105, 189
   Advertisements of Accident and Sickness Insurance Model Regulation, 97–105, 116, 127
   Advertisements of Life Insurance and Annuities Model Regulation, 43–48, 60, 255
   Annuity Disclosure Model Regulation, 255–56
   Assumption Reinsurance Model Act, 156–60
   Consumer Credit Insurance Model Act, 226, 233–45
   Consumer Credit Insurance Model Regulation, 226
   Credit for Reinsurance Model Law, 163–64
   Credit for Reinsurance Model Regulation, 163–64
narrative summary, 51–52
NASD. *See* National Association of Securities Dealers
National Association of Insurance Commissioners. *See* NAIC
National Association of Securities Dealers, 25
negotiated trusteeships, 178
net amount at risk, 19

net premium, 19, 92
network model HMO, 139
network plan, 87, 218–19
net worth, 142
Newborns' and Mothers' Health Protection Act of 1996, 84, 220
new business strain, 162–65
NMHPA. *See* Newborns' and Mothers' Health Protection Act of 1996
noncancellable policy, 81, 123
noncontributory plan, 172
Nondiscrimination in Health Insurance Coverage in the Group Market Model Regulation, 218
nondiscrimination requirements
    retirement plans, 270–71
    under HIPAA, 217
nonduplication of benefits provision, 189
nonforfeiture benefits, 124
nonforfeiture laws, 18
nonforfeiture provision, 7, 12, 184, 186, 253
nonforfeiture values, 18
nonguaranteed elements, 53, 55
nonguaranteed values, 51
non-level premiums, advertising for, 45
nonpreferred provider, 148
nonqualified deferred compensation plans, 256
notice of claim provision, 70–71, 113, 232
notice of transfer, 156–58
notice requirements, COBRA coverage, 206–7
numeric summary, 52

Oo

open contract, 9–10, 68
open-end credit, 230
open-end credit transaction, 227–29
open-enrollment period, 172
open panel HMO, 139
outline of coverage, 107–8, 117, 129–30
overinsurance provision, 73

Pp

paid-up additional insurance option, 12
paid-up long-term care coverage, 124
participating policies, 12
participation requirements, retirement plans, 268–70

patients' rights legislation, 149–50
payment of claims provision, 72, 113, 232
payout period, 251
PBGC. *See* Pension Benefit Guaranty Corporation
Pension Benefit Guaranty Corporation, 272
pension plan, 264, 266–70
performance records, failure to maintain, 41
permanent life insurance, 4
    net amount at risk, 19
    policy reserve levels, 19
personal line of credit, 230
personal selling, 20, 22, 117, 120
physical examinations and autopsy provision, 72, 113, 232
plan administrator, 206–7, 267
plan participant, 267
plan sponsor, 267
point of service plans, 138
policy date, 8
policy definitions, individual health insurance, 75
policy dividends, 48
policy endorsement, 36 n.2
policy face page requirements, 8, 66–67
policy form development, 4–6
    application for insurance, 16
    credit insurance, 231–40
    group insurance, 173
    policy face page requirements, 8
    premium receipts, 17–18
    provisions required, life insurance policies, 9–12
    provisions required, permanent insurance policies, 12
    provisions, optional, 7, 12–15
    provisions, prohibited, 7, 15–16
    readability requirements, 7
policy form filing, 4, 5
policy forms, illustrations used with, 49–50, 54
policy loan provision, 7, 12
policy processing days, 28
policy provisions, 6
    for credit insurance, 232
    group health insurance policies, 184, 186–89
    group life insurance, 183–86
    health insurance, 102–3
    long-term care insurance, 123–25
    optional, 7, 12–15, 72–74
    prohibited, 7, 15–16, 82–83
    required for individual health insurance, 67–72, 81

policy provisions, *continued*
   required for life insurance policies, 7, 9–12
   required for Medicare supplement insurance, 112–13
   required for permanent insurance policies, 12
   universal life insurance, 30–32
   variable life insurance, 27–28
policy requirements, variable life insurance, 26–28
policy reserve, 19
policy rider, 13, 18, 36 n.2
policy standards, minimum
   group insurance, 189–90
   individual health insurance, 74–83
policy summary, 57–58, 130–31
policy termination, remaining responsibility for claims, 81
portfolio, 29
portfolio manager, 29
PPA. *See* preferred provider arrangement
preexisting condition, 83, 114, 123, 124, 208–15
preexisting condition policy provision, 83, 90
preferred provider arrangements, regulation of, 148–49
Preferred Provider Arrangements Model Act, 148–49
preferred provider organizations, 138, 148
pregnancy, 85
pregnancy benefits, 80
Pregnancy Discrimination Act, 200
premium charges, COBRA coverage, 205–6
premium rate filing requirements, health insurance, 93
premium rates
   Medicare supplement policies, 112
   race used as factor in, 61
Premium Rates and Renewability of Coverage for Health Insurance Sold to Small Groups, 192–93
premium receipt, 17–18
premium reduction option, 12
premiums, 19
   changing, 46
   for credit insurance, 229
   non-level, 46
   prima facie, 241, 242
pre-need funeral contract, 60–61
prima facie premium rates, 241, 242
prior approval requirements, reinsurance, 158–60
privacy, 237

probationary period, 82–83, 172
product development
   actuarial considerations, 18–19
   annuities, 250–55
   credit insurance, 231
   distribution method, 20–22
   group insurance, 173–91
   individual health insurance, 66–91
   process, 5
   underwriting considerations, 23
product development team, 3–4
product implementation, 4, 5
product introduction, 5
product regulation
   industrial life insurance, 33–35
   universal life insurance, 30–32
   variable life insurance, 24–30
professional association, 179
profit sharing plan, 266
proofs of loss provision, 71, 113, 232, 233
prospectus, 25, 58–59
provisions, required, long-term care policies, 112, 113
public employee association, 179
Public Health Service Act, 86, 87, 90, 220
pure endowment benefit, 46

Qq

qualified beneficiaries, 202–7
qualified long-term care insurance policy, 122
qualified plan, 267
qualified retirement plans, 271–72
qualifying events, 202–7
quality assessment program, 147
Quality Assessment and Improvement Model Act, 147
quality assurance program, 141
quality rating, 44, 45

Rr

rating agencies, 44, 45
readability requirements, 6, 7, 66
rebating, 40
recapture provision, 160
recurrent disability, 80
reduction, 102

registration statement, 25, 59
regulation
    annuity products, 257–60
    health maintenance organizations, 139–40
    preferred provider arrangements, 148–49
    primary goal with reinsurance, 154
    reinsurance intermediaries, 166–67
    retirement products, 260–72
regulatory jurisdiction, group insurance, 195
regulatory supervision and enforcement, health maintenance organizations, 145
reinstatement provision
    annuities, 253
    credit insurance, 232, 234
    individual health insurance, 69, 70
    individual life insurance, 7, 9, 11–12
    long-term care policies, 113
    Medicare supplement policies, 113
reinstatement, 258
reinsurance, 153
    business purposes for, 162–66
    types of agreements, 154–62
reinsurance allowance, 163
reinsurance commission, 163
reinsurance intermediary, 166–67
reinsurance intermediary—broker (RB), 166–67
reinsurance intermediary—manager (RM), 166–67
Reinsurance Intermediary Model Act, 166–67
reinsurance premiums, 163
reinsurance treaty, 161
reinsurer, 153
renewability, 90
renewal provision, 8, 70, 113, 123–24, 144, 232
replacements, 40, 118, 119–20, 134–35
representation, 10
reserve credit, 163
reserves, 18, 92–93
Restatement of UPPL in Simplified Language, 68
retirement products, regulation, 260–72
Retirement Security Advice Act of 2001, 269
retroceded, 161
retrocessionaires, 161
"Revised Illustration," 54
Ricard, Kathryn, 269
riders, long-term care insurance provided under life insurance policy, 121
risk, underwriting, 23
Roth IRA, 262

Ss

sales illustrations, 48–50, 275–83
    basic elements, 50–51
    considered advertisements, 49
    content of, 50–53
    delivery of, 54
    life insurance, 48–56
    not used in sale of policy, 54
    prohibitions, 50
    reporting requirements, 55–56
    supplemental, content of, 53
savings incentive match plan for employees, 272
scheduled net debt, 236–38, 239
scheduled premium variable life policy, 24
scheduled retention limit, 161
Securities Act of 1933, 25, 59
Securities Exchange Act of 1934, 25
Securities and Exchange Commission, 5, 25, 29, 58–59, 255
Senior Health Insurance Benefits Advisors Program, 128
Senior Health Insurance Program, 128
separate accounts, variable life insurance, 28–29
SEP plan. *See* simplified employee pension plan
settlement options provision, 253
Shopper's Guide to Long-Term Care Insurance, 130
significant break in coverage, 91, 211
SIMPLE. *See* savings incentive match plan for employees
simplified employee pension plan, 272
single employer group, 174–76
single-premium annuity, 251
small employer allocation program, 194
Small Employer Health Insurance Availability Model Act, 192–95
small employer health reinsurance program, 194–95
Small Employer and Individual Health Insurance Availability Model Act, 89–90, 91
small employers, 181, 192
small face amount policies, 61–62
small groups, insurance for, 192–95
Social Security Administration, 205
solicitation disclosure requirements
    health insurance, 105–8
    long-term care insurance, 129–31
solvency, reinsurers, 154
solvency requirements, health maintenance organizations, 142–43

special enrollment period, under HIPAA, 215–17
specified accident coverage, 77, 79
specified disease coverage, 77, 79
specified disease policies, 81
spokesperson, 104–5
staff model HMO, 139
standard benefit plans, Medicare supplement insurance, 114–15
standard health benefit plan, 89
Standard Nonforfeiture Law for Individual Deferred Annuities, 253–54, 257
Standard Nonforfeiture Law for Life Insurance, 12
Standard & Poor's, 32, 45
Standard Valuation Law, 253
standards of suitability, 26
state insurance authority, authority to regulate premium rates, 18
state insurance department, 4
    approval of application, 16
    approval of Medicare supplement policies, 112
    approval of standard group policy provisions, 181–82
    establishing premium refunds for credit insurance, 234
    HMO information required, 144–45
    licensing HMOs, 141
    policy provision review, 9
    role in approving coverage for discretionary groups, 180–81
    role in reinsurance transactions, 159–60
statement of actuarial opinion, interest-indexed universal life policies, 32, 34
state regulation, 40
    annuities, 250
    managed care plans, 145–48
stock bonus plan, 266
structured settlement annuity, 254–55
submission package, 254
    interest-indexed policies, 32
    policy forms, 4, 5
substance abuse, 85
suicide exclusion, universal life insurance, 32
suicide exclusion provision, 7, 15
suitability requirement, 40
suitability standards, long-term care insurance, 131–32
supplemental illustration, 49, 53, 281–83
surplus strain, 162–65

Tt

Taft-Hartley Act, 178
Taft-Hartley trusts, 178
technical product design, 5
temporary insurance agreement, 17
term life insurance, 4
    grace period, 10
    net amount at risk, 19
testimonials, 47, 104–5
Things You Should Know Before You Buy Long-Term Care Insurance, 132
third party administrators, 138
third-party endorsements, 47
thrift and savings plan, 266
TIA. *See* temporary insurance agreement
time limit on certain defenses provision, 68, 69, 83, 113, 124, 232
time of payment of claims provision, 71–72, 113, 232
top-heavy plan, 271–72
traditional IRA, 262
transplants, 80
trust, 174
trust beneficiary, 174
trustee, 174
trust fund, 174
trust property, 174
Truth in Lending Act, 227
twisting, 116, 128

Uu

UETA. *See* Uniform Electronic Transactions Act
unauthorized reinsurer, 164
uncovered expenditures, 142
underwriting, group insurance, 174, 175, 176
underwriting considerations, 23
underwriting guidelines, 23
underwriting philosophy, 23
unearned premium reserves, 93
Unfair Claims Settlement Practices Act, 245
Unfair Trade Practices Act, 39–43, 116, 255
Uniform Electronic Transactions Act, 21
Uniform Individual Accident and Sickness Policy Provision Law, 67–72, 112, 113, 123, 232

Uniform Policy Provision Law. *See* Uniform Individual Accident and Sickness Policy Provision Law
uninsurable individual, 91
unit of coverage, 19
universal life insurance, 4
    grace period, 10
    interest-indexed policies, 32, 34
    periodic reports, 55
    policy, 30
    product regulation, 30–32
    required policy provisions, 30–32
Universal Life Insurance Model Regulation, 30–32
unpaid premiums provision, 73
UPPL. *See* Uniform Individual Accident and Sickness Policy Provision Law
U.S. House of Representatives, 268, 269

Vv

variable annuities, 253, 255, 257
variable life insurance, 4
    application for insurance, 30, 31
    disclosure requirements, 58–60
    insurer qualifications, 24–26
    not covered by Life Insurance Illustrations Model Regulation, 49
    not subject to Life Insurance Disclosure Model Regulation, 56
    periodic disclosure requirements, 58–60
    policy, 24–30
    product regulation, 24–30
    separate accounts, 28–29
    solicitation disclosure requirements, 58–60
    supplemental illustrations used with, 53
Variable Life Insurance Model Regulation, 24–30, 58–60
variable products, registration with the Securities and Exchange Commission, 5
variable universal life insurance, 24
vested, 270
vesting requirements, retirement plans, 270

Ww–Xx

waiting period, 211. *See also* probationary period
waiver of premium coverage, 15
war exclusion provision, 7, 15
warranty, 10
Weiss Ratings, 45
welfare benefit plan, 199, 201
WHCRA. *See* Women's Health and Cancer Rights Act of 1998
whole life insurance, 4, 10
Women's Health and Cancer Rights Act of 1998, 84, 220
World Wide Web, 21, 22

Yy–Zz

yearly renewable term reinsurance method, 161–62
YRT. *See* yearly renewable term reinsurance method